YOUR 15-MONTH CANDID,
COMPLETE AND INDIVIDUAL FORECAST

SCORPIO
1987
SUPER HOROSCOPE
OCT. 23—NOV. 22

ARROW BOOKS LIMITED
62-65 Chandos Place
London WC2N 4NW

CONTENTS

THE PUBLISHERS REGRET THAT THEY CANNOT ANSWER INDIVIDUAL LETTERS REQUESTING PERSONAL HOROSCOPE INFORMATION.

FIRST PUBLISHED IN GREAT BRITAIN BY ARROW BOOKS 1986
© GROSSET & DUNLAP, INC., 1974, 1978, 1979, 1980, 1981, 1982
© CHARTER COMMUNICATIONS, INC., 1983, 1984, 1985
COPYRIGHT © 1986 BY THE BERKLEY PUBLISHING GROUP

PRINTED IN GREAT BRITAIN BY
GUERNSEY PRESS CO. LTD
GUERNSEY C.I.
ISBN 0 09 948740 3

NOTE TO THE CUSP-BORN

First find the year of your birth, and then find the sign under which you were born according to your day of birth. Thus, you can determine if you are a true Scorpio (or Libra or Sagittarius), according to the variations of the dates of the Zodiac. (See also page 7.)

Are you *really* a Scorpio? If your birthday falls during the third to fourth week of October, at the beginning of Scorpio, will you still retain the traits of Libra, the sign of the Zodiac before Scorpio? And what if you were born late in November—are you more Sagittarius than Scorpio? Many people born at the edge, or cusp, of a sign have difficulty determining exactly what sign they are. If you are one of these people, here's how you can figure it out, once and for all.

Consult the following table. It will tell you the precise days on which the Sun entered and left your sign for the year of your birth. If you were born at the beginning or end of Scorpio, yours is a lifetime reflecting a process of subtle transformation. Your life on Earth will symbolize a significant change in consciousness, for you are either about to enter a whole new way of living or are leaving one behind.

If you were born at the beginning of Scorpio, you may want to read the horoscope book for Libra as well as Scorpio, for Libra holds the keys to much of the complexity of your spirit and reflects many of your hidden weaknesses, secret sides and unspoken wishes.

You have a keen way of making someone feel needed and desired, whether you care deeply or not. Sex is a strong directive in your life and you could turn your talents toward superficiality in relationships, merely winning people over with your sexual magnetism and sheer magic.

You can love with an almost fatal obsession, a bigger-than-both-of-you type thing, where you will blind your eyes to facts to keep the peace in a relationship—then suddenly declare war.

No one in the whole Zodiac is as turned on to the passions of life as you. You can survive any crisis, for deep in your spirit lie the seeds of immortality and you know it. Above all you are the symbol that life goes on—the personification of awakening passion.

If you were born at the end of Scorpio, you may want to read the horoscope book for Sagittarius as well as Scorpio. You are the symbol of the human mind awakening to its higher capabilities. What you are leaving behind is greed, blind desire and shallow lust, as you awaken to your own ability to learn, create, understand. You *want* to travel, see new places, see how people live, figure yourself out, acquire knowledge—yet you are often not quite ready to take the plunge. When you shift your behavior patterns significantly and permanently, new worlds open up and you turn on to immortality and the infinite possibilities of your own mind.

DATES SUN ENTERS SCORPIO (LEAVES LIBRA)

October 23 every year from 1900 to 2000, except for the following:

October 24:				October 22:
1902	1911	1923	1943	1992
03	14	27	48	96
06	15	31	51	
07	18	35	55	
10	19	39	59	

DATES SUN LEAVES SCORPIO (ENTERS SAGITTARIUS)

November 22 every year from 1900 to 2000, except for the following:

November 23:			November 21:	
1902	1915	1931	1976	1992
03	19	35	80	93
07	23	39	84	96
10	27	43	88	
11				

HISTORY AND USES
OF ASTROLOGY

Does astrology have a place in the fast-moving, ultra-scientific world we live in today? Can it be justified in a sophisticated society whose outriders are already preparing to step off the moon into the deep space of the planets themselves? Or is it just a hangover of ancient superstition, a psychological dummy for neurotics and dreamers of every historical age?

These are the kind of questions that any inquiring person can be expected to ask when they approach a subject like astrology which goes beyond, but never excludes, the materialistic side of life.

The simple, single answer is that astrology works. It works for tens of millions of people in the western world alone. In the United States there are 10 million followers and in Europe, an estimated 25 million. America has more than 4000 practicing astrologers, Europe nearly three times as many. Even down-under Australia has its hundreds of thousands of adherents. The importance of such vast numbers of people from diverse backgrounds and cultures is recognized by the world's biggest newspapers and magazines who probably devote more of their space to this subject in a year than to any other. In the eastern countries, astrology has enormous followings, again, because it has been proved to work. In countries like India, brides and grooms for centuries have been chosen on the basis of astrological compatibility. The low divorce rate there, despite today's heavy westernizing influence, is attributed largely to this practice.

In the western world, astrology today is more vital than ever before; more practicable because it needs a sophisticated society like ours to understand and develop its contribution to the full; more valid because science itself is confirming the precepts of astrological knowledge with every new exciting step. The ordinary person who daily applies astrology intelligently does not have to wonder whether it is true nor believe in it blindly. He can see it working for himself. And, if he can use it—and this book is designed to help the reader to do just that—he can make living a far richer experience, and become a more developed personality and a better person.

Astrology is the science of relationships. It is not just a study of planetary influences on man and his environment. It is the study of man himself.

We are at the center of our personal universe, of all our rela-

1

tionships. And our happiness or sadness depends on how we act, how we relate to the people and things that surround us. The emotions that we generate have a distinct affect—for better or worse—on the world around us. Our friends and our enemies will confirm this. Just look in the mirror the next time you are angry. In other words, each of us is a kind of sun or planet or star and our influence on our personal universe, whether loving, helpful or destructive, varies with our changing moods, expressed through our individual character.

And to an extent that includes the entire galaxy, this is true of the planetary bodies. Their radiations affect each other, including the earth and all the things on it. And in comparatively recent years, giant constellations called "quasars" have been discovered. These exist far beyond the night stars that we can observe, and science says these quasars are emitting radiating influences more powerful and different than ever recorded on earth. Their effect on man from an astrological point of view is under deep study. Compared with these inter-stellar forces, our personal "radiations" are negligible on the planetary scale. But ours are just as potent in the way they affect our moods, and our ability to control them. To this extent they determine much of the happiness and satisfaction in our lives. For instance, if we were bound and gagged and had to hold some strong emotion within us without being able to move, we would soon start to feel very uncomfortable. We are obviously pretty powerful radiators inside, in our own way. But usually, we are able to throw off our emotion in some sort of action—we have a good cry, walk it off, or tell someone our troubles—before it can build up too far and make us physically ill. Astrology helps us to understand the universal forces working on us, and through this understanding, we can become more properly adjusted to our surroundings and find ourselves coping where others may flounder.

Closely related to our emotions is the "other side" of our personal universe, our physical welfare. Our body, of course, is largely influenced by things around us over which we have very little control. The phone rings, we hear it. The train runs late. We snag our stocking or cut our face shaving. Our body is under a constant bombardment of events that influence our lives to varying degrees.

The question that arises from all this is, what makes each of us act so that we have to involve other people and keep the ball of activity and evolution rolling? This is the question that both science and astrology are involved with. The scientists have attacked it from different angles: anthropology, the study of human evolution as body, mind and response to environment; anatomy, the study of bodily structure; psychology, the science of the human mind; and so on. These studies have produced very impressive classifications and valuable information, but because the approach to the problem is fragmented, so is the result. They remain "branches" of science. Science generally studies effects. It keeps turning up wonderful answers but no lasting solutions. Astrology, on the other hand approaches the question from the broader viewpoint. Astrology began its inquiry with the totality of human experience and saw it as an effect. It then looked to find the cause, or at least the prime movers, and during thousands of years of observation of man and his *universal* environment, came up with the extraordinary principle of planetary influence—or astrology, which, from the Greek, means the science of the stars.

Modern science, as we shall see, has confirmed much of astrology's foundations—most of it unintentionally, some of it reluctantly, but still, indisputably.

It is not difficult to imagine that there must be a connection between outer space and the earth. Even today, scientists are not too sure how our earth was created, but it is generally agreed that it is only a tiny part of the universe. And as a part of the universe, people on earth see and feel the influence of heavenly bodies in almost every aspect of our existence. There is no doubt that the sun has the greatest influence on life on this planet. Without it there would be no life, for without it there would be no warmth, no division into day and night, no cycles of time or season at all. This is clear and easy to see. The influence of the moon, on the other hand, is more subtle, though no less definite.

There are many ways in which the influence of the moon manifests itself here on earth, both on human and animal life. It is a well-known fact, for instance, that the large movements of water on our planet—that is the ebb and flow of the tides—are caused by the moon's gravitational pull. Since this is so, it follows that these water movements do not occur only in the oceans, but that all bodies of water are affected, even down to the tiniest puddle.

The human body, too, which consists of about 70 percent water, falls within the scope of this lunar influence. For example the menstrual cycle of most women corresponds to the lunar month; the period of pregnancy in humans is 273 days, or equal to nine lunar months. Similarly, many illnesses reach a crisis at the change of the moon, and statistics in many countries have shown that the crime rate is highest at the time of the full moon. Even human sexual desire has been associated with the phases of the moon. But, it is in the movement of the tides that we get the clearest demonstration of planetary influence, and the irresistible correspondence between the so-called metaphysical and the physical.

Tide tables are prepared years in advance by calculating the future positions of the moon. Science has known for a long time that the moon is the main cause of tidal action. But only in the last few years has it begun to realize the possible extent of this influence on mankind. To begin with, the ocean tides do not rise and fall as we might imagine from our personal observations of them. The moon as it orbits around the earth, sets up a circular wave of attraction which pulls the oceans of the world after it, broadly in an east to west direction. This influence is like a phantom wave crest, a loop of power stretching from pole to pole which passes over and around the earth like an invisible shadow. It travels with equal effect across the land masses and, as scientists were recently amazed to observe, caused oysters placed in the dark in the middle of the United States where there is no sea, to open their shells to receive the non-existent tide. If the land-locked oysters react to this invisible signal, what effect does it have on us who not so long ago in evolutionary time, came out of the sea and still have its salt in our blood and sweat?

Less well known is the fact that the moon is also the primary force behind the circulation of blood in human beings and animals, and the movement of sap in trees and plants. Agriculturists have established that the moon has a distinct influence on crops, which explains why for centuries people have planted according to moon cycles. The habits of many animals, too, are directed by the movement of the moon. Migratory birds, for instance, depart only at or near the time of the full moon. Just as certain fish, eels in particular, move only in accordance with certain phases of the moon.

Know Thyself—Why?

In today's fast-changing world, everyone still longs to know what the future holds. It is the one thing that everyone has in common: rich and poor, famous and infamous, all are deeply concerned about tomorrow.

But the key to the future, as every historian knows, lies in the past. This is as true of individual people as it is of nations. You cannot understand your future without first understanding your past, which is simply another way of saying that you must first of all know yourself.

The motto "know thyself" seems obvious enough nowadays, but it was originally put forward as the foundation of wisdom by the ancient Greek philosophers. It was then adopted by the "mystery religions" of the ancient Middle East, Greece and Rome, and is still used in all genuine schools of mind training or mystical discipline, both in those of the East, based on yoga, and those of the West. So it is universally accepted now, and has been through the ages.

But how do you go about discovering what sort of person you are? The first step is usually classification into some sort of system of types. Astrology did this long before the birth of Christ. Psychology has also done it. So has modern medicine, in its way.

One system classifies men according to the source of the impulses they respond to most readily: the muscles, leading to direct bodily action; the digestive organs, resulting in emotion, or the brain and nerves. Another such system says that character is determined by the endocrine glands, and gives us labels like "pituitary," "thyroid" and "hyperthyroid" types. These different systems are neither contradictory nor mutually exclusive. In fact, they are very often different ways of saying the same thing.

Very popular and useful classifications were devised by Dr. C. G. Jung, the eminent disciple of Freud. Jung observed among the different faculties of the mind, four which have a predominant influence on character. These four faculties exist in all of us without exception, but not in perfect balance. So when we say, for instance, that a man is a "thinking type," it means that in any situation he tries to be rational. It follows that emotion, which some say is the opposite of thinking, will be his weakest function. This type can be sensible and reasonable, or calculating and unsympathetic. The emotional type, on the other hand, can often be recognized by exaggerated language—everything is either marvelous or terrible—and in extreme cases they even invent dramas and quarrels out of nothing just to make life more interesting.

The other two faculties are intuition and physical sensation. The sensation type does not only care for food and drink, nice clothes and furniture; he is also interested in all forms of physical experience. Many scientists are sensation types as are athletes and nature-lovers. Like sensation, intuition is a form of perception and we all possess it. But it works through that part of the mind which is not under conscious control—consequently it sees meanings and connections which are not obvious to thought or emotion. Inventors and original thinkers are always intuitive, but so, too, are superstitious people who see meanings where none exist.

Thus, sensation tells us what is going on in the world, feeling (that is, emotion) tells us how important it is to ourselves, thinking enables us to interpret it and work out what we should do about it, and intuition tells us what it means to ourselves and others. All four faculties are essential, and all are present in every one of us. But some people are guided chiefly by one, others by another.

Besides these four types, Jung observed a division into extrovert and introvert, which cuts across them. By and large, the introvert is one who finds truth inside himself rather than outside. He is not, therefore, ideally suited to a religion or a political party which tells him what to believe. Original thinkers are almost necessarily introverts. The extrovert, on the other hand, finds truth coming to him from outside. He believes in experts and authorities, and wants to think that nature and the laws of nature really exists, that they are what they appear to be and not just generalities made by men.

A disadvantage of all these systems of classification, is that one cannot tell very easily where to place oneself. Some people are reluctant to admit that they act to please their emotions. So they deceive themselves for years by trying to belong to whichever type they think is the "best." Of course, there is no best; each has its faults and each has its good points.

The advantage of the signs of the Zodiac is that they simplify classification. Not only that, but your date of birth is personal—it is unarguably yours. What better way to know yourself than by going back as far as possible to the very moment of your birth? And this is precisely what your horoscope is all about.

What Is a Horoscope?

If you had been able to take a picture of the heavens at the moment of your birth, that photograph would be your horoscope. Lacking such a snapshot, it is still possible to recreate the picture—and this is at the basis of the astrologer's art. In other words, your horoscope is a representation of the skies with the planets in the exact positions they occupied at the time you were born.

This information, of course, is not enough for the astrologer. He has to have a background of significance to put the photograph on. You will get the idea if you imagine two balls—one inside the other. The inner one is transparent. In the center of both is the astrologer, able to look up, down and around in all directions. The outer sphere is the Zodiac which is divided into twelve approximately equal segments, like the segments of an orange. The inner ball is our photograph. It is transparent except for the images of the planets. Looking out from the center, the astrologer sees the planets in various segments of the Zodiac. These twelve segments are known as the signs or houses.

The position of the planets when each of us is born is always different. So the photograph is always different. But the Zodiac and its signs are fixed.

Now, where in all this are you, the subject of the horoscope?

You, or your character, is largely determined by the sign the sun is in. So that is where the astrologer looks first in your horoscope.

There are twelve signs in the Zodiac and the sun spends approximately one month in each. As the sun's motion is almost perfectly regular, the astrologers have been able to fix the dates governing each sign. There are not many people who do not know which sign of the Zodiac they were born under or who have not been amazed at some time or other at the accuracy of the description of their own character. Here are the twelve signs, the ancient zodiacal symbol, and their dates for the year 1987.*

ARIES	Ram	March 20–April 20
TAURUS	Bull	April 20–May 21
GEMINI	Twins	May 21–June 21
CANCER	Crab	June 21–July 23
LEO	Lion	July 23–August 23
VIRGO	Virgin	August 23–September 23
LIBRA	Scales	September 23–October 23
SCORPIO	Scorpion	October 23–November 22
SAGITTARIUS	Archer	November 22–December 22
CAPRICORN	Sea-Goat	December 22–January 20
AQUARIUS	Water-Bearer	January 20–February 18
PISCES	Fish	February 18–March 20

The time of birth—apart from the date—is important in advanced astrology because the planets travel at such great speed that the patterns they form change from minute to minute. For this reason, each person's horoscope is his and his alone. Further on we will see that the practicing astrologer has ways of determining and reading these minute time changes which dictate the finger character differences in us all.

However, it is still possible to draw significant conclusions and make meaningful predictions based simply on the sign of the Zodiac a person is born under. In a horoscope, the signs do not necessarily correspond with the divisions of the houses. It could be that a house begins half way across a sign. It is the interpretation of such combinations of different influences that distinguishes the professional astrologer from the student and the follower.

However, to gain a workable understanding of astrology, it is not necessary to go into great detail. In fact, the beginner is likely to find himself confused if he attempts to absorb too much too quickly. It should be remembered that this is a science and to become proficient at it, and especially to grasp the tremendous scope of possibilities in man and his affairs and direct them into a worthwhile reading, takes a great deal of study and experience.

*These dates are fluid and change with the motion of the Earth from year to year.

If you do intend to pursue it seriously you will have to learn to figure the exact moment of birth against the degrees of longitude and latitude of the planets at that precise time. This involves adapting local time to Greenwich Mean Time (G.M.T.), reference to tables of houses to establish the Ascendant, as well as making calculations from Ephemeris—the tables of the planets' positions.

After reading this introduction, try drawing up a rough horoscope to get the "feel" of reading some elementary characteristics and natal influences.

Draw a circle with twelve equal segments. Write in counterclockwise the names of the signs—Aries, Taurus, Gemini etc.—one for each segment. Look up an ephemeris for the year of the person's birth and note down the sign each planet was in on the birthday. Do not worry about the number of degrees (although if a planet is on the edge of a sign its position obviously should be considered). Write the name of the planet in the segment/sign on your chart. Write the number 1 in the sign where the sun is. This is the first house. Number the rest of the houses, counterclockwise till you finish at 12. Now you can investigate the probable basic expectation of experience of the person concerned. This is done first of all by seeing what planet or planets is/are in what sign and house. (See also page 72.)

The 12 houses control these functions:

1st.	Individuality, body appearance, general outlook on life	(Personality house)
2nd.	Finance, business	(Money house)
3rd.	Relatives, education, correspondence	(Relatives house)
4th.	Family, neighbors	(Home house)
5th.	Pleasure, children, attempts, entertainment	(Pleasure house)
6th.	Health, employees	(Health house)
7th.	Marriage, partnerships	(Marriage house)
8th.	Death, secret deals, difficulties	(Death house)
9th.	Travel, intellectual affairs	(Travel house)
10th.	Ambition, social standing	(Business and Honor house)
11th.	Friendship, social life, luck	(Friends house)
12th.	Troubles, illness, loss	(Trouble house)

The characteristics of the planets modify the influence of the Sun according to their natures and strengths.

Sun: Source of life. Basic temperament according to sun sign. The will.
Moon: Superficial nature. Moods. Changeable. Adaptive. Mother.
Mercury: Communication. Intellect. Reasoning power. Curiosity. Short travels.
Venus: Love. Delight. Art. Beautiful possessions.
Mars: Energy. Initiative. War. Anger. Destruction. Impulse.
Jupiter: Good. Generous. Expansive. Opportunities. Protection.
Saturn: Jupiter's opposite. Contraction. Servant. Delay. Hardwork. Cold. Privation. Research. Lasting rewards after long struggle.
Uranus: Fashion. Electricity. Revolution. Sudden changes. Modern science.
Neptune: Sensationalism. Mass emotion. Devastation. Delusion.
Pluto: Creates and destroys. Lust for power. Strong obsessions.

Superimpose the characteristics of the planets on the functions of the house in which they appear. Express the result through the character of the birth (sun) sign, and you will get the basic idea of how astrology works.

Of course, many other considerations have been taken into account in producing the carefully worked out predictions in this book: The aspects of the planets to each other; their strength according to position and sign; whether they are in a house of exaltation or decline; whether they are natural enemies or not; whether a planet occupies his own sign; the position of a planet in relation to its own house or sign; whether the planet is male, female or neuter; whether the sign is a fire, earth, water or air sign. These are only a few of the colors on the astrologer's pallet which he must mix with the inspiration of the artist and the accuracy of the mathematician.

The Problem of Love

Love, of course, is never a problem. The problem lies in recognizing the difference between infatuation, emotion, sex and, sometimes, the downright deceit of the other person. Mankind, with its record of broken marriages, despair and disillusionment, is obviously not very good at making these distinctions.

Can astrology help?

Yes. In the same way that advance knowledge can usually help in any human situation. And there is probably no situation as human, as poignant, as pathetic and universal, as the failure of man's love.

Love, of course, is not just between man and woman. It involves love of children, parents, home and so on. But the big problems usually involve the choice of partner.

Astrology has established degrees of compatibility that exist between people born under the various signs of the Zodiac. Because people are individuals, there are numerous variations and modifications and the astrologer, when approached on mate and marriage matters makes allowances for them. But the fact remains that some groups of people are suited for each other and some are not and astrology has expressed this in terms of characteristics which all can study and use as a personal guide.

No matter how much enjoyment and pleasure we find in the different aspects of each other's character, if it is not an overall compatibility, the chances of our finding fulfillment or enduring happiness in each other are pretty hopeless. And astrology can help us to find someone compatible.

History of Astrology

The origins of astrology have been lost far back in history, but we do know that reference is made to it as far back as the first written records of the human race. It is not hard to see why. Even in primitive times, people must have looked for an explanation for the various happenings in their lives. They must have wanted to know why people were different from one to another. And in their search they turned to the regular movements of the sun, moon and stars to see if they could provide an answer.

It is interesting to note that as soon as man learned to use his tools in any type of design, or his mind in any kind of calculation, he turned his attention to the heavens. Ancient cave dwellings reveal dim crescents and circles representative of the sun and moon, rulers of day and night. Mesopotamia and the civilization of Chaldea, in itself the foundation of those of Babylonia and Assyria, show a complete picture of astronomical observation and well-developed astrological interpretation.

Humanity has a natural instinct for order. The study of anthropology reveals that primitive people—even as far back as prehistoric times—were striving to achieve a certain order in their lives. They tried to organize the apparent chaos of the universe. They had the desire to attach meaning to things. This demand for order has persisted throughout the history of man. So that observing the regularity of the heavenly bodies made it logical that primitive peoples should turn heavenwards in their search for an understanding of the world in which they found themselves so random and alone.

And they did find a significance in the movements of the stars. Shepherds tending their flocks, for instance, observed that when the cluster of stars now known as the constellation Aries was in sight, it was the time of fertility and they associated it with the Ram. And they noticed that the growth of plants and plant life corresponded with different phases of the moon, so that certain times were favorable for the planting of crops, and other times were not. In this way, there grew up a tradition of seasons and causes connected with the passage of the sun through the twelve signs of the Zodiac.

Astrology was valued so highly that the king was kept informed of the daily and monthly changes in the heavenly bodies, and the results of astrological studies regarding events of the future. Head astrologers were clearly men of great rank and position, and the office was said to be a hereditary one.

Omens were taken, not only from eclipses and conjunctions of the moon or sun with one of the planets, but also from storms and earthquakes. In the eastern civilizations, particularly, the reverence inspired by astrology appears to have remained unbroken since the very earliest days. In ancient China, astrology, astronomy and religion went hand in hand. The astrologer, who was also an astronomer, was part of the official government service and had his own corner in the Imperial Palace. The duties of the Imperial astrologer, whose office was one of the most important in the land, were clearly defined, as this extract from early records shows:

"This exalted gentleman must concern himself with the stars in the heavens, keeping a record of the changes and movements of the Planets, the Sun and the Moon, in order to examine the movements of the terrestial world with the object of prognosticating good and bad fortune. He divides the territories of the nine regions of the empire in accordance with their dependence on particular celestial bodies. All the fiefs and principalities are connected with the stars and from this their prosperity or misfortune should be ascertained. He makes prognostications according to the twelve years of the Jupiter cycle of good and evil of the terrestial world. From the colors of the five kinds of clouds, he determines the coming of floods or droughts, abundance or famine. From the twelve winds, he draws conclusions about the state of harmony of heaven and earth, and takes note of good and bad signs that result from their accord or disaccord. In general, he concerns himself with five kinds of phenomena so as to warn the Emperor to come to the aid of the government and to allow for variations in the ceremonies according to their circumstances."

The Chinese were also keen observers of the fixed stars, giving them such unusual names as Ghost Vehicle, Sun of Imperial Concubine, Imperial Prince, Pivot of Heaven, Twinkling Brilliance or Weaving Girl. But, great astrologers though they may have been, the Chinese lacked one aspect of mathematics that the Greeks applied to astrology—deductive geometry. Deductive geometry was the basis of much classical astrology in and after the time of the Greeks, and this explains the different methods of prognostication used in the East and West.

Down through the ages the astrologer's art has depended, not so much on the uncovering of new facts, though this is important, as on the interpretation of the facts already known. This is the essence of his skill. Obviously one cannot always tell how people will react (and this underlines the very important difference between astrology and predestination which will be discussed later on) but one can be prepared, be forewarned, to know what to expect.

But why should the signs of the zodiac have any effect at all on the formation of human character? It is easy to see why people thought they did, and even now we constantly use astrological expressions in our everyday speech. The thoughts of "lucky star," "ill-fated," "star-crossed," "mooning around," are interwoven into the very structure of our language.

In the same way that the earth has been created by influences from outside, there remains an indisputable togetherness in the working of the universe. The world, after all, is a coherent structure, for if it were not, it would be quite without order and we would never know what to expect. A dog could turn into an apple, or an elephant sprout wings and fly at any moment without so much as a by your leave. But nature, as we know, functions according to laws, not whims, and the laws of nature are certainly not subject to capricious exceptions.

This means that no part of the universe is ever arbitrarily cut off from any other part. Everything is therefore to some extent linked with everything else. The moon draws an imperceptible tide on every puddle; tiny and trivial events can be effected by outside forces (such as the fall of a feather by the faintest puff of wind). And so it is fair to think that the local events at any moment reflect to a very small extent the evolution of the world as a whole.

From this principle follows the possibility of divination, and also knowledge of events at a distance, provided one's mind were always as perfectly undisturbed, as ideally smooth, as a mirror or unruffled lake. Provided, in other words, that one did not confuse the picture with hopes, guesses, and expectations. When people try to foretell the future by cards or crystal ball gazing they find it much easier to confuse the picture with expectations than to reflect it clearly.

But the present does contain a good deal of the future to which it leads—not all, but a good deal. The diver halfway between bridge and water is going to make a splash; the train whizzing towards the station will pass through it unless interfered with; the burglar breaking a pane of glass has exposed himself to the possibility of a prison sentence. Yet this is not a doctrine of determinism, as was emphasized earlier. Clearly, there are forces already at work in the present, and any one of them could alter the situation in some way. Equally, a change of decision could alter the whole situation as well. So the future depends, not on an irresistible force, but on a small act of free will.

An individual's age, physique, and position on the earth's surface are remote consequences of his birth. Birth counts as the original cause for all that happens subsequently. The horoscope, in this case, means "this person represents the further evolution of the state of the universe pictured in this chart." Such a chart can apply equally to man or woman, dog, ship or even limited company.

If the evolution of an idea, or of a person, is to be understood as a totality, it must continue to evolve from its own beginnings, which is to say, in the terms in which it began. The brown-eyed person will be faithful to brown eyes all his life; the traitor is being faithful to some complex of ideas which has long been evolving in him; and the person born at sunset will always express, as he evolves, the psychological implications or analogies of the moment when the sun sinks out of sight.

This is the doctrine that an idea must continue to evolve in terms of its origin. It is a completely non-materialist doctrine, though it never fails to apply to material objects. And it implies, too, that the individual will continue to evolve in terms of his moment of origin, and therefore possibly of the sign of the Zodiac rising on the eastern horizon at his birth. It also implies that the signs of the Zodiac themselves will evolve in the collective mind of the human race in the same terms that they were first devised and not in the terms in which modern astrologers consciously think they ought to work.

For the human race, like every other kind of animal, has a collective mind, as Professor Jung discovered in his investigation of dreams. If no such collective mind existed, no infant could ever learn anything, for communication would be impossible. Furthermore, it is absurd to suggest that the conscious mind could be older than the "unconscious," for an infant's nervous system functions correctly before it has discovered the difference between "myself" and "something else" or discovered what eyes and hands are for. Indeed, the involuntary muscles function correctly even before birth, and will never be under conscious control. They are part of what we call the "unconscious" which is not really "unconscious" at all. To the contrary, it is totally aware of itself and everything else; it is merely that part of the mind that cannot be controlled by conscious effort.

And human experience, though it varies in detail with every individual, is basically the same for each one of us, consisting of sky and earth, day and night, waking and sleeping, man and woman, birth and death. So there is bound to be in the mind of the human race a very large number of inescapable ideas, which are called our natural archetypes.

There are also, however, artificial or cultural archetypes which are not universal or applicable to everyone, but are nevertheless inescapable within the limits of a given culture. Examples of these are the cross in Christianity, and the notion of "escape from the wheel of rebirth" in India. There was a time when these ideas did not exist. And there was a time, too, when the scheme of the Zodiac did not exist. One would not expect the Zodiac to have any influence on remote and primitive peoples, for example, who have never heard of it. If the Zodiac is only an archetype, their horoscopes probably would not work and it would not matter which sign they were born under.

But where the Zodiac is known, and the idea of it has become worked into the collective mind, then there it could well appear to have an influence, even if it has no physical existence. For ideas do not have a physical existence, anyway. No physical basis has yet been discovered for the telepathy that controls an anthill; young swallows migrate before, not after, their parents; and the weaverbird builds its intricate nest without being taught. Materialists suppose, but cannot prove, that "instinct" (as it is called, for no one knows how it works) is controlled by nucleic acid in the chromosomes. This is not a genuine explanation, though, for it only pushes the mystery one stage further back.

Does this mean, then, that the human race, in whose civilization the idea of the twelve signs of the Zodiac has long been embedded, is divided into only twelve types? Can we honestly believe that it is really as simple as that? If so, there must be pretty wide ranges of variation within each type. And if, to explain the variation, we call in heredity and environment, experiences in early childhood, the thyroid and other glands, and also the four functions of the mind mentioned at the beginning of this introduction, and extroversion and introversion, then one begins to wonder if the original classification was worth making at all. No sensible person believes that his favorite system explains everything. But even so, he will not find it much use at all if it does not even save him the trouble of bothering with the others.

Under the Jungian system, everyone has not only a dominant or principal function, but also a secondary or subsidiary one, so that the four can be arranged in order of potency. In the intuitive type, sensation is always the most inefficient function, but the second most inefficient function can be either thinking (which tends to make original thinkers such as Jung himself) or else feeling (which tends to make artistic people). Therefore, allowing for introversion and extroversion, there are at least four kinds of intuitive types, and sixteen types in all. Furthermore, one can see how the sixteen types merge into each other, so that there are no unrealistic or unconvincingly rigid divisions.

In the same way, if we were to put every person under only one sign of the Zodiac, the system becomes too rigid and unlike life. Besides, it was never intended to be used like that. It may be convenient to have only twelve types, but we know that in practice there is every possible gradation between aggressiveness and timidity, or between conscientiousness and laziness. How, then, do we account for this?

The Tyrant and the Saint

Just as the thinking type of man is also influenced to some extent by sensation and intuition, but not very much by emotion, so a person born under Leo can be influenced to some extent by one or two (but not more) of the other signs. For instance, famous persons born under the sign of Gemini include Henry VIII, whom nothing and no-one could have induced to abdicate, and Edward VIII, who did just that. Obviously, then, the sign Gemini does not fully explain the complete character of either of them.

Again, under the opposite sign, Sagittarius, were both Stalin, who was totally consumed with the notion of power, and Charles V, who freely gave up an empire because he preferred to go into a monastery. And we find under Scorpio, many uncompromising characters such as Luther, de Gaulle, Indira Gandhi and Montgomery, but also Petain, a successful commander whose name later became synonymous with collaboration.

A single sign is therefore obviously inadequate to explain the differences between people; it can only explain resemblances, such as the combativeness of the Scorpio group, or the far-reaching devotion of Charles V and Stalin to their respective ideals—the Christian heaven and the Communist utopia.

But very few people are born under one sign only. As well as the month of birth, as was mentioned earlier, the day matters, and, even more, the hour, which ought, if possible, to be noted to the nearest minute. Without this, it is impossible to have an actual horoscope, for the word horoscope means literally, "a consideration of the hour."

The month of birth tells you only which sign of the Zodiac was occupied by the sun. The day and hour tell you what sign was occupied by the moon. And the minute tells you which sign was rising on the eastern horizon. This is called the Ascendant, and it is supposed to be the most important thing in the whole horoscope.

If you were born at midnight, the sun is then in an important position, although invisible. But at one o'clock in the morning the sun is not important, so the moment of birth will not matter much. The important thing then will be the Ascendant, and possibly one or two of the planets. At a given day and hour, say, dawn on January 1st, or 9:00 p.m. on the longest day, the Ascendant will always be the same at any given place. But the moon and planets alter from day to day, at different speeds and have to be looked up in an astronomical table.

The sun is said to signify one's heart, that is to say, one's deepest desires and inmost nature. This is quite different from the moon, which, as we have seen, signifies one's superficial way of behaving. When the ancient Romans referred to the Emperor Augustus as a Capricornian, they meant that he had the moon in Capricorn; they did not pay much attention to the sun, although he was born at sunrise. Or, to take another example, a modern astrologer would call Disraeli a Scorpion because he had Scorpio rising, but most people would call him Sagittarian because he had the sun there. The Romans would have called him Leo because his moon was in Leo.

The sun, as has already been pointed out, is important if one is born near sunrise, sunset, noon or midnight, but is otherwise not reckoned as the principal influence. So if one does not seem to fit one's birth month, it is always worthwhile reading the other signs, for one may have been born at a time when any of them were rising or occupied by the moon. It also seems to be the case that the influence of the sun develops as life goes on, so that the month of birth is easier to guess in people over the age of forty. The young are supposed to be influenced mainly by their Ascendant which characterizes the body and physical personality as a whole.

It should be clearly understood that it is nonsense to assume that all people born at a certain time will exhibit the same characteristics, or that they will even behave in the same manner. It is quite obvious that, from the very moment of its birth, a child is subject to the effects of its environment, and that this in turn will influence its character and heritage to a decisive extent. Also to be taken into account are education and economic conditions, which play a very important part in the formation of one's character as well.

However, it is clearly established that people born under one sign of the Zodiac do have certain basic traits in their character which are different from those born under other signs. It is obvious to every thinking person that certain events produce different reactions in various people. For instance, if a man slips on a banana skin and falls heavily on the pavement, one passer-by may laugh and find this extremely amusing, while another may just walk on, thinking: "What a fool falling down like that. He should look where he is going." A third might also walk away saying to himself: "It's none of my business—I'm glad it wasn't me." A fourth might walk past and think: "I'm sorry for that man, but I haven't the time to be bothered with helping him." And a fifth might stop to help the fallen man to his feet, comfort him and take him home. Here is just one event which could produce entirely different reactions in different people. And, obviously, there are many more. One that comes to mind immediately is the violently opposed views to events such as wars, industrial strikes, and so on. The fact that people have different attitudes to the same event is simply another way of saying that they have different characters. And this is not something that can be put down to background, for people of the same race, religion, or class, very often express quite different reactions to happenings or events. Similarly, it is often the case that members of the same family, where there is clearly uniform background of economic and social standing, education, race and religion, often argue bitterly among themselves over political and social issues.

People have, in general, certain character traits and qualities which, according to their environment, develop in either a positive or a negative manner. Therefore, selfishness (inherent selfishness, that is) might emerge as unselfishness; kindness and consideration as cruelty and lack of consideration towards others. In the same way, a naturally constructive person, may, through frustration, become destructive, and so on. The latent characteristics with which people are born can, therefore, through environment and good or bad training, become something that would appear to be its opposite, and so give the lie to the astrologer's description of their character. But this is not the case. The true character is still there, but it is buried deep beneath these external superficialities.

Careful study of the character traits of different signs can be immeasurable help, and can render beneficial service to the intelligent person. Undoubtedly, the reader will already have discovered that, while he is able to get on very well with some people, he just "cannot stand" others. The causes sometimes seem inexplicable. At times there is intense dislike, at other times immediate sympathy. And there is, too, the phenomenon of love at first sight, which is also apparently inexplicable. People appear to be either sympathetic or unsympathetic towards each other for no apparent reason.

Now if we look at this in the light of the Zodiac, we find that people born under different signs are either compatible or incompatible with each other. In other words, there are good and bad interrelating factors among the various signs. This does not, of course, mean that humanity can be divided into groups of hostile camps. It would be quite wrong to be hostile or indifferent toward people who happen to be born under an incompatible sign. There is no reason why everybody should not, or cannot, learn to control and adjust their feelings and actions, especially after they are aware of the positive qualities of other people by studying their character analyses, among other things.

Every person born under a certain sign has both positive and negative qualities, which are developed more or less according to his free will. Nobody is entirely good or entirely bad, and it is up to each one of us to learn to control himself on the one hand, and at the same time to endeavor to learn about himself and others.

It cannot be repeated often enough that, though the intrinsic nature of man and his basic character traits are born in him, nevertheless it is his own free will that determines whether he will make really good use of his talents and abilities—whether, in other words, he will overcome his vices or allow them to rule him. Most of us are born with at least a streak of laziness, irritability, or some other fault in our nature, and it is up to each one of us to see that we exert sufficient willpower to control our failings so that they do not harm ourselves or others.

Astrology can reveal our inclinations and tendencies. Our weaknesses should not be viewed as shortcomings that are impossible to change. The horoscope of a man may show him to have criminal leanings, for instance, but this does not mean he will definitely become a criminal.

The ordinary man usually finds it difficult to know himself. He is often bewildered. Astrology can frequently tell him more about himself than the different schools of psychology are able to do. Knowing his failings and shortcomings, he will do his best to overcome them, and make himself a better and more useful member of society and a helpmate to his family and friends. It can also save him a great deal of unhappiness and remorse.

And yet it may seem absurd that an ancient philosophy, something that is known as a "pseudo-science," could be a prop to the men and women of the twentieth century. But below the materialistic surface of modern life, there are hidden streams of feeling and thought. Symbology is reappearing as a study worthy of the scholar; the psychosomatic factor in illness has passed from the writings of the crank to those of the specialist; spiritual healing in all its forms is no longer a pious hope but an accepted phenomenon. And it is into this context that we consider astrology, in the sense that it is an analysis of human types.

Astrology and medicine had a long journey together, and only parted company a couple of centuries ago. There still remain in medical language such astrological terms as "saturnine," "choleric," and "mercurial," used in the diagnosis of physical tendencies. The herbalist, for long the handyman of the medical profession, has been dominated by astrology since the days of the Greeks. Certain herbs traditionally respond to certain planetary influences, and diseases must therefore be treated to ensure harmony between the medicine and the disease.

No one expects the most eccentric of modern doctors to go back to the practices of his predecessors. We have come a long way since the time when phases of the moon were studied in illness. Those days were a medical nightmare, with epidemics that were beyond control, and an explanation of the Black Death sought in conjunction with the planets. Nowadays, astrological diagnosis of disease has literally no parallel in modern life. And yet, age-old symbols of types and of the vulnerability of, say, the Saturnian to chronic diseases or the choleric to apoplexy and blood pressure and so on, are still applicable.

But the stars are expected to foretell and not only to diagnose. The astrological forecaster has a counterpart on a highly conventional level in the shape of the weather prophet, racing tipster and stock market forecaster, to name just three examples. All in their own way are aiming at the same result. They attempt to look a little further into the pattern of life and also try to determine future patterns accurately.

Astrological forecasting has been remarkably accurate, but often it is wide of the mark. The brave man who cares to predict world events takes dangerous chances. Individual forecasting is less clear cut; it can be a help or a disillusionment. Then welcome to the nagging question: if it is possible to foreknow, is it right to foretell? A complex point of ethics on which it is hard to pronounce judgment. The doctor faces the same dilemma if he finds that symptoms of a mortal disease are present in his patient and that he can only prognosticate a steady decline. How much to tell an individual in a crisis is a problem that has perplexed many distinguished scholars. Honest and conscientious astrologers in this modern world, where so many people are seeking guidance, face the same problem.

The ancient cults, the symbols of old religions, are eclipsed for the moment. They may return with their old force within a decade or two. But at present the outlook is dark. Human beings badly need assurance, as they did in the past, that all is not chaos. Somewhere, somehow, there is a pattern that must be worked out. As to the why and wherefore, the astrologer is not expected to give judgment. He is just someone who, by dint of talent and training, can gaze into the future.

Five hundred years ago it was customary to call in a learned man who was an astrologer who was probably also a doctor and a philosopher. By his knowledge of astrology, his study of planetary influences, he felt himself qualified to guide those in distress. The world has moved forward at a fantastic rate since then, and in this twentieth century speed has been the keyword everywhere. Tensions have increased, the spur of ambition has been applied indiscriminately. People are uncertain of themselves. At first sight it seems fantastic in the light of modern thinking that they turn to the most ancient of all studies, and get someone to calculate a horoscope for them. But is it *really* so fantastic if you take a second look? For astrology is concerned with tomorrow, with survival. And in a world such as ours, those two things are the keywords of the time in which we live.

HOW TO USE
THESE PREDICTIONS

A person reading the predictions in this book should understand that they are produced from the daily position of the planets for a group of people and are not, of course, individually specialized. To get the full benefit of them he should relate the predictions to his own character and circumstances, co-ordinate them, and draw his own conclusions from them.

If he is a serious observer of his own life he should find a definite pattern emerge that will be a helpful and reliable guide.

The point is that we always retain our free will. The stars indicate certain directional tendencies but we are not compelled to follow. We can do or not do, and wisdom must make the choice.

We all have our good and bad days. Sometimes they extend into cycles of weeks. It is therefore advisable to study daily predictions in a span ranging from the day before to several days ahead; also to re-read the monthly predictions for similar cycles.

Daily predictions should be taken very generally. The word "difficult" does not necessarily indicate a whole day of obstruction or inconvenience. It is a warning to you to be cautious. Your caution will often see you around the difficulty before you are involved. This is the correct use of astrology.

In another section, detailed information is given about the influence of the moon as it passes through the various signs of the Zodiac. It includes instructions on how to use the Moon Tables. This information should be used in conjunction with the daily forecasts to give a fuller picture of the astrological trends.

THE MOON

Moon is the nearest planet to the earth. It exerts more observable influence on us from day to day than any other planet. The effect is very personal, very intimate, and if we are not aware of how it works it can make us quite unstable in our ideas. And the annoying thing is that at these times we often see our own instability but can do nothing about it. A knowledge of what can be expected may help considerably. We can then be prepared to stand strong against the moon's negative influences and use its positive ones to help us to get ahead. Who has not heard of going with the tide?

Moon reflects, has no light of its own. It reflects the sun—the life giver—in the form of vital movement. Moon controls the tides, the blood rhythm, the movement of sap in trees and plants. Its nature is inconstancy and change so it signifies our moods, our superficial behavior—walking, talking and especially thinking. Being a true reflector of other forces, moon is cold, watery like the surface of a still lake, brilliant and scintillating at times, but easily ruffled and disturbed by the winds of change.

The moon takes 28 ½ days to circle the earth and the Zodiac. It spends just over 2 ¼ days in each sign. During that time it reflects the qualities, energies and characteristics of the sign and, to a degree, the planet which rules the sign. While the moon in its transit occupies a sign incompatible with our own birth sign, we can expect to feel a vague uneasiness, perhaps a touch of irritableness. We should not be discouraged nor let the feeling get us down, or, worse still, allow ourselves to take the discomfort out on others. Try to remember that the moon has to change signs within 55 hours and, provided you are not physically ill, your mood will probably change with it. It is amazing how frequently depression lifts with the shift in the moon's position. And, of course, when the moon is transiting a sign compatible or sympathetic to yours you will probably feel some sort of stimulation or just plain happy to be alive.

In the horoscope, the moon is such a powerful indicator that competent astrologers often use the sign it occupied at birth as the birth sign of the person. This is done particularly when the sun is on the cusp, or edge, of two signs. Most experienced astrologers, however, coordinate both sun and moon signs by reading and confirming from one to the other and secure a far more accurate and personalized analysis.

For these reasons, the moon tables which follow this section (see pages 28–35) are of great importance to the individual. They show the days and the exact times the moon will enter each sign of the Zodiac for the year. Remember, you have to adjust the indicated times to local time. The corrections, already calculated for most of the main cities, are at the beginning of the tables. What follows now is a guide to the influences that will be reflected to the earth by the moon while it transits each of the twelve signs. The influence is at its peak about 26 hours after the moon enters a sign.

MOON IN ARIES

This is a time for action, for reaching out beyond the usual self-imposed limitations and faint-hearted cautions. If you have plans in your head or on your desk, put them into practice. New ventures, applications, new jobs, new starts of any kind—all have a good chance of success. This is the period when original and dynamic impulses are being reflected onto the earth. The energies are extremely vital and favor the pursuit of pleasure and adventure in practically every form. Sick people should feel an improvement. Those who are well will probably find themselves exuding confidence and optimism. People fond of physical exercise should find their bodies growing with tone and well-being. Boldness, strength, determination should characterize most of your activities with a readiness to face up to old challenges. Yesterday's problems may seem petty and exaggerated—so deal with them. Strike out alone. Self-reliance will attract others to you. This is a good time for making friends. Business and marriage partners are more likely to be impressed with the man and woman of action. Opposition will be overcome or thrown aside with much less effort than usual. CAUTION: Be dominant but not domineering.

MOON IN TAURUS

The spontaneous, action-packed person of yesterday gives way to the cautious, diligent, hardworking "thinker." In this period ideas will probably be concentrated on ways of improving finances. A great deal of time may be spent figuring out and going over schemes and plans. It is the right time to be careful with detail. People will find themselves working longer than usual at their desks. Or devoting more time to serious thought about the future. A strong desire to put order into business and financial arrangements may cause extra work. Loved ones may complain of being neglected and may fail to appreciate that your efforts are for their ultimate benefit. Your desire for system may extend to criticism of arrangements in the home and lead to minor upsets. Health may be affected through overwork. Try to secure a reasonable amount of rest and relaxation, although the tendency will be to "keep going" despite good advice. Work done conscientiously in this period should result in a solid contribution to your future security. CAUTION: Try not to be as serious with people as the work you are engaged in.

MOON IN GEMINI

The humdrum of routine and too much work should suddenly end. You are likely to find yourself in an expansive, quicksilver world of change and self-expression. Urges to write, to paint, to experience the freedom of some sort of artistic outpouring, may be very strong. Take full advantage of them. You may find yourself finishing something you began and put aside long ago. Or embarking on something new which could easily be prompted by a chance meeting, a new acquaintance, or even an advertisement. There may be a yearning for a change of scenery, the feeling to visit another country (not too far away), or at least to get away for a few days. This may result in short, quick journeys. Or, if you are planning a single visit, there may be some unexpected changes or detours on the way. Familiar activities will seem to give little satisfaction unless they contain a fresh element of excitement or expectation. The inclination will be towards untried pursuits, particularly those that allow you to express your inner nature. The accent is on new faces, new places. CAUTION: Do not be too quick to commit yourself emotionally.

MOON IN CANCER

Feelings of uncertainty and vague insecurity are likely to cause problems while the moon is in Cancer. Thoughts may turn frequently to the warmth of the home and the comfort of loved ones. Nostalgic impulses could cause you to bring out old photographs and letters and reflect on the days when your life seemed to be much more rewarding and less demanding. The love and understanding of parents and family may be important, and, if it is not forthcoming you may have to fight against a bit of self-pity. The cordiality of friends and the thought of good times with them that are sure to be repeated will help to restore you to a happier frame of mind. The feeling to be alone may follow minor setbacks or rebuffs at this time, but solitude is unlikely to help. Better to get on the telephone or visit someone. This period often causes peculiar dreams and upsurges of imaginative thinking which can be very helpful to authors of occult and mystical works. Preoccupation with the more personal world of simple human needs should overshadow any material strivings. CAUTION: Do not spend too much time thinking—seek the company of loved ones or close friends.

MOON IN LEO

New horizons of exciting and rather extravagant activity open up. This is the time for exhilarating entertainment, glamorous and lavish parties, and expensive shopping sprees. Any merrymaking that relies upon your generosity as a host has every chance of being a spectacular success. You should find yourself right in the center of the fun, either as the life of the party or simply as a person whom happy people like to be with. Romance thrives in this heady atmosphere and friendships are likely to explode unexpectedly into serious attachments. Children and younger people should be attracted to you and you may find yourself organizing a picnic or a visit to a fun-fair, the cinema or the seaside. The sunny company and vitality of youthful companions should help you to find some unsuspected energy. In career, you could find an opening for promotion or advancement. This should be the time to make a direct approach. The period favors those engaged in original research. CAUTION: Bask in popularity but not in flattery.

MOON IN VIRGO

Off comes the party cap and out steps the busy, practical worker. He wants to get his personal affairs straight, to rearrange them, if necessary, for more efficiency, so he will have more time for more work. He clears up his correspondence, pays outstanding bills, makes numerous phone calls. He is likely to make inquiries, or sign up for some new insurance and put money into gilt-edged investment. Thoughts probably revolve around the need for future security—to tie up loose ends and clear the decks. There may be a tendency to be "finicky," to interfere in the routine of others, particularly friends and family members. The motive may be a genuine desire to help with suggestions for updating or streamlining their affairs, but these will probably not be welcomed. Sympathy may be felt for less fortunate sections of the community and a flurry of some sort of voluntary service is likely. This may be accompanied by strong feelings of responsibility on several fronts and health may suffer from extra efforts made. CAUTION: Everyone may not want your help or advice.

MOON IN LIBRA

These are days of harmony and agreement and you should find yourself at peace with most others. Relationships tend to be smooth and sweet-flowing. Friends may become closer and bonds deepen in mutual understanding. Hopes will be shared. Progress by cooperation could be the secret of success in every sphere. In business, established partnerships may flourish and new ones get off to a good start. Acquaintances could discover similar interests that lead to congenial discussions and rewarding exchanges of some sort. Love, as a unifying force, reaches its optimum. Marriage partners should find accord. Those who wed at this time face the prospect of a happy union. Cooperation and tolerance are felt to be stronger than dissension and impatience. The argumentative are not quite so loud in their bellowings, nor as inflexible in their attitudes. In the home, there should be a greater recognition of the other point of view and a readiness to put the wishes of the group before selfish insistence. This is a favorable time to join an art group. CAUTION: Do not be too independent—let others help you if they want to.

MOON IN SCORPIO

Driving impulses to make money and to economize are likely to cause upsets all round. No area of expenditure is likely to be spared the axe, including the household budget. This is a time when the desire to cut down on extravagance can become near fanatical. Care must be exercised to try to keep the aim in reasonable perspective. Others may not feel the same urgent need to save and may retaliate. There is a danger that possessions of sentimental value will be sold to realize cash for investment. Buying and selling of stock for quick profit is also likely. The attention may turn to having a good clean up round the home and at the office. Neglected jobs could suddenly be done with great bursts of energy. The desire for solitude may intervene. Self-searching thoughts could disturb. The sense of invisible and mysterious energies at work could cause some excitability. The reassurance of loves ones may help. CAUTION: Be kind to the people you love.

MOON IN SAGITTARIUS

These are days when you are likely to be stirred and elevated by discussions and reflections of a religious and philosophical nature. Ideas of far-away places may cause unusual response and excitement. A decision may be made to visit someone overseas, perhaps a person whose influence was important to your earlier character development. There could be a strong resolution to get away from present intellectual patterns, to learn new subjects and to meet more interesting people. The superficial may be rejected in all its forms. An impatience with old ideas and unimaginative contacts could lead to a change of companions and interests. There may be an upsurge of religious feeling and metaphysical inquiry. Even a new insight into the significance of astrology and other occult studies is likely under the curious stimulus of the moon in Sagittarius. Physically, you may express this need for fundamental change by spending more time outdoors: sports, gardening or going for long walks. CAUTION: Try to channel any restlessness into worthwhile study.

MOON IN CAPRICORN

Life in these hours may seem to pivot around the importance of gaining prestige and honor in the career, as well as maintaining a spotless reputation. Ambitious urges may be excessive and could be accompanied by quite acquisitive drives for money. Effort should be directed along strictly ethical lines where there is no possibility of reproach or scandal. All endeavors are likely to be characterized by great earnestness, and an air of authority and purpose which should impress those who are looking for leadership or reliability. The desire to conform to accepted standards may extend to sharp criticism of family members. Frivolity and unconventional actions are unlikely to amuse while the moon is in Capricorn. Moderation and seriousness are the orders of the day. Achievement and recognition in this period could come through community work or organizing for the benefit of some amateur group. CAUTION: Dignity and esteem are not always self-awarded.

MOON IN AQUARIUS

Moon in Aquarius is in the second last sign of the Zodiac where ideas can become disturbingly fine and subtle. The result is often a mental "no-man's land" where imagination cannot be trusted with the same certitude as other times. The dangers for the individual are the extremes of optimism and pessimism. Unless the imgination is held in check, situations are likely to be misread, and rosy conclusions drawn where they do not exist. Consequences for the unwary can be costly in career and business. Best to think twice and not speak or act until you think again. Pessimism can be a cruel self-inflicted penalty for delusion at this time. Between the two extremes are strange areas of self-deception which, for example, can make the selfish person think he is actually being generous. Eerie dreams which resemble the reality and even seem to continue into the waking state are also possible. CAUTION: Look for the fact and not just for the image in your mind.

MOON IN PISCES

Everything seems to come to the surface now. Memory may be crystal clear, throwing up long-forgotten information which could be valuable in the career or business. Flashes of clairvoyance and intuition are possible along with sudden realizations of one's own nature, which may be used for self-improvement. A talent, never before suspected, may be discovered. Qualities not evident before in friends and marriage partners are likely to be noticed. As this is a period in which the truth seems to emerge, the discovery of false characteristics is likely to lead to disenchantment or a shift in attachments. However, where qualities are realized it should lead to happiness and deeper feeling. Surprise solutions could bob up for old problems. There may be a public announcement of the solving of a crime or mystery. People with secrets may find someone has "guessed" correctly. The secrets of the soul or the inner self also tend to reveal themselves. Religious and philosophical groups may make some interesting discoveries. CAUTION: Not a time for activities that depend on secrecy.

MOON TABLES

TIME CORRECTIONS FOR
GREENWICH MOON TABLES

London, Glasgow, Dublin, Dakar..Same time

Vienna, Prague, Rome, Kinshasa, Frankfurt,
Stockholm, Brussels, Amsterdam, Warsaw,
Zurich...Add 1 hour

Bucharest, Istanbul, Beirut, Cairo, Johannesburg,
Athens, Cape Town, Helsinki, Tel Aviv.............................Add 2 hours

Dhahran, Baghdad, Moscow, Leningrad, Nairobi,
Addis Ababa, Zanzibar...Add 3 hours

Delhi, Calcutta, Bombay, Colombo....................................Add 5½ hours

Rangoon...Add 6½ hours

Saigon, Bangkok, Chungking...Add 7 hours

Canton, Manila, Hong Kong, Shanghai, Peking...................Add 8 hours

Tokyo, Pusan, Seoul, Vladivostok, Yokohama....................Add 9 hours

Sydney, Melbourne, Guam, Port Moresby...........................Add 10 hours

Azores, Reykjavik...Deduct 1 hour

Rio de Janeiro, Montevideo, Buenos Aires,
Sao Paulo, Recife...Deduct 3 hours

LaPaz, San Juan, Santiago, Bermuda, Caracas,
Halifax...Deduct 4 hours

New York, Washington, Boston, Detroit, Lima,
Havana, Miami, Bogota..Deduct 5 hours

Mexico, Chicago, New Orleans, Houston...........................Deduct 6 hours

San Francisco, Seattle, Los Angeles, Hollywood,
Ketchikan, Juneau...Deduct 8 hours

Honolulu, Fairbanks, Anchorage, Papeete.........................Deduct 10 hours

1987 MOON TABLES—GREENWICH TIME

JANUARY		FEBRUARY		MARCH	
Day Moon Enters		**Day Moon Enters**		**Day Moon Enters**	
1. Aquar.	0:29 pm	1. Pisces		1. Aries	0:42 pm
2. Aquar.		2. Aries	2:31 am	2. Aries	
3. Pisces	1:22 pm	3. Aries		3. Taurus	6:16 pm
4. Pisces		4. Taurus	9:00 am	4. Taurus	
5. Aries	5:17 pm	5. Taurus		5. Taurus	
6. Aries		6. Gemini	7:33 pm	6. Gemini	3:17 am
7. Aries		7. Gemini		7. Gemini	
8. Taurus	1:31 am	8. Gemini		8. Cancer	3:29 pm
9. Taurus		9. Cancer	8:20 am	9. Cancer	
10. Gemini	0:49 pm	10. Cancer		10. Cancer	
11. Gemini		11. Leo	8:48 pm	11. Leo	4:20 am
12. Gemini		12. Leo		12. Leo	
13. Cancer	1:30 am	13. Leo		13. Virgo	3:15 pm
14. Cancer		14. Virgo	7:55 am	14. Virgo	
15. Leo	2:10 pm	15. Virgo		15. Libra	11:48 pm
16. Leo		16. Libra	5:01 pm	16. Libra	
17. Leo		17. Libra		17. Libra	
18. Virgo	1:35 am	18. Libra		18. Scorpio	5:58 am
19. Virgo		19. Scorpio	0:05 am	19. Scorpio	
20. Libra	11:15 am	20. Scorpio		20. Sagitt.	10:46 am
21. Libra		21. Sagitt.	5:03 am	21. Sagitt.	
22. Scorpio	6:23 pm	22. Sagitt.		22. Capric.	1:52 pm
23. Scorpio		23. Capric.	6:42 am	23. Capric.	
24. Sagitt.	10:07 pm	24. Capric.		24. Aquar.	4:40 pm
25. Sagitt.		25. Aquar.	9:08 am	25. Aquar.	
26. Capric.	11:22 pm	26. Aquar.		26. Pisces	6:59 pm
27. Capric.		27. Pisces	10:13 am	27. Pisces	
28. Aquar.	11:26 pm	28. Pisces		28. Aries	10:26 pm
29. Aquar.				29. Aries	
30. Pisces	11:40 pm			30. Aries	
31. Pisces				31. Taurus	3:38 am

1987 MOON TABLES—GREENWICH TIME

APRIL	MAY	JUNE
Day Moon Enters	**Day Moon Enters**	**Day Moon Enters**
1. Taurus	1. Gemini	1. Leo 3:20 am
2. Gemini Noon	2. Cancer 7:25 am	2. Leo
3. Gemini	3. Cancer	3. Virgo 4:11 pm
4. Cancer 11:30 pm	4. Leo 8:09 pm	4. Virgo
5. Cancer	5. Leo	5. Virgo
6. Cancer	6. Leo	6. Libra 2:21 am
7. Leo 0:36 pm	7. Virgo 8:14 am	7. Libra
8. Leo	8. Virgo	8. Scorpio 8:50 am
9. Virgo 11:41 pm	9. Libra 5:19 pm	9. Scorpio
10. Virgo	10. Libra	10. Sagitt. 11:41 am
11. Virgo	11. Scorpio 10:48 pm	11. Sagitt.
12. Libra 8:11 am	12. Scorpio	12. Capric. 0:10 pm
13. Libra	13. Scorpio	13. Capric.
14. Scorpio 1:24 pm	14. Sagitt. 1:14 am	14. Aquar. 11:50 am
15. Scorpio	15. Sagitt.	15. Aquar.
16. Sagitt. 4:56 pm	16. Capric. 2:41 am	16. Pisces 1:31 pm
17. Sagitt.	17. Capric.	17. Pisces
18. Capric. 7:36 pm	18. Aquar. 3:54 am	18. Aries 5:15 pm
19. Capric.	19. Aquar.	19. Aries
20. Aquar. 10:25 pm	20. Pisces 6:51 am	20. Aries
21. Aquar.	21. Pisces	21. Taurus 0:22 am
22. Aquar.	22. Aries 11:49 am	22. Taurus
23. Pisces 1:33 am	23. Aries	23. Gemini 10:14 am
24. Pisces	24. Taurus 6:56 pm	24. Gemini
25. Aries 6:18 am	25. Taurus	25. Cancer 9:29 pm
26. Aries	26. Taurus	26. Cancer
27. Taurus 0:11 pm	27. Gemini 3:53 am	27. Cancer
28. Taurus	28. Gemini	28. Leo 10:00 am
29. Gemini 8:42 pm	29. Cancer 3:01 pm	29. Leo
30. Gemini	30. Cancer	30. Virgo 10:43 pm
	31. Cancer	

1987 MOON TABLES—GREENWICH TIME

JULY		AUGUST		SEPTEMBER	
Day Moon Enters		**Day Moon Enters**		**Day Moon Enters**	
1. Virgo		1. Libra		1. Sagitt.	
2. Virgo		2. Scorpio	0:49 am	2. Capric.	5:03 pm
3. Libra	10:02 am	3. Scorpio		3. Capric.	
4. Libra		4. Sagitt.	6:35 am	4. Aquar.	6:39 pm
5. Scorpio	5:50 pm	5. Sagitt.		5. Aquar.	
6. Scorpio		6. Capric.	8:41 am	6. Pisces	6:59 pm
7. Sagitt.	9:46 pm	7. Capric.		7. Pisces	
8. Sagitt.		8. Aquar.	8:53 am	8. Aries	8:04 pm
9. Capric.	10:36 pm	9. Aquar.		9. Aries	
10. Capric.		10. Pisces	8:32 am	10. Taurus	11:11 pm
11. Aquar.	10:15 pm	11. Pisces		11. Taurus	
12. Aquar.		12. Aries	9:34 am	12. Taurus	
13. Pisces	10:03 pm	13. Aries		13. Gemini	5:49 am
14. Pisces		14. Taurus	1:39 pm	14. Gemini	
15. Pisces		15. Taurus		15. Cancer	4:37 pm
16. Aries	0:21 am	16. Gemini	9:52 pm	16. Cancer	
17. Aries		17. Gemini		17. Cancer	
18. Taurus	6:09 am	18. Gemini		18. Leo	5:18 am
19. Taurus		19. Cancer	9:25 am	19. Leo	
20. Gemini	3:35 pm	20. Cancer		20. Virgo	5:40 pm
21. Gemini		21. Leo	10:24 pm	21. Virgo	
22. Gemini		22. Leo		22. Virgo	
23. Cancer	3:29 am	23. Leo		23. Libra	3:56 am
24. Cancer		24. Virgo	10:37 am	24. Libra	
25. Leo	4:13 pm	25. Virgo		25. Scorpio	0:22 pm
26. Leo		26. Libra	9:22 pm	26. Scorpio	
27. Leo		27. Libra		27. Sagitt.	6:28 pm
28. Virgo	4:32 am	28. Libra		28. Sagitt.	
29. Virgo		29. Scorpio	6:34 am	29. Capric.	10:57 pm
30. Libra	3:55 pm	30. Scorpio		30. Capric.	
31. Libra		31. Sagitt.	1:04 pm		

1987 MOON TABLES—GREENWICH TIME

OCTOBER	NOVEMBER	DECEMBER
Day Moon Enters	**Day Moon Enters**	**Day Moon Enters**
1. Capric.	1. Pisces	1. Aries
2. Aquar. 2:00 am	2. Aries 1:45 pm	2. Taurus 0:58 am
3. Aquar.	3. Aries	3. Taurus
4. Pisces 4:04 am	4. Taurus 6:02 pm	4. Gemini 8:08 am
5. Pisces	5. Taurus	5. Gemini
6. Aries 5:48 am	6. Taurus	6. Cancer 5:07 pm
7. Aries	7. Gemini 0:10 am	7. Cancer
8. Taurus 9:04 am	8. Gemini	8. Cancer
9. Taurus	9. Cancer 9:17 am	9. Leo 4:37 am
10. Gemini 3:01 pm	10. Cancer	10. Leo
11. Gemini	11. Leo 8:52 pm	11. Virgo 5:27 pm
12. Gemini	12. Leo	12. Virgo
13. Cancer 0:35 am	13. Leo	13. Virgo
14. Cancer	14. Virgo 9:48 am	14. Libra 5:19 am
15. Leo 1:00 pm	15. Virgo	15. Libra
16. Leo	16. Libra 9:09 pm	16. Scorpio 2:34 pm
17. Leo	17. Libra	17. Scorpio
18. Virgo 1:30 am	18. Libra	18. Sagitt. 7:16 pm
19. Virgo	19. Scorpio 4:44 am	19. Sagitt.
20. Libra 0:11 pm	20. Scorpio	20. Capric. 9:18 pm
21. Libra	21. Sagitt. 9:14 am	21. Capric.
22. Scorpio 7:31 pm	22. Sagitt.	22. Aquar. 9:45 pm
23. Scorpio	23. Capric. 11:50 am	23. Aquar.
24. Scorpio	24. Capric.	24. Pisces 10:48 pm
25. Sagitt. 0:47 am	25. Aquar. 1:31 pm	25. Pisces
26. Sagitt.	26. Aquar.	26. Pisces
27. Capric. 4:34 am	27. Pisces 3:51 pm	27. Aries 1:17 am
28. Capric.	28. Pisces	28. Aries
29. Aquar. 7:35 am	29. Aries 7:37 pm	29. Taurus 6:38 am
30. Aquar.	30. Aries	30. Taurus
31. Pisces 10:19 am		31. Gemini 2:29 pm

1987 PHASES OF THE MOON—GREENWICH TIME

New Moon	First Quarter	Full Moon	Last Quarter
(1986)	Jan. 6	Jan. 15	Jan. 22
Jan. 29	Feb. 5	Feb. 13	Feb. 21
Feb. 28	March 7	March 15	March 22
March 29	April 6	April 14	April 20
April 28	May 6	May 13	May 20
May 27	June 4	June 11	June 18
June 26	July 4	July 11	July 17
July 25	Aug. 2	Aug. 9	Aug. 16
Aug. 24	Sept. 1	Sept. 7	Sept. 14
Sept. 23	Sept. 30	Oct. 7	Oct. 14
Oct. 22	Oct. 29	Nov. 5	Nov. 13
Nov. 20	Nov. 28	Dec. 5	Dec. 13
Dec. 20	Dec. 27	(1988)	(1988)

Summer time to be considered where applicable.

1987 PLANTING GUIDE

	Aboveground Crops	Root Crops	Pruning	Weeds-Pests
January	4-8-9-13-14-31	21-22-23-24-27-28	23-24	16-17-18-19-25-26
February	1-4-5-9-10-28	17-18-19-20-23-24	19-20	14-15-21-22-25-26
March	4-5-9-10-31	16-17-18-19-23-27-28	18-19-27-28	21-25
April	1-5-6-12-13-28	14-15-19-20-23-24	15-23-24	17-21-22-25-26
May	2-3-10-11-12-30-31	16-17-20-21-25-26	20-21	14-15-18-19-23
June	6-7-8-9-26-27	13-17-21-22	17	15-19-20-24
July	4-5-6-10-31	11-14-15-18-19-23-24	14-15-23-24	12-13-16-17-21-22
August	1-2-3-6-7-27-28-29-30	10-11-15-19-20-21	10-11-19-20-21	12-13-17-18-22-23
September	3-23-24-25-26-30	11-12-16-17	16-17	9-10-13-14-18-19-20-21-22
October	1-4-5-23-24-27-28	8-9-13-14-21	13-14	7-11-12-16-17-18-19
November	1-24-28	6-9-10-17-18-19	9-10-19	7-8-12-13-14-15
December	2-3-21-25-26-29-30	7-8-14-15-16-17	7-8-17	5-9-10-11-12-13-19

1987 FISHING GUIDE

	Good	Best
January	6-12-15-16-17-18-29	13-14-22
February	11-12-13-14-15-16-21	5-10-28
March	7-12-13-14-15-22-29	16-17-18
April	11-16-17	6-12-13-14-15-20-28
May	6-14-15-27	10-11-12-13-16-20
June	4-10-11-12-14-18	8-9-13-26
July	8-9-12-13-17-25	4-10-11-14
August	8-9-12-16-24	2-6-7-10-11
September	1-4-5-6-8-9-10-14	7-23-30
October	6-7-10-29	4-5-8-9-14-22
November	2-3-4-7-8-13	5-6-20-28
December	4-5-6-13-20-27	2-3-7-8

MOON'S INFLUENCE OVER DAILY AFFAIRS

The Moon makes a complete transit of the Zodiac every 27 days 7 hours and 43 minutes. In making this transit the Moon forms different aspects with the planets and consequently has favorable or unfavorable bearings on affairs and events for persons according to the sign of the Zodiac under which they were born.

Whereas the Sun exclusively represents fire, the Moon rules water. The action of the Moon may be described as fluctuating, variable, absorbent and receptive. It is well known that the attraction to the Moon in combination with the movement of the Earth is responsible for the tides. The Moon has a similar effect on men. A clever navigator will make use of the tides to bring his ship to the intended destination. You also can reach your "destination" better by making use of your tides.

When the Moon is in conjunction with the Sun it is called a New Moon; when the Moon and Sun are in opposition it is called a Full Moon. From New Moon to Full Moon, first and second quarter—which takes about two weeks—the Moon is increasing or waxing. From Full Moon to New Moon, third and fourth quarter, the Moon is said to be decreasing or waning. The Moon Table indicates the New Moon and Full Moon and the quarters.

ACTIVITY	MOON IN
Business	
buying and selling	Sagittarius, Aries, Gemini, Virgo
new, requiring public support	1st and 2nd quarter
meant to be kept quiet	3rd and 4th quarter
Investigation	3rd and 4th quarter
Signing documents	1st & 2nd quarter, Cancer, Scorpio, Pisces
Advertising	2nd quarter, Sagittarius
Journeys and trips	1st & 2nd quarter, Gemini, Virgo
Renting offices, etc.	Taurus, Leo, Scorpio, Aquarius
Painting of house/apartment	3rd & 4th quarter, Taurus, Scorpio, Aquarius
Decorating	Gemini, Libra, Aquarius
Buying clothes and accessories	Taurus, Virgo
Beauty salon or barber shop visit	1st & 2nd quarter, Taurus, Leo, Libra, Scorpio, Aquarius
Weddings	1st & 2nd quarter

MOON'S INFLUENCE OVER YOUR HEALTH

ARIES	Head, brain, face, upper jaw
TAURUS	Throat, neck, lower jaw
GEMINI	Hands, arms, lungs, shoulders, nervous system
CANCER	Esophagus, stomach, breasts, womb, liver
LEO	Heart, spine
VIRGO	Intestines, liver
LIBRA	Kidneys, lower back
SCORPIO	Sex and eliminative organs
SAGITTARIUS	Hips, thighs, liver
CAPRICORN	Skin, bones, beeth, knees
AQUARIUS	Circulatory system, lower legs
PISCES	Feet, tone of being

Try to avoid work being done on that part of the body when the Moon is in the sign governing that part.

MOON'S INFLUENCE OVER PLANTS

Centuries ago it was established that seeds planted when the Moon is in certain signs and phases called "fruitful" will produce more than seeds planted when the Moon is in a Barren sign.

FRUITFUL SIGNS	*BARREN SIGNS*	*DRY SIGNS*
Taurus	Aries	Aries
Cancer	Gemini	Gemini
Libra	Leo	Sagittarius
Scorpio	Virgo	Aquarius
Capricorn	Sagittarius	
Pisces	Aquarius	

ACTIVITY	MOON IN
Mow lawn, trim plans	Fruitful sign, 1st & 2nd quarter
Plant flowers	Fruitful sign, 2nd quarter; best in Cancer and Libra
Prune	Fruitful sign, 3rd & 4th quarter
Destroy pests; spray	Barren sign, 4th quarter
Harvest potatoes, root crops	Dry sign, 3rd & 4th quarter; Taurus, Leo, and Aquarius

THE SIGNS: DOMINANT CHARACTERISTICS

March 21–April 20

The Positive Side of Aries

The Arien has many positive points to his character. People born under this first sign of the Zodiac are often quite strong and enthusiastic. On the whole, they are forward-looking people who are not easily discouraged by temporary setbacks. They know what they want out of life and they go out after it. Their personalities are strong. Others are usually quite impressed by the Arien's way of doing things. Quite often they are sources of inspiration for others traveling the same route. Aries men and women have a special zest for life that is often contagious; for others, they are often the example of how life should be lived.

The Aries person usually has a quick and active mind. He is imaginative and inventive. He enjoys keeping busy and active. He generally gets along well with all kinds of people. He is interested in mankind, as a whole. He likes to be challenged. Some would say he thrives on opposition, for it is when he is set against that he often does his best. Getting over or around obstacles is a challenge he generally enjoys. All in all, the Arien is quite positive and young-thinking. He likes to keep abreast of new things that are happening in the world. Ariens are often fond of speed. They like things to be done quickly and this sometimes aggravates their slower colleagues and associates.

The Aries man or woman always seems to remain young. Their whole approach to life is youthful and optimistic. They never say die, no matter what the odds. They may have an occasional setback, but it is not long before they are back on their feet again.

The Negative Side of Aries

Everybody has his less positive qualities—and Aries is no exception. Sometimes the Aries man or woman is not very tactful in communicating with others; in his hurry to get things done he is apt to

be a little callous or inconsiderate. Sensitive people are likely to find him somewhat sharp-tongued in some situations. Often in his eagerness to achieve his aims, he misses the mark altogether. At times the Arien is too impulsive. He can occasionally be stubborn and refuse to listen to reason. If things do not move quickly enough to suit the Aries man or woman, he or she is apt to become rather nervous or irritable. The uncultivated Arien is not unfamiliar with moments of doubt and fear. He is capable of being destructive if he does not get his way. He can overcome some of his emotional problems by steadily trying to express himself as he really is, but this requires effort.

April 21–May 20

The Positive Side of Taurus

The Taurus person is known for his ability to concentrate and for his tenacity. These are perhaps his strongest qualities. The Taurus man or woman generally has very little trouble in getting along with others; it's his nature to be helpful toward people in need. He can always be depended on by his friends, especially those in trouble.

The Taurean generally achieves what he wants through his ability to persevere. He never leaves anything unfinished but works on something until it has been completed. People can usually take him at his word; he is honest and forthright in most of his dealings. The Taurus person has a good chance to make a success of his life because of his many positive qualities. The Taurean who aims high seldom falls short of his mark. He learns well by experience. He is thorough and does not believe in short-cuts of any kind. The Taurean's thoroughness pays off in the end, for through his deliberateness he learns how to rely on himself and what he has learned. The Taurus person tries to get along with others, as a rule. He is not overly critical and likes people to be themselves. He is a tolerant person and enjoys peace and harmony—especially in his home life.

The Taurean is usually cautious in all that he does. He is not a person who believes in taking unnecessary risks. Before adopting any one line of action, he will weigh all of the pros and cons. The

Taurus person is steadfast. Once his mind is made up it seldom changes. The person born under this sign usually is a good family person—reliable and loving.

The Negative Side of Taurus

Sometimes the Taurus man or woman is a bit too stubborn. He won't listen to other points of view if his mind is set on something. To others, this can be quite annoying. The Taurean also does not like to be told what to do. He becomes rather angry if others think him not too bright. He does not like to be told he is wrong, even when he is. He dislikes being contradicted.

Some people who are born under this sign are very suspicious of others—even of those persons close to them. They find it difficult to trust people fully. They are often afraid of being deceived or taken advantage of. The Taurean often finds it difficult to forget or forgive. His love of material things sometimes makes him rather avaricious and petty.

May 21–June 20

The Positive Side of Gemini

The person born under this sign of the Heavenly Twins is usually quite bright and quick-witted. Some of them are capable of doing many different things. The Gemini person very often has many different interests. He keeps an open mind and is always anxious to learn new things.

The Geminian is often an analytical person. He is a person who enjoys making use of his intellect. He is governed more by his mind than by his emotions. He is a person who is not confined to one view; he can often understand both sides to a problem or question. He knows how to reason; how to make rapid decisions if need be.

He is an adaptable person and can make himself at home almost anywhere. There are all kinds of situations he can adapt to. He is a person who seldom doubts himself; he is sure of his talents and his

ability to think and reason. The Geminian is generally most satisfied when he is in a situation where he can make use of his intellect. Never short of imagination, he often has strong talents for invention. He is rather a modern person when it comes to life; the Geminian almost always moves along with the times—perhaps that is why he remains so youthful throughout most of his life.

Literature and art appeal to the person born under this sign. Creativity in almost any form will interest and intrigue the Gemini man or woman.

The Geminian is often quite charming. A good talker, he often is the center of attraction at any gathering. People find it easy to like a person born under this sign because he can appear easygoing and usually has a good sense of humor.

The Negative Side of Gemini

Sometimes the Gemini person tries to do too many things at one time—and as a result, winds up finishing nothing. Some Geminians are easily distracted and find it rather difficult to concentrate on one thing for too long a time. Sometimes they give in to trifling fancies and find it rather boring to become too serious about any one thing. Some of them are never dependable, no matter what they promise.

Although the Gemini man or woman often appears to be well-versed on many subjects, this is sometimes just a veneer. His knowledge may be only superficial, but because he speaks so well he gives people the impression of erudition. Some Geminians are sharp-tongued and inconsiderate; they think only of themselves and their own pleasure.

June 21–July 20

The Positive Side of Cancer

The Cancerians's most positive point is his understanding nature. On the whole, he is a loving and sympathetic person. He would never go out of his way to hurt anyone. The Cancer man or woman

is often very kind and tender; they give what they can to others. They hate to see others suffering and will do what they can to help someone in less fortunate circumstances than themselves. They are often very concerned about the world. Their interest in people generally goes beyond that of just their own families and close friends; they have a deep sense of brotherhood and respect humanitarian values. The Cancerian means what he says, as a rule; he is honest about his feelings.

The Cancer man or woman is a person who knows the art of patience. When something seems difficult, he is willing to wait until the situation becomes manageable again. He is a person who knows how to bide his time. The Cancerian knows how to concentrate on one thing at a time. When he has made his mind up he generally sticks with what he does, seeing it through to the end.

The Cancerian is a person who loves his home. He enjoys being surrounded by familiar things and the people he loves. Of all the signs, Cancer is the most maternal. Even the men born under this sign often have a motherly or protective quality about them. They like to take care of people in their family—to see that they are well loved and well provided for. They are usually loyal and faithful. Family ties mean a lot to the Cancer man or woman. Parents and in-laws are respected and loved. The Cancerian has a strong sense of tradition. He is very sensitive to the moods of others.

The Negative Side of Cancer

Sometimes the Cancerian finds it rather hard to face life. It becomes too much for him. He can be a little timid and retiring, when things don't go too well. When unfortunate things happen, he is apt to just shrug and say, "Whatever will be will be." He can be fatalistic to a fault. The uncultivated Cancerian is a bit lazy. He doesn't have very much ambition. Anything that seems a bit difficult he'll gladly leave to others. He may be lacking in initiative. Too sensitive, when he feels he's been injured, he'll crawl back into his shell and nurse his imaginary wounds. The Cancer woman often is given to crying when the smallest thing goes wrong.

Some Cancerians find it difficult to enjoy themselves in environments outside their homes. They make heavy demands on others, and need to be constantly reassured that they are loved.

July 21–August 21

The Positive Side of Leo

Often Leos make good leaders. They seem to be good organizers and administrators. Usually they are quite popular with others. Whatever group it is that he belongs to, the Leo man is almost sure to be or become the leader.

The Leo person is generous most of the time. It is his best characteristic. He or she likes to give gifts and presents. In making others happy, the Leo person becomes happy himself. He likes to splurge when spending money on others. In some instances it may seem that the Leo's generosity knows no boundaries. A hospitable person, the Leo man or woman is very fond of welcoming people to his house and entertaining them. He is never short of company.

The Leo person has plenty of energy and drive. He enjoys working toward some specific goal. When he applies himself correctly, he gets what he wants most often. The Leo person is almost never unsure of himself. He has plenty of confidence and aplomb. He is a person who is direct in almost everything he does. He has a quick mind and can make a decision in a very short time.

He usually sets a good example for others because of his ambitious manner and positive ways. He knows how to stick to something once he's started. Although the Leo person may be good at making a joke, he is not superficial or glib. He is a loving person, kind and thoughtful.

There is generally nothing small or petty about the Leo man or woman. He does what he can for those who are deserving. He is a person others can rely upon at all times. He means what he says. An honest person, generally speaking, he is a friend that others value.

The Negative Side of Leo

Leo, however, does have his faults. At times, he can be just a bit too arrogant. He thinks that no one deserves a leadership position except him. Only he is capable of doing things well. His opinion of himself is often much too high. Because of his conceit, he is sometimes rather unpopular with a good many people. Some Leos are too materialistic; they can only think in terms of money and profit.

Some Leos enjoy lording it over others—at home or at their place of business. What is more, they feel they have the right to. Egocentric to an impossible degree, this sort of Leo cares little about how others think or feel. He can be rude and cutting.

August 22–September 22

The Positive Side of Virgo

The person born under the sign of Virgo is generally a busy person. He knows how to arrange and organize things. He is a good planner. Above all, he is practical and is not afraid of hard work.

The person born under this sign, Virgo, knows how to attain what he desires. He sticks with something until it is finished. He never shirks his duties, and can always be depended upon. The Virgo person can be thoroughly trusted at all times.

The man or woman born under this sign tries to do everything to perfection. He doesn't believe in doing anything half-way. He always aims for the top. He is the sort of a person who is constantly striving to better himself—not because he wants more money or glory, but because it gives him a feeling of accomplishment.

The Virgo man or woman is a very observant person. He is sensitive to how others feel, and can see things below the surface of a situation. He usually puts this talent to constructive use.

It is not difficult for the Virgoan to be open and earnest. He believes in putting his cards on the table. He is never secretive or under-handed. He's as good as his word. The Virgo person is generally plain-spoken and down-to-earth. He has no trouble in expressing himself.

The Virgo person likes to keep up to date on new developments in his particular field. Well-informed, generally, he sometimes has a keen interest in the arts or literature. What he knows, he knows well. His ability to use his critical faculties is well-developed and sometimes startles others because of its accuracy.

The Virgoan adheres to a moderate way of life; he avoids excesses. He is a responsible person and enjoys being of service.

The Negative Side of Virgo

Sometimes a Virgo person is too critical. He thinks that only he can do something the way it should be done. Whatever anyone else does is inferior. He can be rather annoying in the way he quibbles over insignificant details. In telling others how things should be done, he can be rather tactless and mean.

Some Virgos seem rather emotionless and cool. They feel emo-

tional involvement is beneath them. They are sometimes too tidy, too neat. With money they can be rather miserly. Some try to force their opinions and ideas on others.

September 23–October 22

The Positive Side of Libra

Librans love harmony. It is one of their most outstanding character traits. They are interested in achieving balance; they admire beauty and grace in things as well as in people. Generally speaking, they are kind and considerate people. Librans are usually very sympathetic. They go out of their way not to hurt another person's feelings. They are outgoing and do what they can to help those in need.

People born under the sign of Libra almost always make good friends. They are loyal and amiable. They enjoy the company of others. Many of them are rather moderate in their views; they believe in keeping an open mind, however, and weighing both sides of an issue fairly before making a decision.

Alert and often intelligent, the Libran, always fair-minded, tries to put himself in the position of the other person. They are against injustice; quite often they take up for the underdog. In most of their social dealings, they try to be tactful and kind. They dislike discord and bickering, and most Libras strive for peace and harmony in all their relationships.

The Libra man or woman has a keen sense of beauty. They appreciate handsome furnishings and clothes. Many of them are artistically inclined. Their taste is usually impeccable. They know how to use color. Their homes are almost always attractively arranged and inviting. They enjoy entertaining people and see to it that their guests always feel at home and welcome.

The Libran gets along with almost everyone. He is well-liked and socially much in demand.

The Negative Side of Libra

Some people born under this sign tend to be rather insincere. So eager are they to achieve harmony in all relationships that they will even go so far as to lie. Many of them are escapists. They find facing

the truth an ordeal and prefer living in a world of make-believe.

In a serious argument, some Librans give in rather easily even when they know they are right. Arguing, even about something they believe in, is too unsettling for some of them.

Librans sometimes care too much for material things. They enjoy possessions and luxuries. Some are vain and tend to be jealous.

October 23–November 22

The Positive Side of Scorpio

The Scorpio man or woman generally knows what he or she wants out of life. He is a determined person. He sees something through to the end. The Scorpion is quite sincere, and seldom says anything he doesn't mean. When he sets a goal for himself he tries to go about achieving it in a very direct way.

The Scorpion is brave and courageous. They are not afraid of hard work. Obstacles do not frighten them. They forge ahead until they achieve what they set out for. The Scorpio man or woman has a strong will.

Although the Scorpion may seem rather fixed and determined, inside he is often quite tender and loving. He can care very much for others. He believes in sincerity in all relationships. His feelings about someone tend to last; they are profound and not superficial.

The Scorpio person is someone who adheres to his principles no matter what happens. He will not be deterred from a path he believes to be right.

Because of his many positive strengths, the Scorpion can often achieve happiness for himself and for those that he loves.

He is a constructive person by nature. He often has a deep understanding of people and of life, in general. He is perceptive and unafraid. Obstacles often seem to spur him on. He is a positive person who enjoys winning. He has many strengths and resources; challenge of any sort often brings out the best in him.

The Negative Side of Scorpio

The Scorpio person is sometimes hypersensitive. Often he imagines injury when there is none. He feels that others do not bother to

recognize him for his true worth. Sometimes he is given to excessive boasting in order to compensate for what he feels is neglect

The Scorpio person can be rather proud and arrogant. They can be rather sly when they put their minds to it and they enjoy outwitting persons or institutions noted for their cleverness.

Their tactics for getting what they want are sometimes devious and ruthless. They don't care too much about what others may think. If they feel others have done them an injustice, they will do their best to seek revenge. The Scorpion often has a sudden, violent temper; and this person's interest in sex is sometimes quite unbalanced or excessive.

November 23–December 20

The Positive Side of Sagittarius

People born under this sign are often honest and forthright. Their approach to life is earnest and open. The Sagittarian is often quite adult in his way of seeing things. They are broadminded and tolerant people. When dealing with others the person born under the sign of Sagittarius is almost always open and forthright. He doesn't believe in deceit or pretension. His standards are high. People who associate with the Sagittarian, generally admire and respect him.

The Sagittarian trusts others easily and expects them to trust him. He is never suspicious or envious and almost always thinks well of others. People always enjoy his company because he is so friendly and easy-going. The Sagittarius man or woman is often good-humored. He can always be depended upon by his friends, family, and co-workers.

The person born under this sign of the Zodiac likes a good joke every now and then; he is keen on fun and this makes him very popular with others.

A lively person, he enjoys sports and outdoor life. The Sagittarian is fond of animals. Intelligent and interesting, he can begin an animated conversation with ease. He likes exchanging ideas and discussing various views.

He is not selfish or proud. If someone proposes an idea or plan that is better than his, he will immediately adopt it. Imaginative yet practical, he knows how to put ideas into practice.

He enjoys sport and game, and it doesn't matter if he wins or loses. He is a forgiving person, and never sulks over something that has not worked out in his favor.

He is seldom critical, and is almost always generous.

The Negative Side of Sagittarius

Some Sagittarians are restless. They take foolish risks and seldom learn from the mistakes they make. They don't have heads for money and are often mismanaging their finances. Some of them devote much of their time to gambling.

Some are too outspoken and tactless, always putting their feet in their mouths. They hurt others carelessly by being honest at the wrong time. Sometimes they make promises which they don't keep. They don't stick close enough to their plans and go from one failure to another. They are undisciplined and waste a lot of energy.

December 21–January 19

The Positive Side of Capricorn

The person born under the sign of Capricorn is usually very stable and patient. He sticks to whatever tasks he has and sees them through. He can always be relied upon and he is not averse to work.

An honest person, the Capricornian is generally serious about whatever he does. He does not take his duties lightly. He is a practical person and believes in keeping his feet on the ground.

Quite often the person born under this sign is ambitious and knows how to get what he wants out of life. He forges ahead and never gives up his goal. When he is determined about something, he almost always wins. He is a good worker—a hard worker. Although things may not come easy to him, he will not complain, but continue working until his chores are finished.

He is usually good at business matters and knows the value of money. He is not a spendthrift and knows how to put something away for a rainy day; he dislikes waste and unnecessary loss.

The Capricornian knows how to make use of his self-control. He

can apply himself to almost anything once he puts his mind to it. His ability to concentrate sometimes astounds others. He is diligent and does well when involved in detail work.

The Capricorn man or woman is charitable, generally speaking, and will do what is possible to help others less fortunate. As a friend, he is loyal and trustworthy. He never shirks his duties or responsibilities. He is self-reliant and never expects too much of the other fellow. He does what he can on his own. If someone does him a good turn, then he will do his best to return the favor.

The Negative Side of Capricorn

Like everyone, the Capricornian, too, has his faults. At times, he can be over-critical of others. He expects others to live up to his own high standards. He thinks highly of himself and tends to look down on others.

His interest in material things may be exaggerated. The Capricorn man or woman thinks too much about getting on in the world and having something to show for it. He may even be a little greedy.

He sometimes thinks he knows what's best for everyone. He is too bossy. He is always trying to organize and correct others. He may be a little narrow in his thinking.

January 20–February 18

The Positive Side of Aquarius

The Aquarius man or woman is usually very honest and forthright. These are his two greatest qualities. His standards for himself are generally very high. He can always be relied upon by others. His word is his bond.

The Aquarian is perhaps the most tolerant of all the Zodiac personalities. He respects other people's beliefs and feels that everyone is entitled to his own approach to life.

He would never do anything to injure another's feelings. He is never unkind or cruel. Always considerate of others, the Aquarian is always willing to help a person in need. He feels a very strong tie between himself and all the other members of mankind.

The person born under this sign is almost always an individualist. He does not believe in teaming up with the masses, but prefers going his own way. His ideas about life and mankind are often quite advanced. There is a saying to the effect that the average Aquarian is fifty years ahead of his time.

He is broadminded. The problems of the world concern him greatly. He is interested in helping others no matter what part of the globe they live in. He is truly a humanitarian sort. He likes to be of service to others.

Giving, considerate, and without prejudice, Aquarians have no trouble getting along with others.

The Negative Side of Aquarius

The Aquarian may be too much of a dreamer. He makes plans but seldom carries them out. He is rather unrealistic. His imagination has a tendency to run away with him. Because many of his plans are impractical, he is always in some sort of a dither.

Others may not approve of him at all times because of his unconventional behavior. He may be a bit eccentric. Sometimes he is so busy with his own thoughts, that he loses touch with the realities of existence.

Some Aquarians feel they are more clever and intelligent than others. They seldom admit to their own faults, even when they are quite apparent. Some become rather fanatic in their views. Their criticism of others is sometimes destructive and negative.

February 19–March 20

The Positive Side of Pisces

The Piscean can often understand the problems of others quite easily. He has a sympathetic nature. Kindly, he is often dedicated in the way he goes about helping others. The sick and the troubled often turn to him for advice and assistance.

He is very broadminded and does not criticize others for their faults. He knows how to accept people for what they are. On the whole, he is a trustworthy and earnest person. He is loyal to his

friends and will do what he can to help them in time of need. Generous and good-natured, he is a lover of peace; he is often willing to help others solve their differences. People who have taken a wrong turn in life often interest him and he will do what he can to persuade them to rehabilitate themselves.

He has a strong intuitive sense and most of the time he knows how to make it work for him; the Piscean is unusually perceptive and often knows what is bothering someone before that person, himself, is aware of it. The Pisces man or woman is an idealistic person, basically, and is interested in making the world a better place in which to live. The Piscean believes that everyone should help each other. He is willing to do more than his share in order to achieve cooperation with others.

The person born under this sign often is talented in music or art. He is a receptive person; he is able to take the ups and downs of life with philosophic calm.

The Negative Side of Pisces

Some Pisceans are often depressed; their outlook on life is rather glum. They may feel that they have been given a bad deal in life and that others are always taking unfair advantage of them. The Piscean sometimes feel that the world is a cold and cruel place. He is easily discouraged. He may even withdraw from the harshness of reality into a secret shell of his own where he dreams and idles away a good deal of his time.

The Piscean can be rather lazy. He lets things happen without giving the least bit of resistance. He drifts along, whether on the high road or on the low. He is rather short on willpower.

Some Pisces people seek escape through drugs or alcohol. When temptation comes along they find it hard to resist. In matters of sex, they can be rather permissive.

THE SIGNS AND
THEIR KEY WORDS

		POSITIVE	NEGATIVE
ARIES	self	courage, initiative, pioneer instinct	brash rudeness, selfish impetuosity
TAURUS	money	endurance, loyalty, wealth	obstinacy, gluttony
GEMINI	mind	versatility	capriciousness, unreliability
CANCER	family	sympathy, homing instinct	clannishness, childishness
LEO	children	love, authority, integrity	egotism, force
VIRGO	work	purity, industry, analysis	fault-finding, cynicism
LIBRA	marriage	harmony, justice	vacillation, superficiality
SCORPIO	sex	survival, regeneration	vengeance, discord
SAGITTARIUS	travel	optimism, higher learning	lawlessness
CAPRICORN	career	depth	narrowness, gloom
AQUARIUS	friends	human fellowship, genius	perverse unpredictability
PISCES	confine- ment	spiritual love, universality	diffusion, escapism

THE ELEMENTS AND QUALITIES OF THE SIGNS

ELEMENT	SIGN	QUALITY	SIGN
FIRE...............	ARIES LEO SAGITTARIUS	CARDINAL.........	ARIES LIBRA CANCER CAPRICORN
EARTH............	TAURUS VIRGO CAPRICORN	FIXED...............	TAURUS LEO SCORPIO AQUARIUS
AIR.................	GEMINI LIBRA AQUARIUS	MUTABLE.........	GEMINI VIRGO SAGITTARIUS PISCES
WATER...........	CANCER SCORPIO PISCES		

Every sign has both an element and a quality associated with it. The element indicates the basic makeup of the sign, and the quality describes the kind of activity associated with each.

Signs can be grouped together according to their *element* and *quality*. Signs of the same element share many basic traits in common. They tend to form stable configurations and ultimately harmonious relationships. Signs of the same quality are often less harmonious, but they share many dynamic potentials for growth as well as profound fulfillment.

THE FIRE SIGNS

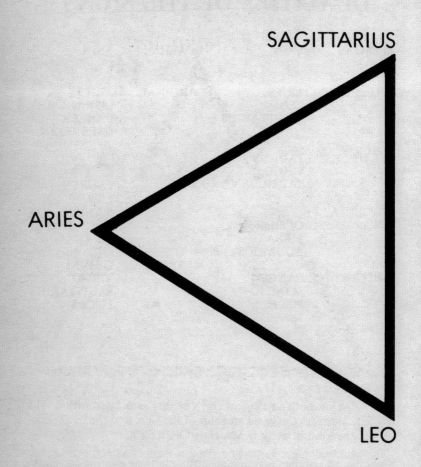

This is the fire group. On the whole these are emotional, volatile types, quick to anger, quick to forgive. They are adventurous, powerful people and.act as a source of inspiration for everyone. They spark into action with immediate exuberant impulses. They are intelligent, self-involved, creative and idealistic. They all share a certain vibrancy and glow that outwardly reflects an inner flame and passion for living.

THE EARTH SIGNS

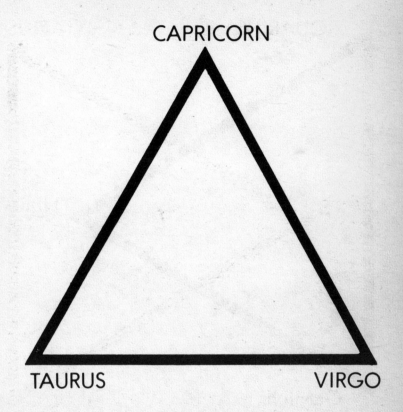

This is the earth group. They are in constant touch with the material world and tend to be conservative. Although they are all capable of spartan self-discipline, they are earthy, sensual people who are stimulated by the tangible, elegant and luxurious. The thread of their lives is always practical, but they do fantasize and are often attracted to dark, mysterious, emotional people. They are like great cliffs overhanging the sea, forever married to the ocean but always resisting erosion from the dark, emotional forces that thunder at their feet.

THE AIR SIGNS

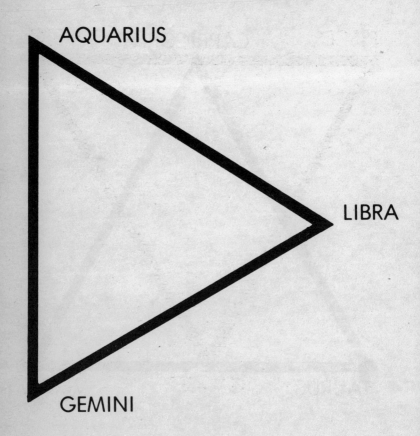

AQUARIUS

LIBRA

GEMINI

This is the air group. They are light, mental creatures desirous of contact, communication and relationship. They are involved with people and the forming of ties on many levels. Original thinkers, they are the bearers of human news. Their language is their sense of word, color, style and beauty. They provide an atmosphere suitable and pleasant for living. They add change and versatility to the scene, and it is through them that we can explore new territory of human intelligence and experience.

THE WATER SIGNS

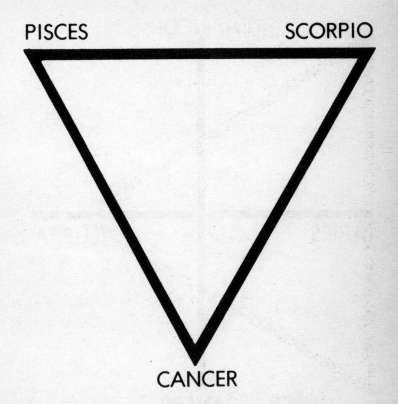

PISCES   SCORPIO

CANCER

This is the water group. Through the water people, we are all joined together on emotional, non-verbal levels. They are silent, mysterious types whose magic hypnotizes even the most determined realist. They have uncanny perceptions about people and are as rich as the oceans when it comes to feeling, emotion or imagination. They are sensitive, mystical creatures with memories that go back beyond time. Through water, life is sustained. These people have the potential for the depths of darkness or the heights of mysticism and art.

THE CARDINAL SIGNS

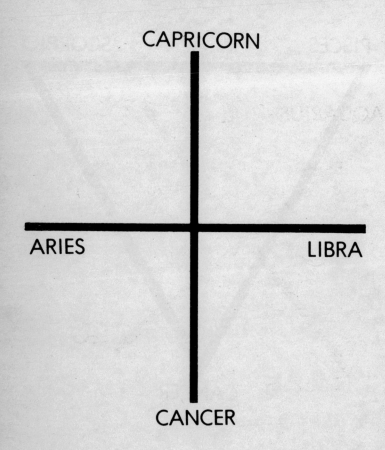

Put together, this is a clear-cut picture of dynamism, activity, tremendous stress and remarkable achievement. These people know the meaning of great change since their lives are often characterized by significant crises and major successes. This combination is like a simultaneous storm of summer, fall, winter and spring. The danger is chaotic diffusion of energy; the potential is irrepressible growth and victory.

THE FIXED SIGNS

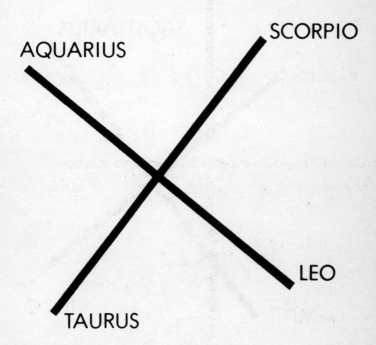

Fixed signs are always establishing themselves in a given place or area of experience. Like explorers who arrive and plant a flag, these people claim a position from which they do not enjoy being deposed. They are staunch, stalwart, upright, trusty, honorable people, although their obstinacy is well-known. Their contribution is fixity, and they are the angels who support our visible world.

THE MUTABLE SIGNS

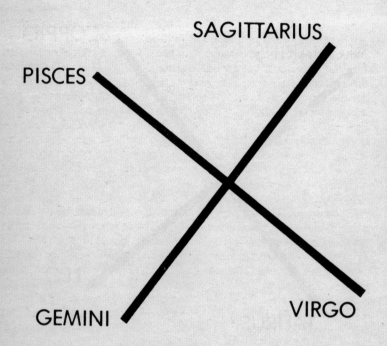

Mutable people are versatile, sensitive, intelligent, nervous and deeply curious about life. They are the translators of all energy. They often carry out or complete tasks initiated by others. Combinations of these signs have highly developed minds; they are imaginative and jumpy and think and talk a lot. At worst their lives are a Tower of Babel. At best they are adaptable and ready creatures who can assimilate one kind of experience and enjoy it while anticipating coming changes.

HOW TO APPROXIMATE YOUR RISING SIGN

Apart from the month and day of birth, the exact *time* of birth is another vital factor in the determination of an accurate horoscope. Not only do the planets move with great speed, but one must know how far the Earth has turned during the day. That way you can determine exactly where the planets are located with respect to the precise birthplace of an individual. This makes *your* horoscope *your* horoscope. In addition to these factors, another grid is laid upon that of the Zodiac and the planets: the houses. After all three have been considered, specific planetary relationships can be measured and analyzed in accordance with certain ordered procedures. It is the skillful translation of all this complex astrological language that a serious astrologer strives for in his attempt at coherent astrological synthesis. Keep this in mind.

The horoscope sets up a kind of framework around which the life of an individual grows like wild ivy, this way and that, weaving its way around the trellis of the natal positions of the planets. The year of birth tells us the positions of the distant, slow-moving planets like Jupiter, Saturn, Uranus and Pluto. The month of birth indicates the Sun sign, or birth sign as it is commonly called, as well as indicating the positions of the rapidly moving planets like Venus, Mercury and Mars. The day of birth locates the position of our Moon, and the moment of birth determines the houses through what is called the Ascendant, or Rising Sign.

As the Earth rotates on its axis once every 24 hours, each one of the twelve signs of the Zodiac appears to be "rising" on the horizon, with a new one appearing about every two hours. Actually it is the turning of the Earth that exposes each sign to view, but you will remember that in much of our astrological work we are discussing "apparent" motion. This *Rising Sign* marks the Ascendant and it colors the whole orientation of a horoscope. It indicates the sign governing the first house of the chart, and will thus determine which signs will govern all the other houses. The idea is a bit complicated at first, and we needn't dwell on complications in this introduction, but if you can imagine two color wheels with twelve divisions superimposed upon each other, one moving slowly and the other remaining still, you will have some idea of how the signs keep shifting the "color" of the houses as the Rising Sign continues to change every two hours.

The important point is that the birth chart, or horoscope, actually does define specific factors of a person's makeup. It contains a picture of being, much the way the nucleus of a tiny cell contains the potential for an entire elephant, or a packet of seeds contains a rosebush. If there were no order or continuity to the world, we could plant roses and get elephants. This same order that gives continuous flow to our lives often annoys people if it threatens to determine too much of their lives. We must grow from what we were planted, and there's no reason why we can't do that magnificently. It's all there in the horoscope. Where there is limitation, there is breakthrough; where there is crisis, there is transformation. Accurate analysis of a horoscope can help you find these points of breakthrough and transformation, and it requires knowledge of subtleties and distinctions that demand skillful judgment in order to solve even the simplest kind of personal question.

It is still quite possible, however, to draw some conclusions based upon the sign occupied by the Sun alone. In fact, if you're just being introduced to this vast subject, you're better off keeping it simple. Otherwise it seems like an impossible jumble, much like trying to read a novel in a foreign language without knowing the basic vocabulary. As with anything else, you can progress in your appreciation and understanding of astrology in direct proportion to your interest. To become really good at it requires study, experience, patience and above all—and maybe simplest of all—a fundamental understanding of what is actually going on right up there in the sky over your head. It is a vital living process you can observe, contemplate and ultimately understand. You can start by observing sunrise, or sunset, or even the full Moon.

In fact you can do a simple experiment after reading this introduction. You can erect a rough chart by following the simple procedure below:

1. Draw a circle with twelve equal segments.

2. Starting at what would be the nine o'clock position on a clock, number the segments, or houses, from 1 to 12 in a *counterclockwise direction.*

3. Label house number 1 in the following way: 4 A.M.-6 A.M.

4. In a counterclockwise direction, label the rest of the houses: 2 A.M.-4 A.M., MIDNIGHT-2 A.M., 10 P.M-MIDNIGHT, 8 P.M.-10 P.M., 6 P.M.-8 P.M., 4 P.M.-6 P.M., 2 P.M.-4 P.M., NOON-2 P.M., 10 A.M.-NOON, 8 A.M.-10 A.M., and 6 A.M.-8 A.M.

5. Now find out what time you were born and place the sun in the appropriate house.

6. Label the edge of that house with your Sun sign. You now have a description of your basic character and your fundamental drives. You can also see in what areas of life on Earth you will be most likely to focus your constant energy and center your activity.

7. If you are really feeling ambitious, label the rest of the houses with the signs, starting with your Sun sign, in order, still in a *counterclockwise direction*. When you get to Pisces, start over with Aries and keep going until you reach the house behind the Sun.

8. Look to house number 1. The sign that you have now labeled and attached to house number 1 is your Rising sign. It will color your self-image, outlook, physical constitution, early life and whole orientation to life. Of course this is a mere approximation, since there are many complicated calculations that must be made with respect to adjustments for birth time, but if you read descriptions of the sign preceding and the sign following the one you have calculated in the above manner, you may be able to identify yourself better. In any case, when you get through labeling all the houses, your drawing should look something like this:

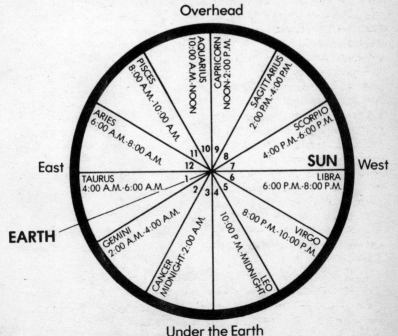

*Basic chart illustrating the position of the Sun in Scorpio,
with the Ascendant Taurus as the Rising Sign.*

This individual was born at 5:15 P.M. on October 31 in New York City. The Sun is in Scorpio and is found in the 7th house. The Rising sign, or the sign governing house number 1, is Taurus, so this person is a blend of Scorpio and Taurus.

Any further calculation would necessitate that you look in an ephemeris, or table of planetary motion, for the positions of the rest of the planets for your particular birth year. But we will take the time to define briefly all the known planets of our Solar System and the Sun to acquaint you with some more of the astrological vocabulary that you will be meeting again and again. (See page 21 for a full explanation of the Moon in all the Signs.)

THE PLANETS AND SIGNS THEY RULE

The signs of the Zodiac are linked to the planets in the following way. Each sign is governed or ruled by one or more planets. No matter where the planets are located in the sky at any given moment, they still rule their respective signs, and when they travel through the signs they rule, they have special dignity and their effects are stronger.

Following is a list of the planets and the signs they rule. After looking at the list, go back over the definitions of the planets and see if you can determine how the planet ruling *your* Sun sign has affected your life.

SIGNS	RULING PLANETS
Aries	Mars, Pluto
Taurus	Venus
Gemini	Mercury
Cancer	Moon
Leo	Sun
Virgo	Mercury
Libra	Venus
Scorpio	Mars, Pluto
Sagittarius	Jupiter
Capricorn	Saturn
Aquarius	Saturn, Uranus
Pisces	Jupiter, Neptune

THE PLANETS
OF THE
SOLAR SYSTEM

Here are the planets of the Solar System. They all travel around the Sun at different speeds and different distances. Taken with the Sun, they all distribute individual intelligence and ability throughout the entire chart.

The planets modify the influence of the Sun in a chart according to their own particular natures, strengths and positions. Their positions must be calculated for each year and day, and their function and expression in a horoscope will change as they move from one area of the Zodiac to another.

Following, you will find brief statements of their pure meanings.

THE SUN

SUN

This is the center of existence. Around this flaming sphere all the planets revolve in endless orbits. Our star is constantly sending out its beams of light and energy without which no life on Earth would be possible. In astrology it symbolizes everything we are trying to become, the center around which all of our activity in life will always revolve. It is the symbol of our basic nature and describes the natural and constant thread that runs through everything that we do from birth to death on this planet.

To early astrologers, the sun seemed to be another planet because it crossed the heavens every day, just like the rest of the bodies in the sky.

It is the only star near enough to be seen well—it is, in fact, a dwarf star. Approximately 860,000 miles in diameter, it is about ten times as wide as the giant planet Jupiter. The next nearest star is nearly 300,000 times as far away, and if the Sun were located as far away as most of the bright stars, it would be too faint to be seen without a telescope.

Everything in the horoscope ultimately revolves around this singular body. Although other forces may be prominent in the charts of some individuals, still the Sun is the total nucleus of being and symbolizes the complete potential of every human being alive. It is vitality and the life force. Your whole essence comes from the position of the Sun.

You are always trying to express the Sun according to its position by house and sign. Possibility for all development is found in the Sun, and it marks the fundamental character of your personal radiations all around you.

It is the symbol of strength, vigor, wisdom, dignity, ardor and generosity, and the ability for a person to function as a mature individual. It is also a creative force in society. It is consciousness of the gift of life.

The underdeveloped solar nature is arrogant, pushy, undependable and proud, and is constantly using force.

MERCURY

Mercury is the planet closest to the Sun. It races around our star, gathering information and translating it to the rest of the system. Mercury represents your capacity to understand the desires of your own will and to translate those desires into action.

In other words it is the planet of Mind and the power of communication. Through Mercury we develop an ability to think, write, speak and observe—to become aware of the world around us. It colors our attitudes and vision of the world, as well as our capacity to communicate our inner responses to the outside world. Some people who have serious disabilities in their power of verbal communication have often wrongly been described as people lacking intelligence.

Although this planet (and its position in the horoscope) indicates your power to communicate your thoughts and perceptions to the world, intelligence is something deeper. Intelligence is distributed throughout all the planets. It is the relationship of the planets to each other that truly describes what we call intelligence. Mercury rules speaking, language, mathematics, draft and design, students, messengers, young people, offices, teachers and any pursuits where the mind of man has wings.

VENUS

Venus is beauty. It symbolizes the harmony and radiance of a rare and elusive quality: beauty itself. It is refinement and delicacy, softness and charm. In astrology it indicates grace, balance and the aesthetic sense. Where Venus is we see beauty, a gentle drawing in of energy and the need for satisfaction and completion. It is a special touch that finishes off rough edges. It is sensitivity, and affection, and it is always the place for that other elusive phenomenon: love. Venus describes our sense of what is beautiful and loving. Poorly developed, it is vulgar, tasteless and self-indulgent. But its ideal is the flame of spiritual love—Aphrodite, goddess of love, and the sweetness and power of personal beauty.

MARS

This is raw, crude energy. The planet next to Earth but outward from the Sun is a fiery red sphere that charges through the horoscope with force and fury. It represents the way you reach out for new adventure and new experience. It is energy and drive, initiative, courage and daring. The power to start something and see it through. It can be thoughtless, cruel and wild, angry and hostile, causing cuts, burns, scalds and wounds. It can stab its way through a chart, or it can be the symbol of healthy spirited adventure, well-channeled constructive power to begin and keep up the drive. If you have trouble starting things, if you lack the get-up-and-go to start the ball rolling, if you lack aggressiveness and self-confidence, chances are there's another planet influencing your Mars. Mars rules soldiers, butchers, surgeons, salesmen—any field that requires daring, bold skill, operational technique or self-promotion.

JUPITER

This is the largest planet of the Solar System. Scientists have recently learned that Jupiter reflects more light than it receives from the Sun. In a sense it is like a star itself. In astrology it rules good luck and good cheer, health, wealth, optimism, happiness, success and joy. It is the symbol of opportunity and always opens the way for new possibilities in your life. It rules exuberance, enthusiasm, wisdom, knowledge, generosity and all forms of expansion in general. It rules actors, statesmen, clerics, professional people, religion, publishing and the distribution of many people over large areas.

Sometimes Jupiter makes you think you deserve everything, and you become sloppy, wasteful, careless and rude, prodigal and lawless, in the illusion that nothing can ever go wrong. Then there is the danger of over-confidence, exaggeration, undependability and over-indulgence.

Jupiter is the minimization of limitation and the emphasis on spirituality and potential. It is the thirst for knowledge and higher learning.

SATURN

Saturn circles our system in dark splendor with its mysterious rings, forcing us to be awakened to whatever we have neglected in the past. It will present real puzzles and problems to be solved, causing delays, obstacles and hindrances. By doing so, Saturn stirs our own sensitivity to those areas where we are laziest.

Here we must patiently develop *method,* and only through painstaking effort can our ends be achieved. It brings order to a horoscope and imposes reason just where we are feeling least reasonable. By creating limitations and boundary, Saturn shows the consequences of being human and demands that we accept the changing cycles inevitable in human life. Saturn rules time, old age and sobriety. It can bring depression, gloom, jealousy and greed, or serious acceptance of responsibilities out of which success will develop. With Saturn there is nothing to do but face facts. It rules laborers, stones, granite, rocks and crystals of all kinds.

The Outer Planets

The following three are the outer planets. They liberate human beings from cultural conditioning, and in that sense are the law breakers. In early times it was thought that Saturn was the last planet of the system—the outer limit beyond which we could never go. The discovery of the next three planets ushered in new phases of human history, revolution and technology.

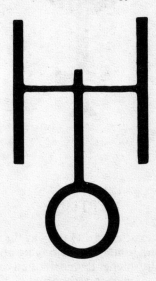

URANUS

Uranus rules unexpected change, upheaval, revolution. It is the symbol of total independence and asserts the freedom of an individual from all restriction and restraint. It is a breakthrough planet and indicates talent, originality and genius in a horoscope. It usually causes last-minute reversals and changes of plan, unwanted separations, accidents, catastrophes and eccentric behavior. It can add irrational rebelliousness and perverse bohemianism to a personality or a streak of unaffected brilliance in science and art. It rules technology, aviation and all forms of electrical and electronic advancement. It governs great leaps forward and topsy-turvy situations, and *always* turns things around at the last minute. Its effects are difficult to ever really predict, since it rules sudden last-minute decisions and events that come like lightning out of the blue.

NEPTUNE

Neptune dissolves existing reality the way the sea erodes the cliffs beside it. Its effects are subtle like the ringing of a buoy's bell in the fog. It suggests a reality higher than definition can usually describe. It awakens a sense of higher responsibility often causing guilt, worry, anxieties or delusions. Neptune is associated with all forms of escape and can make things seem a certain way so convincingly that you are absolutely sure of something that eventually turns out to be quite different.

It is the planet of illusion and therefore governs the invisible realms that lie beyond our ordinary minds, beyond our simple factual ability to prove what is "real." Treachery, deceit, disillusionment and disappointment are linked to Neptune. It describes a vague reality that promises eternity and the divine, yet in a manner so complex that we cannot really fathom it at all. At its worst Neptune is a cheap intoxicant; at its best it is the poetry, music and inspiration of the higher planes of spiritual love. It has dominion over movies, photographs and much of the arts.

PLUTO

Pluto lies at the outpost of our system and therefore rules finality in a horoscope—the final closing of chapters in your life, the passing of major milestones and points of development from which there is no return. It is a final wipeout, a closeout, an evacuation. It is a distant, subtle but powerful catalyst in all transformations that occur. It creates, destroys, then recreates. Sometimes Pluto starts its influence with a minor event or insignificant incident that might even go unnoticed. Slowly but surely, little by little, everything changes, until at last there has been a total transformation in the area of your life where Pluto has been operating. It rules mass thinking and the trends that society first rejects, then adopts and finally outgrows.

Pluto rules the dead and the underworld—all the powerful forces of creation and destruction that go on all the time beneath, around and above us. It can bring a lust for power with strong obsessions.

It is the planet that rules the metamorphoses of the caterpillar into a butterfly, for it symbolizes the capacity to change totally and forever a person's life style, way of thought and behavior.

FAMOUS PERSONALITIES

ARIES: Hans Christian Andersen, Pearl Bailey, Marlon Brando, Wernher Von Braun, Charlie Chaplin, Joan Crawford, Da Vinci, Bette Davis, Doris Day, W. C. Fields, Alec Guinness, Adolf Hitler, Billie Holiday, Thomas Jefferson, Nikita Khrushchev, Elton John, Arturo Toscanini, J. P. Morgan, Paul Robeson, Gloria Steinem, Lowell Thomas, Vincent van Gogh, Tennessee Williams

TAURUS: Fred Astaire, Charlote Brontë, Carol Burnett, Irving Berlin, Bing Crosby, Salvador Dali, Tchaikovsky, Queen Elizabeth II, Duke Ellington, Ella Fitzgerald, Henry Fonda, Sigmund Freud, Orson Welles, Joe Louis, Lenin, Karl Marx, Golda Meir, Eva Peron, Bertrand Russell, Shakespeare, Kate Smith, Benjamin Spock, Barbra Streisand, Shirley Temple, Harry Truman

GEMINI: Mikhail Baryshnikov, Boy George, Igor Stravinsky, Carlos Chavez, Walt Whitman, Bob Dylan, Ralph Waldo Emerson, Judy Garland, Paul Gauguin, Allen Ginsberg, Benny Goodman, Bob Hope, Burl Ives, John F. Kennedy, Peggy Lee, Marilyn Monroe, Joe Namath, Cole Porter, Laurence Olivier, Harriet Beecher Stowe, Queen Victoria, John Wayne, Frank Lloyd Wright

CANCER: "Dear Abby," David Brinkley, Yul Brynner, Pearl Buck, Marc Chagall, Jack Dempsey, Mildred (Babe) Zaharias, Mary Baker Eddy, Henry VIII, John Glenn, Ernest Hemingway, Lena Horne, Oscar Hammerstein, Helen Keller, Ann Landers, George Orwell, Nancy Reagan, Rembrandt, Richard Rodgers, Ginger Rogers, Rubens, Jean-Paul Sartre, O. J. Simpson

LEO: Neil Armstrong, Russell Baker, James Baldwin, Emily Brontë, Wilt Chamberlain, Julia Child, Cecil B. De Mille, Ogden Nash, Amelia Earhart, Edna Ferber, Arthur Goldberg, Dag Hammarskjöld, Alfred Hitchcock, Mick Jagger, George Meany, George Bernard Shaw, Napoleon, Jacqueline Onassis, Henry Ford, Francis Scott Key, Andy Warhol, Mae West, Orville Wright

VIRGO: Ingrid Bergman, Warren Burger, Maurice Chevalier, Agatha Christie, Sean Connery, Lafayette, Peter Falk, Greta Garbo, Althea Gibson, Arthur Godfrey, Goethe, Buddy Hackett, Michael Jackson, Lyndon Johnson, D. H. Lawrence, Sophia Loren, Grandma Moses, Arnold Palmer, Queen Elizabeth I, Walter Reuther, Peter Sellers, Lily Tomlin, George Wallace

LIBRA: Brigitte Bardot, Art Buchwald, Truman Capote, Dwight D. Eisenhower, William Faulkner, F. Scott Fitzgerald, Gandhi, George Gershwin, Micky Mantle, Helen Hayes, Vladimir Horowitz, Doris Lessing, Martina Navratalova, Eugene O'Neill, Luciano Pavarotti, Emily Post, Eleanor Roosevelt, Bruce Springsteen, Margaret Thatcher, Gore Vidal, Barbara Walters, Oscar Wilde

SCORPIO: Vivien Leigh, Richard Burton, Art Carney, Johnny Carson, Billy Graham, Grace Kelly, Walter Cronkite, Marie Curie, Charles de Gaulle, Linda Evans, Indira Gandhi, Theodore Roosevelt, Rock Hudson, Katherine Hepburn, Robert F. Kennedy, Billie Jean King, Martin Luther, Georgia O'Keeffe, Pablo Picasso, Jonas Salk, Alan Shepard, Robert Louis Stevenson

SAGITTARIUS: Jane Austen, Louisa May Alcott, Woody Allen, Beethoven, Willy Brandt, Mary Martin, William F. Buckley, Maria Callas, Winston Churchill, Noel Coward, Emily Dickinson, Walt Disney, Benjamin Disraeli, James Doolittle, Kirk Douglas, Chet Huntley, Jane Fonda, Chris Evert Lloyd, Margaret Mead, Charles Schulz, John Milton, Frank Sinatra, Steven Spielberg

CAPRICORN: Muhammad Ali, Isaac Asimov, Pablo Casals, Dizzy Dean, Marlene Dietrich, James Farmer, Ava Gardner, Barry Goldwater, Cary Grant, J. Edgar Hoover, Howard Hughes, Joan of Arc, Gypsy Rose Lee, Martin Luther King, Jr., Rudyard Kipling, Mao Tse-tung, Richard Nixon, Gamal Nasser, Louis Pasteur, Albert Schweitzer, Stalin, Benjamin Franklin, Elvis Presley

AQUARIUS: Marian Anderson, Susan B. Anthony, Jack Benny, Charles Darwin, Charles Dickens, Thomas Edison, John Barrymore, Clark Gable, Jascha Heifetz, Abraham Lincoln, John McEnroe, Yehudi Menuhin, Mozart, Jack Nicklaus, Ronald Reagan, Jackie Robinson, Norman Rockwell, Franklin D. Roosevelt, Gertrude Stein, Charles Lindbergh, Margaret Truman

PISCES: Edward Albee, Harry Belafonte, Alexander Graham Bell, Frank Borman, Chopin, Adelle Davis, Albert Einstein, Jackie Gleason, Winslow Homer, Edward M. Kennedy, Victor Hugo, Mike Mansfield, Michelangelo, Edna St. Vincent Millay, Liza Minelli, John Steinbeck, Linus Pauling, Ravel, Diana Ross, William Shirer, Elizabeth Taylor, George Washington

SCORPIO

CHARACTER ANALYSIS

People born under the sign of Scorpio are usually gifted with a very strong personality. Of all the signs, they are perhaps the most goal-directed and relentless. Often they are quite dominating. Some people find them hard to like or appreciate. Scorpio people are not afraid of being disliked. They just do not want to be ignored. They know what they want, generally speaking, and do not give up the struggle until they have it. They can be quite belligerent in stating their views; they aren't afraid of conflict or disapproval.

He has his own way of doing things—his own laws to follow. As long as he is true to himself, he is happy; he seldom dances to someone else's tune. The Scorpio is a person who perseveres. It may take some time before he achieves his ends, but he'll wait. He pushes ahead, ignoring the setbacks, the disappointments.

The person born under this sign often sees life as one big fight. Often he controls himself like a soldier. He is willing to undergo self-discipline in order to win out. He trains himself so that he is bound to be the victor. Defeat is something the Scorpio man or woman cannot accept. They do their best to see to it that it never comes about. People born under this eighth sign of the Zodiac are fighters. Generally, they are gifted with brains and know how to put them to use. They can be clever and shrewd when the occasion calls for it. The Scorpion could hardly be called sensitive. Most of the time he is not terribly interested in how others might feel or react to his behavior. His nature is not a soft one; he can't be buttered up and sugared over. The Scorpio person generally says what he means. He can be quite cutting and when forced to can reduce his adversary to a pitiful state by just saying a few words. He is not the kind of person who encourages others with words of hope and best wishes. He is too concerned with his own aims for that.

Many people find it difficult to understand the personality of the person born under the sign of Scorpio. It is rather a subtle combination of intelligence and ruthlessness. Quite often people of this sign are seized by profound and revealing thoughts that are too complex to express. At such moments, the Scorpio is likely to draw within himself and remain silent. He may spend most of his quiet moments within his own private world—a realm with its own rules and regulations. He is quite interested in the mysteries of life. Some Scorpios have a deep almost intuitive understanding of life and death.

Scorpios tend to be consistent in all that they do. They never do things halfway. They are not afraid of conflict situations or emergencies. Under duress they can be relied upon to handle things in a calm manner. He is generally constructive and positive in the way he channels his forces. He is against waste and feels committed to make every gesture—every action—count.

In spite of his good sense of purpose and direction, the person born under the sign of Scorpio is sometimes the victim of his conflicting moods. He may contradict himself several times a day without feeling that he is being untrue to himself and his beliefs. He believes that every moment has its own truth. He feels his moods strongly and believes that it is necessary to obey them in order to remain the person he is. The Scorpio is an organizer. He likes to have things his own way or not at all. On the whole, he is what you would call a principled person. He holds fast to his ideals.

His understanding of life is sometimes remarkable. He is not short on insight and often can analyze a human situation accurately long before others. His knowledge of things in general is often superior to that of others. In spite of the intelligence he has at his disposal he is not the kind of person to take the easy way toward a goal. He seems to have a penchant for argumentation. In some instances, he seems to bring about quarrels just for the enjoyment he derives from crossing swords.

The Scorpio's ability to fly into a rage is considerable. People sometimes wind up disliking him intensely after having witnessed one of his fits of temper. This does not bother him, however. If he loses a friend or two along his way in life he is not apt to let it upset him. He keeps moving on—his ultimate goal always in sight. He is capable of being angry at someone quite abruptly but it never lasts very long. He has more important things to do in life besides holding grudges.

He does not believe in using fancy or complicated language; he is to the point—not really caring how blunt he may sound to sensitive ears. Power—and how to get it—is what is most important to him in life; he does not try to hide this fact.

In spite of him being straight-off-the-shoulder in most of his dealings, the Scorpio man or woman is capable of holding back a fact or two—especially if it is to his or her advantage.

Health

On the whole, the person born under this sign is quite healthy. His constitution is generally strong; he seldom has to worry about common ailments. He is capable of great spurts of energy. He can apply himself to a strenuous task for a long period of time without tiring. The Scorpio person rather enjoys stress and strain; it proves his mettle. As has already been mentioned, the Scorpio man or woman is seldom bothered by illnesses; their resistance is remarkably strong. When, however, he does become ill—really ill—he has to give in in order to recuperate. Illness is a sort of weakness or frailty to him. He is ashamed of himself when he is sick and does all he can to quickly recover. If he tries to fight it—that is, act as if he weren't incapacitated—he often winds up worse off than when he began. It is difficult at times for the Scorpio to realize that even he has limits.

In spite of the fact that he can take on a lot, it is also important that the person born under the sign of Scorpio learn how to relax. Often, Scorpio people push themselves to the limit—and sometimes there are serious consequences to pay. Overworked Scorpios are highly susceptible to breakdowns of various sorts. It is the cultivated Scorpio man or woman who knows when and how to relax. Because of their serious attitude toward most things, the Scorpio when young often seems much older than what he really is.

The Scorpio man or woman is often sturdily built. There is usually something massive about them—they are often largeboned and have deep set interesting eyes. In general, they could best be described as sensuous in their appearance and behavior. Scorpio women are often beautiful in a seductive way. Their voices are sometimes husky and rather sexy.

The weakest part of the Scorpio's anatomy is his digestive system. Whenever he becomes ill this is the area usually affected. The sensible person born under this sign pays attention to minor warnings of an oncoming illness and does something about it while there is still time. Some people born under this sign pick up infections rather easily.

Occupation

The Scorpio man or woman is a very industrious person. He enjoys keeping busy and he always finishes what he starts. He does not believe in turning out slipshod work; he's a professional. The Scorpio is not a person lacking in push or energy. He takes his work seriously and does what he can to be recognized for his deeds.

Quite often the person born under the sign of Scorpio dislikes heavy work. He would much rather leave that to someone else. He is goal-directed. It is important for him to achieve what he desires . . . in some instances, it does not matter how. When he sets his mind to it—and he usually does—he can accomplish almost anything he wishes. Obstacles do not frighten him; in fact, the threat of opposition seems to spur him on. He is no quitter. He'll hang on until the bitter end. His never-say-die attitude helps him to scan heights that would frighten others. He's confident of himself and of the moves he makes.

The Scorpio person is ambitious. He can make work even when there isn't any—just to keep busy. Idleness tends to bore him and make him disagreeable. He is fascinated by difficult tasks. He enjoys figuring out ways of how to attack a project or a chore. He doesn't always choose the easiest route—but the most challenging. In short he's a fighter.

His intellectual ability is quite superior. There is almost no subject that would stump him. He is not afraid of learning something new and is quite capable of applying himself to new or different trains of thought if he feels they will help him achieve his ends.

Generally speaking Scorpio people prefer to work for themselves—they don't like to share tasks, but will if it is absolutely necessary. People who work with them are not apt to find this relationship an enjoyable one, for the Scorpio is always ready to bring about a quarrel or argument if things are not going exactly the way he likes.

Often people born under this sign do extremely well in the field of medicine or science. They have a deep interest in exploration of all sorts and are willing to devote their whole lives to something that is somewhat elusive and mysterious. The Scorpio has an open mind and this helps him to succeed in the things he does. He likes to make tests; to prove things through experimentation. He isn't afraid of taking risks. He is always sure of himself—sure that he'll come out a winner. Some people born under the sign of Scorpio make good detectives and lawyers.

The Scorpio person feels deeply whenever he is engaged socially. He can either hate someone or love them; there is no middle of the road. He cannot afford to be indifferent. He'll admire someone if he feels that person deserves to be admired. He makes a strong leader. The people working under him may dislike him rather intensely but they will not try to usurp his authority. He won't put up with any nonsense from his subordinates and he lets them know that right from the start.

In whatever he undertakes, he forges ahead with no thought of quitting until the goal has been reached. His powers of concentration are amazingly strong. He seldom allows himself to be distracted from the path he has chosen. He expects the people work-ing under him to have the same sort of devotion to purpose that he has. He can be quite a driver at times. If others are not up to his standards, he won't waste time by pampering them—he'll simply discard them and take on new people.

Some Scorpios have a bit of the genius in them. They are quite perceptive and often can accurately guess what someone else is thinking—particularly in a conflict situation.

People born under this sign are basically materialists. They are quite fond of money and what it can do and make no effort to dis-guise their interest. They are extremely power-oriented. Money seldom presents a problem to them. One way or another, they almost always come by the finances they feel they need or deserve. They are fond of luxuries as well, of course; and are sometimes deeply involved in such power-games as "keeping up with the Joneses;" in most instances the Joneses wind up trying to keep up with them.

The Scorpio person is careful in the way he handles his fi-nances. He doesn't believe in waste, although at times he is given to being extravagent. When he is wealthy, he can be a bit of a show-off about it. He can easily detect a false friend—someone who associates with him for the gain he is likely to derive from the relationship.

Home and Family

In general, the person born under the sign of Scorpio is not terri-bly interested in an intense domestic life. He does not like to feel tied down by home and family. However, he is adaptable and will be willing to sacrifice some of his freedoms for the comforts and conveniences a home life can provide. Routine, though, bores him and is apt to put him in a bad mood. He enjoys a home life that has a surprise in it now and again. Day-in day-out monotony is something he refuses to tolerate.

He is as efficient and forceful in his homemaking as he is in other things. He likes to see to it that everything runs well. His home may be quite glamorous in an ostentatious way. He is fond of a show of luxury. His tastes in furnishings is likely to be some-what outspoken. It is likely to offend someone who has refined or cultivated taste.

The Scorpio man is proud. He enjoys showing off his posses-sions. His family is important to him. He likes his wife and chil-dren to support him in his interests and attitudes. Keeping his home attractive and luxurious is a full-time activity for many

Scorpios. They are interested in having the latest appliances and the best trademark.

The Scorpio person likes to rule his own roost. His mate had better not try to take the head position. He wears the pants in the family and is apt to make that unmistakably clear before the marriage has taken place. All of the major decisions must be made by him. He'll listen to another's point of view but will hardly take it into consideration when making up his mind.

Luxury helps the Scorpio man or woman to feel successful. It has definite psychological influence. The Scorpio in shabby surroundings is apt to be quite difficult to get along with. A show of affluence brightens his spirits and helps him to feel that he is on the right road.

The Scorpio person is often fond of large families. He may not be as responsible as he should be in caring for them. Quite often he is a strict parent and tolerates no misbehavior from his offspring. The children may resent his iron hand—especially when they are young—but as they reach adulthood they are likely to be thankful for his firmness. The Scorpio is only concerned with instilling those values in his children which will help them to go far in the battlefield of life. He can be quite a disciplinarian. Some of them are quite possessive of their children.

Scorpios as children are often very affectionate. As a rule, they are sensitive children and should be handled in a considerate and loving way. Emotionally, they may not be as strong as children born under other signs. The observant and sensitive parent should have no trouble in bringing him up in such a way that he is able to develop his personality along natural lines as he reaches a stage of independence.

At times the Scorpio child may be difficult to manage. He may be delinquent at times and cause some trouble at school. In spite of this, he is apt to show strong creative or artistic talent during his growing-up period. The wise parent or guardian will do what he can to foster this interest in such a way that it develops along satisfactory lines.

Social Relationships

Scorpio people are deeply interested in sex. They enjoy being physically involved with the people they feel themselves attracted to. They are often given to experimentation in sex; they are curious and want to know all there is to discover. They are, by and large, intensely passionate and intensely emotional. Life without love is difficult for them to imagine. It is important to them that their sex life is well arranged and interesting. They may spend a great deal of time getting involved sexually with all kinds of people before they are satisfied and can concentrate their attention on just one person.

LOVE AND MARRIAGE

The Scorpio can be quite a flirt. He may have quite a number of affairs before he thinks about settling down. In every romantic adventure he is quite sincere. He does not believe in being false or untrue when involved with someone. However, his interest may dissolve after he feels he has discovered everything there was to find out about a particular person. He is not very interested in light romances. He means business when it comes to love. He expects his lover to be as honest in his affections as he is.

The Scorpio is in need of someone who is as passionate and understanding as he is. His romances may be rather violent at times; an element of struggle may be quite definite in them—in fact, it is this quality that will perhaps keep his interest alive in a love affair. He likes to be admired and complimented by his partner. He hates criticism and is apt to become rather difficult if his lover finds fault with him.

He does what he can to make his loved one comfortable and happy. He can be rather generous when in love and is never without a gift or some token of his affection. He likes to impress his loved one with a show of luxury. Often his gifts are quite expensive.

It is important to the Scorpio person that the object of his affections be true during the relationship. He is very jealous and possessive. If he suspects deceit, he can be violent.

The best partner for a Scorpio person is one who can compliment his character. Someone who does not mind being agreeable and supportive. Someone who does not mind letting him make all of the decisions both large and small. A quiet, retiring sort of person sometimes makes the ideal mate for the man or woman born under Scorpio. Two Scorpios often clash; however, if they are cultivated and understand themselves well, they can go far together—helping each other out in various ways.

When the Scorpio man or woman sets his sights on someone he generally wins them. He can be quite demonstrative when dealing with someone who tries to stand between him and his loved one. He will do everything in his power to win the person who interests him. Some people born under this sign will stop at nothing in order to eliminate competition. Others are rather jealous and suspicious when they really have no cause to be.

In married life, the Scorpio person seldom gives himself completely—even though he may expect this of his partner. There is always a corner of himself which he does not give away. In general, the person born under this sign is faithful to his mate. However, if home life is rather dull, he will do what he can not to spend too much time there. He'll see to it that outside interests keep him occupied as much as possible.

The Scorpio person marries for keeps. He is not the kind of person who shouts "divorce!" as soon as something goes wrong. Marriage is important to him and he is willing to do whatever is necessary to keep the relationship alive and fruitful.

Romance and the Scorpio Woman

The Scorpio woman is generally quite attractive and is often sought after by the opposite sex. Her attractiveness is sometimes more suggestive than real. Her voice is rather rough and mellow— her mannerisms not without charm. She can be quite passionate when in love. She may be too much to handle for the man of moderate romantic interests. She does what she can to make a success of her love life. When in love, she does not hold back her affections. She expects the same honesty from her partner.

She is always serious when in love. She may have a great number of affairs before actually settling down. Romance is important to her. But more important is that she find a man that is compatible to her interests and needs. The man she desires, she usually wins. She is sure of herself in matters of the heart and can be very persuasive when necessary. Men find her difficult to ignore or resist. She may be rather jealous and possessive. If she suspects her lover of not being true, she can become quite angry and vindictive.

She is usually accurate when sizing up someone who interests her. She seldom choses the wrong man. She is usually very faithful when married. She does all she can to help her man get ahead in his career. She supports him in all his interests and often is able to supply him with some very good advice. She will never let her husband down even in difficult times. She will fight for her husband if it is necessary.

The Scorpio woman is a bit old-fashioned when it comes to attitudes about marriage. She is often contented with her role as housewife and mother. She does everything she can to keep the household in order.

Although others may not think her suitable material for a mother because of her emotional and sometimes explosive outbursts, she does what she can to bring up her children correctly. She is rather strict, especially when they are young. They understand her better though, as they grow older.

Romance and the Scorpio Man

The Scorpio man is often popular with women. There is something magnetic about his charm. He is protective and adventurous. His passionate way in love often sweeps women off their feet. Love—in each affair—is a matter of life and death. He does not believe in being lighthearted.

As a rule, he is warm and generous. He knows how to make a woman feel loved and wanted. He expects his loved one to be as demonstrative as he is in expressing her love. By nature, he is possessive and resents another's interest in his woman. He can easily become jealous. His anger can be quite frightening to a sensitive woman.

The Scorpio man makes a good husband and father. He is a good provider, most often, and sees to it that his family has everything it needs. His married life is apt to be full of ups and downs. He is affectionate though and true in his desire to be a good husband; this sometimes makes it easier for his wife to accept his changeable nature. He is faithful. Once settled down he is apt to stay true to his wife. The cultivated Scorpio man is often successful in marriage. He knows how to withhold his negative traits so that they do not seriously affect the relationship.

He is fond of large families. Even though he may father one himself, he may not have enough interest in his offspring—especially when they are young—to make them feel secure and well loved. As the children grow older, however, and reach an adult stage, his interest is likely to increase considerably. At any rate, he will always see to it that they never want for anything.

Woman—Man

SCORPIO WOMAN
ARIES MAN

Although it's possible that you could find happiness with a man born under the sign of the Ram, it's uncertain as to how long that happiness would last.

An Aries who has made his mark in the world and is somewhat

steadfast in his outlooks and attitudes could be quite a catch for you. On the other hand, men under this sign are often swift-footed and quick-minded; their industrious mannerisms may fail to impress you, especially if you feel that much of their get-up-and-go often leads nowhere.

When it comes to a fine romance, you want someone with a nice, broad shoulder to lean on. You are likely to find a relationship with someone who doesn't like to stay put for too long somewhat upsetting.

The Aries man may have a little trouble in understanding you, too . . . at least, in the beginning of the relationship. He may find you a bit too shy and moody. Aries men tend to speak their minds; he's liable to criticize you at the drop of a hat.

You may find a man born under this sign too demanding. He may give you the impression that he expects you to be at his beck and call. You have a lot of patience at your disposal and he may try every last bit of it. He is apt to be not as thorough as you in everything he does. In order to achieve success or a goal quickly, he is liable to overlook small but important details—and regret it when it is too late.

Being married to an Aries does not mean that you'll have a secure and safe life as far as finances are concerned. Not all Aries are rash with cash, but they lack the sound head you perhaps have for putting away something for that inevitable rainy day. He'll do his best, however, to see that you're adequately provided for—even though his efforts may leave something to be desired as far as you're concerned.

With an Aries man for a mate, you'll find yourself constantly among people. Aries people generally have many friends—and you may not heartily approve of them all. People born under this sign are often more interested in "interesting" people than they are in influential ones. Although there may be a family squabble from time to time, you are stable enough to be able to take it in your stride.

Aries men love children. They make wonderful fathers. Kids take to them like ducks to water. Their quick minds and behavior appeal to the young.

SCORPIO WOMAN
TAURUS MAN

If you've got your heart set on a man born under the sign of Taurus, you'll have to learn the art of being patient. Taureans take their time about everything—even love.

The steady and deliberate Taurus man is a little slow on the draw; it may take him quite a while before he gets around to popping that question. For the woman who doesn't mind twiddling her thumbs, the waiting and anticipating almost always pays off. Taurus men want to make sure that every step they take is a good one —particularly, if they feel that the path they're on leads to the altar.

If you are in the mood for a whirlwind romance, you had better cast your net in shallower waters. Moreover, most Taureans prefer to do the angling themselves. They are not keen on women taking the lead; once she does, he's liable to drop her like a dead fish. If you let yourself get caught on his terms, you'll find that he's fallen for you—hook, line, and sinker.

The Taurus man is fond of a comfortable homelife. It is very important to him. If you keep those home fires burning you will have no trouble keeping that flame in your Taurean's heart aglow. You have a talent for homemaking; use it. Your taste in furnishings is excellent. You know how to make a house come to life with colors and decorations.

Taurus, the strong, steady, and protective Bull may not be your idea of a man on the move, still he's reliable. Perhaps he could be the anchor for your dreams and plans. He could help you to acquire a more balanced outlook and approach to your life. If you're given to impulsiveness, he could help you to curb it. He's the man who is always there when you need him.

When you tie the knot with a man born under Taurus, you can put away fears about creditors pounding on the door. Taureans are practical about everything including bill-paying. When he carries you over that threshold, you can be certain that the entire house is paid for, not only the doorsill.

As a housewife, you won't have to worry about putting aside your many interests for the sake of back-breaking house chores. Your Taurus hubby will see to it that you have all the latest time-saving appliances and comforts.

Your children will be obedient and orderly. Your Taurus husband will see to that.

SCORPIO WOMAN
GEMINI MAN

Gemini men, in spite of their charm and dashing manner, may make your skin crawl. They may seem to lack the sort of common sense you set so much store in. Their tendency to start something then, out of boredom, never finish it, may do nothing more than exasperate you.

You may be inclined to interpret a Gemini's jumping around

from here to there as childish if not downright neurotic. A man born under this sign will seldom stay put and if you should take it upon yourself to try and make him sit still, he's liable to resent it strongly.

On the other hand, the Gemini man is liable to think you're an old slowpoke—someone far too interested in security and material things. He's attracted to things that sparkle and dazzle; you, with your practical way of looking at things most of the time, are likely to seem a little dull and uninteresting to this gadabout. If you're looking for a life of security and permanence, you'd better look elsewhere for your Mr. Right.

Chances are you'll be taken by his charming ways and facile wit—few women can resist Gemini magic—but after you've seen through his live-for-today, gossamer facade, you'll most likely be very happy to turn your attention to someone more stable, even if he is not as interesting. You want a man who is there when you need him. You need someone on whom you can fully rely. Keeping track of a Gemini's movements will make you dizzy. Still, if you are a patient woman, you should be able to put up with someone contrary—especially if you feel the experience may be well worth the effort.

A successful and serious Gemini could make you a very happy woman, perhaps if you gave him half a chance. Although you may think he's got bats in his belfry, the Gemini man generally has a good brain and can make good use of it when he wants. Some Geminis who have learned the importance of being diligent have risen to great heights, professionally. President Kennedy was a Gemini as was Thomas Mann and William Butler Yeats. Once you can convince yourself that not all people born under the sign of the Twins are witless grasshoppers, you'll find that you've come a long way in trying to understand them.

Life with a Gemini man can be more fun than a barrel of clowns. You'll never experience a dull moment. He's always the life of the party. He's a little scatterbrained when it comes to handling money most of the time. You'd better handle the budgeting and bookkeeping.

In ways, he's like a child and perhaps that is why he can get along so well with the younger generation.

SCORPIO WOMAN
CANCER MAN

The man born under the sign of Cancer may very well be the man after your own heart. Generally, Cancer people are steady. They are interested in security and practicality. Despite their seemingly grouchy exterior, men born under the sign of the Crab are rather sensitive and kind individuals. They are amost always hard workers and are very interested in becoming successful in business as well as in society. You'll find that his conservative outlook on many things often agrees with yours. He'll be a man on whom you can depend come rain or shine. He 'll never shirk his responsibilities as a provider and he'll always see to it that his wife and family never want.

Your patience will come in handy if you decide it's a Cancer may you want for a mate. He isn't the type that rushes headlong into romance. He wants to be sure about love as you do. If after the first couple of months of dating, he suggests that you take a walk with him down lovers' lane, don't jump to the conclusion that he's about to make his "great play." Chances are he'll only hold your hand and seriously observe the stars. Don't let his coolness fool you, though. Beneath his starched reserve lies a very warm heart. He's just not interested in showing off as far as affection is concerned. Don't think his interest is wandering if he doesn't kiss you goodnight at the front door; that just isn't his style. For him, affection should only be displayed for two sets of eyes—yours and his. He's passionate only in private.

He will never step out of line. He's too much of a gentleman for that. When you're alone with him and there's no chance of you being disturbed or spied upon, he'll pull out an engagement ring (that used to belong to his grandmother) and slip it on your trembling finger.

Speaking of relatives, you'll have to get pretty much used to the fact that Cancer men are overly fond of their mothers. When he says his mother is the most wonderful woman in the world, you'd better agree with him—that is, if you want to become his wife.

He'll always be a faithful husband; Cancer men never play around after they've taken that marriage vow. They don't take marriage responsibilities lightly. He'll see to it that everything in the house runs smoothly and that bills are paid promptly—never put aside. He's liable to take all kinds of insurance policies out on his family and property. He'll arrange it so that when retirement time rolls around, you'll both be very well off.

Men under this sign make patient and understanding fathers.

SCORPIO WOMAN
LEO MAN

To know a man born under the sign of the Lion is not necessarily to love him—even though the temptation may be great. When he fixes most girls with his leonine double-whammy, it causes their hearts to pitter-pat and their minds to cloud over.

You are a little too sensible to allow yourself to be bowled over by a regal strut and a roar. Still, there's no denying that Leo has a way with women—even sensible women like yourself. Once he's swept a girl off her feet, it may be hard for her to scramble upright again. However, you are no pushover for romantic charm—especially if you feel it's all show.

He'll wine you and dine you in the fanciest places. He'll croon to you under the moon and shower you with diamonds if he can get a hold of them . . . but, it would be wise to find out just how long that shower is going to last before consenting to be his wife.

Lions in love are hard to ignore, let alone brush off. Your no's will have a way of nudging him on until he feels he has you completely under his spell. Once mesmerized by this romantic powerhouse, you will most likely find yourself doing things you never dreamed of. Leos can be like vain pussycats when involved romantically. They like to be cuddled, curried, and tickled under the chin. This may not be your cup of tea exactly, still when you're romantically dealing with a man born under the sign of Leo, you'll find yourself doing all kinds of things to make him purr.

Although he may be big and magnanimous while trying to win you, he'll let out a blood-curdling roar if he thinks he's not getting the tender love and care he feels is his due. If you keep him well supplied with affection, you can be sure his eyes will never look for someone else and his heart will never wander.

Leo men often tend to be authoritarian—they are born to lord it over others in one way or another, it seems. If he is the top banana at his firm, he'll most likely do everything he can to stay on top. If he's not number one, he's most likely working on it and will be sitting on the throne before long.

You'll have more security than you can use if he is in a position to support you in the manner to which he feels you should be accustomed. He is apt to be too lavish, at least by your standards.

You'll always have plenty of friends when you have a Leo for a mate. He's a natural-born friend-maker and entertainer. He loves to kick up his heels at a party.

As fathers, Leos tend to spoil their children no end.

SCORPIO WOMAN
VIRGO MAN

Although the Virgo man may be a bit of a fuss-budget at times, his seriousness and dedication to common sense may help you to overlook his tendency to sometimes be overcritical about minor things.

Virgo men are often quiet, respectable types who set great store in conservative behavior and level-headedness. He'll admire you for your practicality and tenacity—perhaps even more than for your good looks. He's seldom bowled over by a glamour-puss. When he gets his courage up, he turns to a serious and reliable girl for romance. He'll be far from a Valentino while dating. In fact, you may wind up making all the passes. Once he does get his motor running, however, he can be a warm and wonderful fellow—to the right girl.

He's gradual about love. Chances are your romance with him will most likely start out looking like an ordinary friendship. Once he's sure you're no fly-by-night flirt and have no plans of taking him for a ride, he'll open up and rain sunshine all over your heart.

Virgo men tend to marry late in life. He believes in holding out until he's met the right girl. He may not have many names in his little black book; in fact, he may not even have a black book. He's not interested in playing the field; leave that to men of the more flamboyant signs. The Virgo man is so particular that he may remain romantically inactive for a long period. His girl has to be perfect or it's no go. If you find yourself feeling weak-kneed for a Virgo man, do your best to convince him that perfect is not so important when it comes to love; help him to realize that he's missing out on a great deal by not considering the near-perfect or whatever it is you consider yourself to be. With your sure-fire perseverance, you will most likely be able to make him listen to reason and he'll wind up reciprocating your romantic interests.

The Virgo man is no block of ice. He'll respond to what he feels to be the right feminine flame. Once your love-life with a Virgo man starts to bubble, don't give it a chance to fall flat. You may never have a second chance at winning his heart.

If you should ever have a falling out with him, forget about patching up. He'd prefer to let the pieces lie scattered. Once married, though, he'll stay that way—even if it hurts. He's too conscientious to try to back out of a legal deal of any sort.

The Virgo man is as neat as a pin. He's thumbs down on sloppy housekeeping. Keep everything bright, neat, and shiny . . . and that goes for the children, too, at least by the time he gets home from work. Chocolate-coated kisses from Daddy's little girl go over like a lead balloon with him.

SCORPIO WOMAN
LIBRA MAN

You are apt to find men born under the sign of Libra too wrapped up in their own private dreams to be really interesting as far as love and romance are concerned. Quite often, he is a difficult person to bring back down to earth; it is hard for him to face reality at times. Although he may be very cautious about weighing both sides of an argument, he may never really come to a reasonable decision about anything. Decision-making is something that often makes the Libra man uncomfortable; he'd rather leave that job to someone else. Don't ask him why for he probably doesn't know himself.

Qualities such as permanance and constancy are important to you in a love relationship. The Libra man may be quite a puzzle for you. One moment he comes on hard and strong with declarations of his love; the next moment you find he's left you like yesterday's mashed potatoes. It does no good to wonder what went wrong. Chances are: nothing, really. It's just one of Libra's strange ways.

He is not exactly what you would call an ambitious person; you are perhaps looking for a mate or friend with more drive and fidelity. You are the sort of person who is interested in getting ahead—in making some headway in the areas that interest you; the Libran is often contented just to drift along. He does have drive, however, but it's not the long-range kind. It is not that he's shiftless or lazy. He's interested in material things; he appreciates luxuries and the like, but he may not be willing to work hard enough to obtain them. Beauty and harmony interest him. He'll dedicate a lot of time arranging things so that they are aesthetically pleasing. It would be difficult to accuse the Libra man of being practical; nine times out of ten, he isn't.

If you do begin a relationship with a man born under this sign, you will have to coax him now and again to face various situations in a realistic manner. You'll have your hands full, that's for sure. But if you love him, you'll undoubtedly do your best to understand him—no matter how difficult this may be.

If you take up with a Libra man, either temporarily or permanently, you'd better take over the task of managing his money. Often he has little understanding of financial matters; he tends to spend without thinking, following his whims.

SCORPIO WOMAN
SCORPIO MAN

Many find the Scorpio's sting a fate worse than death. When his anger breaks loose, you had better clear out of the vicinity.

The average Scorpio may strike you as a brute. He'll stick pins into the balloons of your plans and dreams if they don't line up with what he thinks is right. If you do anything to irritate him—

just anything—you'll wish you hadn't. He'll give you a sounding out that would make you pack your bags and go back to Mother—if you were that kind of a girl.

The Scorpio man hates being tied down to home life—he would rather be out on the battlefield of life, belting away at whatever he feels is a just and worthy cause, instead of staying home nestled in a comfortable armchair with the evening paper. If you are a girl who has a homemaking streak—don't keep those home fires burning too brightly too long; you may just run out of firewood.

As passionate as he is in business affairs and politics, the Scorpio man still has plenty of pep and ginger stored away for lovemaking.

Most women are easily attracted to him—perhaps you are no exception. Those who allow a man born under this sign to sweep them off their feet, shortly find that they're dealing with a pepper pot of seething excitement. The Scorpio man is passionate with a capital P, you can be sure of that. But he's capable of dishing out as much pain as pleasure. Damsels with fluttering hearts who, when in the emrrace of a Scorpio, think "This is it," had better be in a position moments later to realize that "Perhaps this isn't it."

Scorpios are blunt. An insult is likely to whiz out of his mouth quicker than a compliment.

If you're the kind of woman who can keep a stiff upper lip, take it on the chin, turn a deaf ear, and all of that, because you feel you are still under his love spell in spite of everything: lots of luck.

If you have decided to take the bitter with the sweet, prepare yourself for a lot of ups and downs. Chances are you won't have as much time for your own affairs and interests as you'd like. The Scorpio's love of power may cause you to be at his constant beck and call.

Scorpios like fathering large families. They love children but quite often they fail to live up to their responsibilities as a parent.

SCORPIO WOMAN
SAGITTARIUS MAN

Sagittarius men are not easy to catch. They get cold feet whenever visions of the altar enter the romance. You'll most likely be attracted to the Sagittarian because of his sunny nature. He's lots of laughs and easy to get along with, but as soon as the relationship begins to take on a serious hue, you may feel yourself a little letdown.

Sagittarians are full of bounce; perhaps too much bounce to suit you. They are often hard to pin down; they dislike staying put. If he ever has a chance to be on-the-move, he'll latch onto it without so much as a how-do-you-do. Sagittarians are quick people—both in mind and spirit. If ever they do make mistakes, it's because of their zip; they leap before they look.

If you offer him good advice, he most likely won't follow it. Saigittarians like to rely on their own wits and ways.

His up-and-at-'em manner about most things is likely to drive you up the wall. He's likely to find you a little too slow and deliberate. "Get the lead out of your shoes," he's liable to tease when you're accompanying him on a stroll or jogging through the park with him on Sunday morning. He can't abide a slowpoke.

At times you'll find him too much like a kid—too breezy. Don't mistake his youthful zest for premature senility. Sagittarians are equipped with first-class brain power and know how to use it. They are often full of good ideas and drive. Generally, they are very broadminded people and very much concerned with fair play and equality.

In the romance department, he's quite capable of loving you wholeheartedly while treating you like a good pal. His hail-fellow-well-met manner in the arena of love is likely to scare off a dainty damsel. However, a woman who knows that his heart is in the right place won't mind it too much if, once in a while, he slaps her (lightly) on the back instead of giving her a gentle embrace.

He's not so much of a homebody. He's got ants in his pants and enjoys being on the move. Humdrum routine—especially at home—bores him silly. At the drop of a hat, he may ask you to whip off your apron and dine out for a change. He's a past-master in the instant surprise department. He'll love to keep you guessing. His friendly, candid nature will win him many friends. He'll expect his friends to be yours, and vice-versa.

Sagittarians make good fathers when the children become older; with little shavers, they feel all thumbs.

SCORPIO WOMAN
CAPRICORN MAN

The Capricorn man is quite often not the romantic kind of lover that attracts most women. Still, with his reserve and calm, he is capable of giving his heart completely once he has found the right girl. The Capricorn man is thorough and deliberate in all that he does; he is slow and sure.

He doesn't believe in flirting and would never lead a heart on a merry chase just for the game of it. If you win his trust, he'll give you his heart on a platter. Quite often, it is the woman who has to take the lead when romance is in the air. As long as he knows you're making the advances in earnest, he won't mind—in fact, he'll probably be grateful. Don't get to thinking he's all cold fish; he isn't. While some Capricorns are indeed quite capable of expressing passion, others often have difficulty in trying to display affection. He should have no trouble in this area, however, once he has found a patient and understanding girl.

The Capricorn man is very interested in getting ahead. He's quite ambitious and usually knows how to apply himself well to whatever task he undertakes. He's far from being a spendthrift. Like you, he knows how to handle money with extreme care. You, with your knack for putting away pennies for that rainy day, should have no difficulty understanding his way with money. The Capricorn man thinks in terms of future security. He wants to make sure that he and his wife have something to fall back on when they reach retirement. There's nothing wrong with that; in fact, it's a plus quality.

The Capricorn man will want you to handle household matters efficiently. Most Capricorn-oriented women will have no trouble in doing this. If he should check up on you from time to time, don't let it irritate you. Once you assure him that you can handle it all to his liking, he'll leave you alone.

The Capricorn man likes to be liked. He may seem dull to some, but underneath his reserve there is sometimes an adventurous streak that has never had a chance to express itself. He may be a real daredevil in his heart of hearts. The right woman—the affectionate, adoring woman can bring out that hidden zest in his nature.

He makes a loving, dutiful father, even though he may not understand his children completely.

SCORPIO WOMAN
AQUARIUS MAN

You are liable to find the Aquarius man the most broadminded man you have ever met; on the other hand, you are also liable to find him the most impractical. Oftentimes, he's more of a dreamer than a doer. If you don't mind putting up with a man whose heart and mind are as wide as the Missouri but whose head is almost always up in the clouds, then start dating that Aquarian who has somehow captured your fancy.

He's no dumbbell; make no mistake about that. He can be busy making some very complicated and idealistic plans when he's got that out-to-lunch look in his eyes. But more than likely, he'll never execute them. After he's shared one or two of his progressive ideas with you, you are liable to ask yourself, "Who is this nut?" But don't go jumping to conclusions. There's a saying that Aquarians are a half-century ahead of everybody else in the thinking department.

If you decide to answer "Yes" to his "Will you marry me?", you'll find out how right his zany whims are on or about your 50th anniversary. Maybe the waiting will be worth it. Could be that you have an Einstein on your hands—and heart.

Life with an Aquarian won't be one of total dispair if you can learn to temper his airiness. The Aquarian always maintains an open mind; he'll entertain the ideas and opinions of everybody although he may not agree with all of them.

His broadmindedness doesn't stop when it comes to you and your personal freedom. You won't have to give up any of your hobbies or projects after you're married; he'll encourage you to continue in your interests.

He'll be a kind and generous husband. He'll never quibble over petty things. Keep track of the money you both spend. He can't. Money burns a hole in his pockets.

At times, you may feel like calling it quits because he fails to satisfy your intense feelings. Chances are, though, that you'll always give him another chance.

He's a good family man. He understands children as much as he loves them.

SCORPIO WOMAN
PISCES MAN

The Pisces man could be the man you've looked for high and low and thought never existed. He's terribly sensitive and terribly romantic. Still, he has a very strong individual character and is well aware that the moon is not made of green cheese. He'll be very considerate of your every wish and will do his best to see to it that your relationship is a happy one.

The Pisces man is great for showering the object of his affection with all kinds of little gifts and tokens of his love.

He's just the right mixture of dreamer and realist; he's capable of pleasing most women's hearts. When it comes to earning bread and butter, the strong Pisces will do all right in the world. Quite often they are capable of rising to the very top. Some do extremely well as writers or psychiatrists. He'll be as patient and understanding with you as you will undoubtedly be with him. One thing a Pisces man dislikes is pettiness; anyone who delights in running another into the ground is almost immediately crossed off his list of possible mates. If you have any small grievances with your girl-friends, don't tell him. He couldn't care less and will think less of you if you do.

If you fall in love with a weak kind of Piscean, don't give up your job at the office before you get married. Better hang onto it until a good time after the honeymoon; you may still need it. A funny thing about the man born under this sign is that he can be content almost anywhere. This is perhaps because he is quite inner-directed and places little value on material things. In a shack or a palace, the Pisces man is capable of making the best of all possible adjustments. He won't kick up a fuss if the roof leaks and if the fence is in sad need of repair, he's liable just to shrug his shoulders. He's got more important things on his mind, he'll tell you. At this point, you'll most likely feel like giving him a piece of your mind. Still and all, the Pisces man is not shiftless or aimless; it is important to understand that material gain is never a direct goal for someone born under this sign.

Pisces men have a way with the sick and troubled. He can listen to one hard-luck story after another without seeming to tire. He often knows what's bothering someone before that someone knows it himself.

As a lover, he'll be quite attentive. You'll never have cause to doubt his intentions or sincerity. Everything will be above-board in his romantic dealings with you.

Children are delighted with Pisces men because of their permissiveness.

Man—Woman

SCORPIO MAN
ARIES WOMAN

The Aries woman may be a little too bossy and busy for you. Generally speaking, Aries are ambitious creatures. They can become a little impatient with people who are more thorough and deliberate than they are—especially if they feel they're taking too much time. The Aries woman is a fast worker. Sometimes she's so fast she forgets to look where she's going. When she stumbles or falls, it would be nice if you were there to catch her. Aries are proud women. They don't like to be told "I told you so" when they err. Tongue lashings can turn them into blocks of ice. Don't begin to think that the Aries woman frequently gets tripped up in her plans. Quite often they are capable of taking aim and hitting the bull's-eye. You'll be flabbergasted at times by their accuracy as well as by their ambition. On the other hand, you're apt to spot a flaw in the Aries woman's plans before she does.

You are perhaps somewhat slower than the Aries in attaining your goals. Still, you are not apt to make mistakes along the way; you're almost always well prepared.

The Aries woman is rather sensitive. She likes to be handled with gentleness and respect. Let her know that you love her for her brains as well as for her good looks. Never give her cause to become jealous. Handle her with tender love and care and she's yours.

The Aries woman can be giving if she feels her partner is deserving. She is no iceberg; she responds to the proper masculine flame. She needs a man she can look up to and feel proud of. If the shoe fits, put it on. If not, better put your sneakers back on and quietly tiptoe out of her sight. She can cause you plenty of heartache if you've made up your mind about her but she hasn't made up hers about you. Aries women are at times very demanding. Some of them tend to be high-strung; they can be difficult if they feel their independence is being hampered.

The cultivated Aries woman makes a wonderful homemaker and hostess. You'll find she's very clever in decorating and using color. Your house will be tastefully furnished; she'll see to it that it radiates harmony. The Aries wife knows how to make guests feel at home.

Although the Aries woman may not be keen on burdensome responsibilities, she is fond of children and the joy they bring.

SCORPIO MAN
TAURUS WOMAN

The woman born under the sign of Taurus may lack a little of the sparkle and bubble you often like to find in a woman. The Taurus woman is generally down-to-earth and never flighty. It's important to her that she keep both feet flat on the ground. She is not fond of bounding all over the place, especially if she's under the impression that there's no profit in it.

On the other hand, if you hit it off with a Taurus woman, you won't be disappointed in romance. The Taurus woman is all woman and proud of it too. She can be very devoted and loving once she decides that her relationship with you is no fly-by-night romance. Basically, she's a passionate person. In sex, she's direct and to-the-point. If she really loves you, she'll let you know she's yours—and without reservations. Better not flirt with other women once you've committed yourself to her. She is capable of being jealous and possessive.

She'll stick by you through thick and thin. It's almost certain that if the going ever gets rough, she'll not go running home to her mother. She can adjust to hard times just as graciously as she can to the good times.

Taureans are, on the whole, even-tempered. They like to be treated with kindness. Pretty things and soft things make them purr like kittens.

You may find her a little slow and deliberate. She likes to be safe and sure about everything. Let her plod along if she likes; don't coax her but just let her take her own sweet time. Everything she does is done thoroughly and, generally, without mistakes. Don't ride her for being a slowpoke. It could lead to flying pots and pans and a fireworks display that would put Bastille Day to shame. The Taurus woman doesn't anger readily but when prodded enough, she's capable of letting loose with a cyclone of anger. If you treat her with kindness and consideration, you'll have no cause for complaint.

The Taurean loves doing things for her man. She's a whiz in the kitchen and can whip up feasts fit for a king if she thinks they'll be royally appreciated. She may not fully understand you, but she'll adore you and be faithful to you if she feels you're worthy of it.

The woman born under Taurus will make a wonderful mother. She knows how to keep her children well-loved, cuddled, and warm. She may find them difficult to manage, however, when they are teen-agers.

SCORPIO MAN
GEMINI WOMAN

The Gemini woman may be too much of a flirt to ever strike your heart seriously. Then again, it depends on what kind of mood she's in. Gemini women can change from hot to cold quicker than a cat can wink it's eye. Chances are her fluctuations will tire you, and you'll pick up your heart—if it's not already broken into small pieces—and go elsewhere. Women born under the sign of the Twins have the talent of being able to change their moods and attitudes as frequently as they change their party dresses.

Sometimes, Gemini girls like to whoop it up. Some of them are good-time girls who love burning the candle at both ends. You'll see them at parties and gatherings, surrounded by men of all types, laughing gaily and kicking up their heels. Wallflowers, they're not. The next day you may bump into the same girl at the neighborhood library and you'll hardly recognize her for her "sensible" attire. She'll probably have five or six books under her arm—on five or six different subjects. In fact, she may even work there. If you think you've met the twin sister of Dr. Jekyll and Mr. Hyde, you're most likely right.

You'll probably find her a dazzling and fascinating creature—for a time, at any rate. Most men do. But when it comes to being serious about love you may find that that sparkling Eve leaves quite a bit to be desired. It's not that she has anything against being serious, it's just that she might find it difficult trying to be serious with you.

At one moment, she'll be capable of praising you for your steadfast and patient ways; the next moment she'll tell you in a cutting way that you're an impossible stick in the mud.

Don't even begin to fathom the depths of her mercurial soul—it's full of false bottoms. She'll resent close investigation, anyway, and will make you rue the day you ever took it into your head to try to learn more about her than she feels is necessary. Better keep the relationship full of fun and fancy free until she gives you the go-ahead. Take as much of her as she is willing to give; don't ask for more. If she does take a serious interest in you, then she'll come across with the goods.

There will come a time when the Gemini girl will realize that she can't spend her entire life at the ball and that the security and warmth you have to offer is just what she needs to be a happy, complete woman.

As a mother, she's easy-going with her children. She likes to spoil them as much as she can.

SCORPIO MAN
CANCER WOMAN

The girl born under Cancer needs to be protected from the cold, cruel world. She'll love you for your masculine yet gentle manner; you make her feel safe and secure. You don't have to pull any he-man or heroic stunts to win her heart; that's not what interests her. She's more likely to be impressed by your sure, steady ways—that way you have of putting your arm around her and making her feel that she's the only girl in the world. When she's feeling glum and tears begin to well up in her eyes, you have that knack of saying just the right thing—you know how to calm her fears, no matter how silly some of them may seem.

The girl born under this sign is inclined to have her ups and downs. You have that talent for smoothing out the ruffles in her sea of life. She'll most likely worship the ground you walk on or put you on a terribly high pedestal. Don't disappoint her if you can help it. She'll never disappoint you. This is the kind of woman who will take great pleasure in devoting the rest of her natural life to you. She'll darn your socks, mend your overalls, scrub floors, wash windows, shop, cook, and do just about anything short of murder in order to please you and to let you know that she loves you. Sounds like that legendary good old-fashioned girl, doesn't it? Contrary to popular belief, there are still a good number of them around—and many of them are Cancer people.

Of all the signs of the Zodiac, the women under the Cancer sign are the most maternal. In caring for and bringing up children, they know just how to combine the right amount of tenderness with the proper dash of discipline. A child couldn't ask for a better mother. Cancer women are sympathetic, affectionate, and patient with their children.

While we're on the subject of motherhood, there's one thing you should be warned about: never be unkind to your mother-in-law. It will be the only golden rule your Cancer wife will probably expect you to live up to. No mother-in-law jokes in the presence of your wife, please. With her, they'll go over like a lead balloon. Mother is something pretty special for her. She may be the crankiest, noisiest old bat this side of the Great Divide, still she's your wife's mother; you'd better treat her like she's one of the landed gentry. Sometimes this may be difficult to swallow, but if you want to keep your home together and your wife happy, you'd better learn to grin and bear it.

Treat your Cancer wife like a queen and she'll treat you royally.

SCORPIO MAN
LEO WOMAN

If you can manage a girl who likes to kick up her heels every now and again, then the Leo woman was made for you. You'll have to learn to put away jealous fears—or at least forget about them—when you take up with a woman born under this sign, because she's often the kind that makes heads turn and tongues wag. You don't necessarily have to believe any of what you hear—it's most likely just jealous gossip or wishful thinking. Take up with a Leo woman and you'll be taking off on a romance full of fire and ice; be prepared to take the good things with the bad—the bitter with the sweet.

The Leo girl has more than a fair share of grace and glamor. She is aware of her charms and knows how to put them to good use. Needless to say, other women in her vicinity turn green with envy and will try anything short of shoving her into the nearest lake, in order to put her out of commission.

If she's captured your heart and fancy, woo her intensely if your intention is to eventually win her. Shower her with expensive gifts and promise her the moon—if you're in a position to go that far—then you'll find her resistance beginning to weaken. It's not that she's difficult, she'll probably make a fuss over you once she's decided you're the man for her, but she does enjoy a lot of attention. What's more: she feels she's entitled to it. Her mild arrogance, though, is becoming. The Leo woman knows how to transform the crime of excessive pride into a very charming misdemeanor. It sweeps most men right off their feet. Those who do not succumb to her leonine charm are few and far between.

If you've got an important business deal to clinch and you have doubts as to whether or not it will go over well, bring your Leo girl along to that business luncheon and it's a cinch that that contract will be yours. She won't have to do or say anything—just be there, at your side. The grouchiest oil magnate can be transformed into a gushing, obedient schoolboy if there's a Leo woman in the room.

If you're rich and want to stay that way, don't give your Leo mate a free hand with the charge accounts and credit cards. If you're poor, the luxury-loving Leo will most likely never enter your life.

She makes a strict yet easy-going mother. She loves to pal around with her children.

SCORPIO MAN
VIRGO WOMAN

The Virgo woman may be a little too difficult for you to understand at first. Her waters run deep. Even when you think you know her, don't take any bets on it. She's capable of keeping things hidden in the deep recesses of her womanly soul—things she'll only release when she's sure that you're the man she's been looking for. It may take her some time to come around to this decision. Virgo girls are finicky about almost everything; everything has to be letter-perfect before they're satisfied. Many of them have the idea that the only people who can do things right are Virgos.

Nothing offends a Virgo woman more than slovenly dress, sloppy character, or a careless display of affection. Make sure your tie is not crooked and your shoes sport a bright shine before you go calling on this lady. Keep your off-color jokes for the locker-room, she'll have none of that. Take her arm when crossing the street. Don't rush the romance. Trying to corner her in the back of a cab may be one way of striking out. Never criticize the way she looks—in fact, the best policy would be to agree with her as much as possible. Still, there's just so much a man can take; all those dos and don'ts you'll have to follow if you want to get to first base. After a few dates, you may come to the conclusion that she just isn't worth all that trouble. However, the Virgo woman is mysterious enough generally speaking, to keep her men running back for more. Chances are you'll be intrigued by her airs and graces.

If love-making means a lot to you, you'll be disappointed at first in the cool ways of your Virgo woman. However, under her glacial facade there lies a caldron of seething excitement. If you're patient and artful in your romantic approach, you'll find that all that caution was well worth the trouble. When Virgos love, they don't stint. It's all or nothing as far as they're concerned. Once they're convinced that they love you, they go all the way, right off the bat—tossing caution to the wind.

One thing a Virgo woman can't stand in love is hypocrisy. They don't give a hoot about what the neighbors say, if their hearts tell them "Go ahead!" They're very concerned with human truths . . . so much so that if their hearts stumble upon another fancy, they're liable to be true to that new heart-throb and leave you standing in the rain. She's honest to her heart and will be as true to you as you are with her, generally. Do her wrong once, however, and it's farewell.

Both strict and tender, she tries to bring out the best in her children.

SCORPIO MAN
LIBRA WOMAN

As the old saying goes: It's a woman's prerogative to change her mind. Whoever said it must have had the Libra woman in mind. Her changeability, in spite of its undeniable charm (sometimes) could actually drive even a man of your patience up the wall. She's capable of smothering you with love and kisses one day and on the next, avoid you like the plague. If you think you're a man of steel nerves then perhaps you can tolerate her sometime-ness without suffering too much. However, if you own up to the fact that you're only a mere mortal who can only take so much, then you'd better fasten your attention on a girl who's somewhat more constant.

But don't get the wrong idea: a love affair with a Libra is not bad at all. In fact, it can have an awful lot of plusses to it. Libra women are soft, very feminine, and warm. She doesn't have to vamp all over the place in order to gain a man's attention. Her delicate presence is enough to warm the cockles of any man's heart. One smile and you're like a piece of putty in the palm of her hand.

She can be fluffy and affectionate—things you like in a girl. On the other hand, her indecision about which dress to wear, what to cook for dinner, or whether to redo the rumpus room or not could make you tear your hair out. What will perhaps be more exasperating is her flat denial to the accusation that she cannot make even the simplest decision. The trouble is that she wants to be fair or just in all matters; she'll spend hours weighing pros and cons. Don't make her rush into a decision; that will only irritate her.

The Libra woman likes to be surrounded by beautiful things. Money is not object where beauty is concerned. There will always be plenty of flowers in the house. She'll know how to arrange them tastefully, too. Women under this sign are fond of beautiful clothes and furnishings. They will run up bills without batting an eye—if given the chance.

Once she's cottoned to you, the Libra woman will do everything in her power to make you happy. She'll wait on you hand and foot when you're sick and bring you breakfast in bed on Sundays. She'll be very thoughtful and devoted. If anyone dares suggest you're not the grandest man in the world, your Libra wife will give that person a piece of her mind.

Libras work wonders with children. Gentle persuasion and affection are all she uses in bringing them up. It works.

SCORPIO MAN
SCORPIO WOMAN

The Scorpio woman can be a whirlwind of passion—perhaps too much passion to really suit you. When her temper flies, you'd better lock up the family heirlooms and take cover. When she chooses to be sweet, you're apt to think that butter wouldn't melt in her mouth—but, of course, it would.

The Scorpio woman can be as hot as a tamale or as cool as a cucumber, but whatever mood she's in, she's in it for real. She does not believe in posing or putting on airs.

The Scorpio woman is often sultry and seductive—her femme fatale charm can pierce through the hardest of hearts like a laser ray. She may not look like Mata Hari (quite often Scorpios resemble the tomboy next door) but once she's fixed you with her tantalizing eyes, you're a goner.

Life with the Scorpio woman will not be all smiles and smooth-sailing; when prompted, she can unleash a gale of venom. Generally, she'll have the good grace to keep family battles within the walls of your home. When company visits, she's apt to give the impression that married life with you is one great big joyride. It's just one of her ways of expressing her loyalty to you—at least in front of others. She may fight you tooth and nail in the confines of your living room, but at a ball or during an evening out, she'll hang onto your arm and have stars in her eyes.

Scorpio women are good at keeping secrets. She may even keep a few buried from you.

Never cross her on even the smallest thing. When it comes to revenge, she's an eye-for-an-eye woman. She's not too keen on forgiveness—especially if she feels she's been wronged unfairly. You'd be well advised not to give her any cause to be jealous, either. When the Scorpio woman sees green, your life will be made far from rosy. Once she's put you in the doghouse, you can be sure that you're going to stay there a while.

You may find life with a Scorpio woman too draining. Although she may be full of the old paprika, it's quite likely that she's not the kind of girl you'd like to spend the rest of your natural life with. You'd prefer someone gentler and not so hot-tempered . . . someone who can take the highs with the lows and not bellyache . . . someone who is flexible and understanding. A woman born under Socrpio can be heavenly, but she can also be the very devil when she chooses.

As a mother, a Scorpio is protective and encouraging.

SCORPIO MAN
SAGITTARIUS WOMAN

The Sagittarius woman is hard to keep track of: first she's here, then she's there. She's a woman with a severe case of itchy feet. She's got to keep on the move.

People generally like her because of her hail-fellow-well-met manner and breezy charm. She is constantly good-natured and almost never cross. She is the kind of girl you're likely to strike up a palsy-walsy relationship with; you might not be interested in letting it go any farther. She probably won't sulk if you leave it on a friendly basis, either. Treat her like a kid sister and she'll eat it up like candy.

She'll probably be attracted to you because of your restful, self-assured manner. She'll need a friend like you to help her over the rough spots in her life; she'll most likely turn to you for advice.

There is nothing malicious about a girl born under this sign. She is full of bounce and good cheer. Her sunshiny disposition can be relied upon on even the rainiest of days. No matter what she says or does, you'll always know that she means well. Sagittarians are sometimes short on tact. Some of them say anything that comes into their pretty little heads, no matter what the occasion. Sometimes the words that tumble out of their mouths seem downright cutting and cruel; they mean well but often everything they say comes out wrong. She's quite capable of losing her friends—and perhaps even yours—through a careless slip of the lip. Always remember that she is full of good intentions. Stick with her if you like her and try to help her mend her ways.

She's not a girl that you'd most likely be interested in marrying, but she'll certainly be lots of fun to pal around with. Quite often, Sagittarius women are outdoor types. They're crazy about things like fishing, camping, and mountain climbing. They love the wide open spaces. They are fond of all kinds of animals. Make no mistake about it: this busy little lady is no slouch. She's full of pep and ginger.

She's great company most of the time; she's more fun than a three-ring circus when she's in the right company. You'll like her for her candid and direct manner. On the whole, Sagittarians are very kind and sympathetic women.

If you do wind up marrying this girl-next-door type, you'd better see to it that you handle all of the financial matters. Sagittarians often let money run through their fingers like sand.

As a mother, she'll smother her children with love and give them all of the freedom *they* think they need.

SCORPIO MAN
CAPRICORN WOMAN

The Capricorn may not be the most romantic woman of the Zodiac, but she's far from frigid when she meets the right man. She believes in true love; she doesn't appreciate getting involved in flings. To her, they're just a waste of time. She's looking for a man who means "business'—in life as well as in love. Although she can be very affectionate with her boyfriend or mate, she tends to let her head govern her heart. That is not to say she is a cool, calculating cucumber. On the contrary, she just feels she can be more honest about love if she consults her brains first. She wants to size-up the situation before throwing her heart in the ring. She wants to make sure it won't get stepped on.

The Capricorn woman is faithful, dependable, and systematic in just about everything she undertakes. She is quite concerned with security and sees to it that every penny she spends is spent wisely. She is very economical about using her time, too. She does not believe in whittling away her energy on a scheme that is not going to pay off.

Ambitious themselves, they are quite often attracted to ambitious men—men who are interested in getting somewhere in life. If a man of this sort wins her heart, she'll stick by him and do all she can to help him get to the top.

The Capricorn woman is almost always diplomatic. She makes an excellent hostess. She can be very influential when your business acquaintances come to dinner.

The Capricorn woman is likely to be very concerned, if not downright proud, about her family tree. Relatives are pretty important to her, particularly if they're socially prominent. Never say a cross word about one of her family. That can really go against her grain and she'll punish you by not talking to you for days.

She's generally thorough in whatever she does. Capricorn women are well-mannered and gracious, no matter what their backgrounds. They seem to have it in their natures to always behave properly.

If you should marry a woman born under this sign, you need never worry about her going on a wild shopping spree. They understand the value of money better than most women. If you turn over your paycheck to her at the end of the week, you can be sure that a good hunk of it will wind up in the bank.

The Capricorn mother is loving and correct.

SCORPIO MAN
AQUARIUS WOMAN

If you find that you've fallen head over heels for a woman born under the sign of the Water Bearer, you'd better fasten your safety belt. It may take you quite a while to actually discover what this girl is like—and even then, you may have nothing to go on but a string of vague hunches. The Aquarian is like a rainbow, full of bright and shining hues; she's like no other girl you've ever known. There is something elusive about her—something delightfully mysterious. You'll most likely never be able to put your finger on it. It's nothing calculated, either; Aquarians don't believe in phony charm.

There will never be a dull moment in your life with this Water Bearing woman; she seems to radiate adventure and magic. She'll most likely be the most open-minded and tolerant woman you've ever met. She has a strong dislike for injustice and prejudice. Narrow-mindedness runs against her grain.

She is very independent by nature and quite capable of shifting for herself if necessary. She may receive many proposals for marriage from all sorts of people without ever really taking them seriously. Marriage is a very big step for her; she wants to be sure she knows what she's getting into. If she thinks that it will seriously curb her independence and love of freedom, she's liable to shake her head and give the man his engagement ring back—if indeed she's let the romance get that far.

The line between friendship and romance is a pretty fuzzy one for an Aquarian. It's not difficult for her to remain buddy-buddy with an ex-lover. She's tolerant, remember? So, if you should see her on the arm of an old love, don't jump to any hasty conclusions.

She's not a jealous person herself and doesn't expect you to be, either. You'll find her pretty much of a free spirit most of the time. Just when you think you know her inside-out, you'll discover that you don't really know her at all.

She's a very sympathetic and warm person; she can be helpful to people in need of assistance and advice.

She'll seldom be suspicious even if she has every right to be. If the man she loves slips and allows himself a little fling, chances are she'll just turn her head the other way. Her tolerance does have its limits, however, and her man should never press his luck at hanky-panky.

She makes a big-hearted mother; her good qualities rub off on her children.

SCORPIO MAN
PISCES WOMAN

The Pisces woman places great value on love and romance. She's gentle, kind, and romantic. Perhaps she's that girl you've been dreaming about all these years. Like you, she has very high ideals; she will only give her heart to a man who she feels can live up to her expectations.

She will never try to wear the pants in the family. She's a staunch believer in the man being the head of the house. Quite often Pisces women are soft and cuddly. They have a feminine, domestic charm that can win the heart of just about any man.

Generally, there's a lot more to her than just a pretty exterior and womanly ways. There's a brain ticking behind that gentle face. You may not become aware of it—that is, until you've married her. It's no cause for alarm, however; she'll most likely never use it against you. But if she feels you're botching up your married life through careless behavior or if she feels you could be earning more money than you do, she'll tell you about it. But any wife would, really. She'll never try to usurp your position as head and bread-winner of the family. She'll admire you for your ambition and drive. If anyone says anything against you in her presence, she'll probably break out into tears. Pisces women are usually very sensitive and their reaction to frustration or anger is often just a plain good old-fashioned cry. They can weep buckets when inclined.

She'll prepare an extra-special dinner for you when you've made a new conquest in your profession. Don't bother to go into the details though at the dinner table; she doesn't have much of a head for business matters, usually, and is only too happy to leave that up to you.

She is a wizard in decorating a home. She's fond of soft and beautiful things. There will always be a vase of fresh flowers on the dining room table. She'll see to it that you always have plenty of socks and underwear in the top dresser drawer.

Treat her with tenderness and your relationship will be an enjoyable one. Pisces women are generally fond of sweets, so keep her in chocolates (and flowers, of course) and you'll have a happy wife. Never forget birthdays or anniversaries; she won't.

If you have a talent for patience and gentleness, it will certainly pay off in your relationship with a Pisces woman. Chances are she'll never make you regret that you placed that band of gold on her finger.

There is usually a strong bond between a Pisces mother and her children. She'll try to give them things she never had as a child and is apt to spoil them as a result.

SCORPIO

SCORPIO

YEARLY FORECAST: 1987

Forecast for 1987 Concerning Business and
Financial Matters, Job Prospects,
Travel, Health, Romance and Marriage
for Those Born with the Sun
in the Zodiacal Sign of Scorpio.
October 23–November 22

This is a year when you determined and strong-willed Scorpio people will apply yourselves with great success and personal satisfaction. It is a time for deepening your interests and your attitude to life. Superficial activities and pastimes will have little appeal for you. Even pleasure pursuits can seem less necessary. Your enthusiasm and energy for work will be greatly increased. You may feel an urgency to increase your financial resources through additional efforts in employment affairs, whether you have money problems or not. And such efforts are likely to be well rewarded. Most business and outside activities can be made more profitable. The personal contribution that Scorpio people make in their line of work will favorably increase their reputations. Health problems are much less likely to occur, and those that do afflict you will clear up rapidly. Romance will not be so high a priority on your list this year but there will be no shortage of chances for meeting new partners if you so desire. And well-established relationships can be put on even firmer ground. Travel can be less successful. It will be easier to make journeys that consume much time and expense, but that are unproductive. Only essential trips should be undertaken.

You should try to bring as much originality and freshness as possible to regular work and business matters in the first two months of the year. You will handle new projects and enterprises with an adventurous spirit. Your willingness to stick your neck out can pay dividends. But before you borrow money to finance new programs, you must be virtually certain of their success. Cash can be pumped into projects that are destined never to achieve lift-off. Beware of pessimistic people who try to throw cold water on your urges to break out in new directions. Valuable chances can be lost because of doubt introduced by such people. You are likely to get official encouragement and permission for entertainment projects or work involving children between February 19 and March 20. From March 2 onward, employment affairs should settle into a more steady and favorable period. You will be able to make better use of your talents and energies, which will be personally advantageous and helpful to others. Scorpio people who employ others can count on a more positive response from the work force. You should get plenty of cooperation and hard work and a minimum of dissent. Anything Scorpio bosses can do to improve working conditions will help to make for happier and more productive employees. Working procedures can be streamlined through the introduction of new equipment and methods with profitable results. The attention of a wider public can be brought to your products and services through lively and engaging publicity. Scorpio people can set their sights high in career affairs with every chance of achieving their targets. Personal efforts can bring about undreamed of successes. The most sensitive period for dealing with employees will be between January 8 and February 19. A heavy-handed approach to personnel can produce widespread unrest. But between July 6 and August 22 conditions will be supportive of efforts to win much greater profits and to improve your personal standing in the eyes of other people.

Money matters are likely to take a turn for the better in 1987. Scorpio people who tended to squander hard-earned cash last year will bring a more responsible attitude to financial affairs this year. In fact, you may be left with no alternative but to adopt a commonsense approach if banks and moneylenders start calling in earnest for repayment of debts, as they are likely to do. But there is nothing like a challenge to get a Scorpio person going so you are likely to respond to any financial problems constructively. Early on in March, employment matters will enter a very productive phase, which should soon reflect well in your bank account. Scorpio people will be more appreciative of regular jobs and wages and the financial security they bring. But this should not be an excuse for complacency. Keep a constant eye out for work that draws more of your innate talents out of you, with increased wages that should accompany the taking on of extra responsibilities. Look for opportunities to stretch yourself. You will be more fulfilled in a job that tests your capabilities.

If you get into a tight corner financially it is older people who are best turned to for help. Parents can give generous support. But you will gain much more satisfaction from self-reliance. Borrowing should only be considered a last resort. New ideas and innovations are the best means to greater earning power. Especially lucrative areas of activity are those connected with publishing, philosophy, higher education, and distant people and places. Keep close tabs on tax and insurance matters between May 21 and June 20. Any rearrangements affecting mutual funds should also be made in this period. But your personal efforts are likely to show the most profitable returns in the time from November 22 to December 21.

Where employment is concerned, January 8 to February 19 is a good period for earning more from overtime and for making a real thrust toward winning promotion and pay raises. Your ability to approach problems with originality and to take responsibility for whatever you tackle will be favorably noticed by employers, as will your consistent hard work. Such qualities are bound to be well rewarded. Don't be content with familiar jobs or positions if you think you can do better. Keep your antennae out for jobs that have brighter future prospects, are more solid, and pay better wages. Your own judgment in such matters will be good, although a second opinion from people who have relevant experience can be useful. But the advice of people who have a strictly nonprofessional relationship to important employment decisions must be listened to guardedly. They can easily get matters totally wrong from your point of view. There will be times when colleagues and fellow workers can be unreliable and uncooperative, particularly in the first 19 days and the last ten days of the year. The more you can be independent of others the better. Solo efforts can produce tremendous results without any aggravations.

The most sensitive period for the health of Scorpios will be from January 8 to February 19. This is when you are likely to run into the most obstructions and difficulties and have to make extra exertions to overcome them. Exhaustion and strain are possible. It will be essential then to offset any overdoing with plenty of rest and relaxation. You must ensure that your tanks are refilled. It would be dangerous to run on empty for even short periods. But things will be looking up, healthwise, from March 2 onward. Your ability to get over illness will be great from then on, and symptoms are likely to disappear completely, even when they had been accepted as lifelong companions. A benevolent influence will guard your general health but will not protect you from the adverse effects of overeating, overdrinking, smoking too much, or not getting enough sleep. Any weight problems should be countered with sensible dieting, carried out with discipline. A sound and tested approach to health is important; untried or fanciful methods can be dangerous and not worth risking.

Affairs of the heart will be on the crest of a wave up to March 1. The first week of January and the period between February 5 and

28 will be especially exciting. These are excellent times for making new romantic partnerships and planning marriages. Scorpios will be more able to balance their heavy and serious side with greater lightheartedness, so that others find them more agreeable companions. Their intense natures will be less onerous to partners.

But from the beginning of March other interests may take priority over romance. You may want to devote more time to work, where successes and rewards are more clear-cut. Your sense of identity is more likely to come from employment and business achievements than from romance, and you may be reluctant to sacrifice working time for leisure. But there will be two periods of heightened romantic interest, one from March 28 to April 21, and the other from October 10 to November 2. Existing relationships can take on a new lease of life then, and new partnerships begun. The best time for marriages, and for established unions, is between May 17 and June 10.

It will be important not to waste time and money on nonessential journeys this year. Other possibilities will be missed if you are away too much. Holidays and long trips will be most successful between February 19 and March 20 and between June 21 and July 22. But Scorpios may prefer to keep up with work schedules than to take a vacation this year. The very early days and the last few days of the year are the best times for keeping in circulation and renewing contacts with friends and associates. But right through 1987, short trips are not likely to come up to expectations, largely due to the shortcomings of other people.

DAILY FORECAST
January–December 1987
JANUARY

1. THURSDAY. Quiet.   You may be very pleased that the day and the year get off to such a slow and unpressured start. You will have plenty of time to get your bearings. If you overdid it somewhat during New Year's Eve celebrations, the quiet morning will be much to your liking. Take it easy while you have the chance. No need to go looking for chores and problems just yet. Working routines will swing into action soon enough. Later on the atmosphere will become less peaceful. Conditions at home, in particular, can become tense and uneasy. Family members can be argumentative and may be unhappy about plans you have made. Scorpio people may have to make concessions to restore domestic harmony.

2. FRIDAY. Good.   Today marks the beginning of a fortunate, though short, period for Scorpios. Recent tensions at home should have blown over by now. In fact, family members will be in a more cooperative mood, especially where domestic finances are concerned. If there is a need to introduce some home-economy measures, you can count on the support of loved ones. Scorpio people will be wily adversaries in any business dealings. Your quick thinking will give you a great advantage over other parties in negotiations. Conditions are especially favorable for buying and selling property. Efforts given to home improvements will work out to your advantage. Good news can come in the mail.

3. SATURDAY. Splendid.   There will be no shortage of creative energies or mental concentration now. Artists, writers, and those involved in study and research should have a field day. Your mind will abound with original and lively ideas. It will be easier to find fresh solutions to old problems. The day is good for reading and intellectual pursuits. Keep an open mind on what relatives have to tell you. They can have valuable information to pass on. Productive short trips can be made. You can meet people who put more business your way, or who inform you of important events.

Scorpios will still have the advantage in transactions. Love affairs will be most favored; it will be easier to form new attachments.

4. SUNDAY. Positive. This is one of those days when much good can come from sticking your neck out in financial and business matters. Calculated risks and gambles can be well worth taking. Opportunities can be missed if you decide to play everything safe. Speculation can pay off handsomely. Pleasure pursuits can offer delightful experiences, especially if loved ones are involved. Outings with sweethearts or spouses are more than likely to come up to expectations. Close relationships can be strengthened by happy times spent together. This is a good time for catching up on correspondence and sending off letters of inquiry. It is likely that you will receive informative responses in the near future.

5. MONDAY. Variable. In stark contrast to yesterday, this is definitely not a day for living dangerously. Any gambling with money, opportunities, or romance can give extremely undesirable results. Tread gingerly. But Scorpios may be more in the mood to take the bull by the horns. In fact there is a strong risk that you will use overly forceful means and upset other people. Love affairs can go through a nasty stormy period as a result. Try to counter your own intensity with more diplomacy and tolerance. Resentment is bound to build up if you attempt to hammer others into submission. There will be opportunities at work for increasing incomes. This is not a good day for property dealing.

6. TUESDAY. Difficult. It won't be easy to see eye-to-eye with bosses and superiors now. Differences can develop over relatively minor matters. Scorpios are advised to step back and not take a stand on details. Mountains can grow from molehills if you try to push a point of principle. It is by keeping your nose to the grindstone and demonstrating your ability to work hard that pay raises are most likely to be awarded. Your past record will stand you in good stead. Employers will not overlook your loyalty and consistent efforts. Conditions continue to be discouraging for property deals. If you are involved in real estate transactions be extra cautious. There may be some domestic disharmony.

7. WEDNESDAY. Challenging. Unexpectedly, opportunities can come your way at work. Conditions will be much to your liking. Pay raises can be offered out of the blue. The advances you make now in your career will give cause for great personal satisfaction. It will be mostly owing to your own past efforts that you achieve such an advantageous position. But there is no room for smugness over any gains you may make. Keep pushing ahead. There may be calls for your particular skills that can be applied with highly lucrative results. Your mind is likely to brimming over with good ideas. Any health problems that have been bothering you can suddenly disappear.

8. THURSDAY. Mixed. Your plans are likely to get a boost from sources close to home. Relatives can come forward with just the facts and information you have been waiting for. What you learn now can put you in a strong position to advance your ambitions and aspirations. Letters both sent and received can be beneficial. Keep abreast of the mail; don't allow any backlog of unanswered letters to build up. It will be easier to reach favorable agreements with other parties in negotiations and discussions. This is a constructive time for thrashing out problems. But at home, Scorpios may have to trim their sails where personal hopes and wishes are concerned. Loved ones will probably raise objections.

9. FRIDAY. Excellent. Conditions bode extremely well for teamwork and all cooperative efforts. Fortune will be with Scorpio people who have to rely on others to further their interests in employment and business. This is the perfect time to pool your energies and financial resources with others in order to undertake commercial operations. Business partnerships formed now can have highly profitable long-term prospects. It will be good also for discussions with bankers, who will be in a sympathetic mood. It will be easier to resolve any difficulties with relatives or neighbors. Take this opportunity to reach new understandings with them. You will have less trouble in winning the help of influential people.

10. SATURDAY. Fair. You may really have to stretch yourself to reach your targets today or complete work you have been set. But with determination you can achieve your ends and win both personal satisfaction and financial rewards as well. Don't be content with halfway measures; go the whole hog. Scorpios will enjoy rising to the challenges that this day presents them. But you will have to keep a firm hand on affairs connected with joint financial projects. Costs associated with such agreements can rise sharply. They will get out of hand if allowed to run up unattended. It may also be the job of Scorpios to rein in free-spending loved ones. They may be adopting a rather casual attitude to your cash now.

11. SUNDAY. Disturbing. Money matters can be subject to worrying ups and downs. It would be unwise to rush into any important moves where finances are concerned. Give yourself plenty of time to assess all the possibilities before making irreversible decisions. There may be a need to spend unexpected sums on relatives. Their health, travel, or other special factors can leave them in straitened circumstances. Problems that you have dealt with more than once in the past can come up again now and require yet more attention. Neighbors, in particular, can be a source of trouble or complaint. Scorpios will be more prone to depression now and news about someone's health won't lift your spirits.

12. MONDAY. Mixed. Scorpio thinking will be precise and crystal clear. Your ability to handle mental problems will be tip-top. Your grasp of situations will be so thorough that influential people will have no hesitation backing your ideas and schemes. You will be able to present your case persuasively. All reading, writing, and study activities will go like a dream. You will cover much ground in intellectual pursuits. Today will be good for dealing with complicated documents and putting your signature to important agreements. But no independent moves should be made with funds that others have a stake in. You must have the full support of other owners in such matters as losses are possible.

13. TUESDAY. Deceptive. You cannot afford to let your heart rule your head now. A calm and clear approach is necessary to steer you through today's rapids. People and situations may not be quite what they seem on first acquaintance. It will generally be more difficult to make sound judgments. You will only add further to the uncertain conditions if you make emotionally based decisions. This is not a good time for pooling financial resources with others to fund new commercial enterprises. But it is likely that some additional attention given to established joint financial projects will boost their profitability. It is where you have the most at stake that your decisions can be most faulty.

14. WEDNESDAY. Variable. It will be easier for feelings to boil over in any contacts you have with relatives or neighbors. It may be in the longer-term interest of Scorpio people to hold back any antagonism they feel. They should definitely avoid any provocative behavior or comment. Facts and information that come your way now should be rechecked before you act on them. There may be mistakes in what you are told. Any difficulties in a love affair can be eased by the intervention of distant people or those who come from far away. But this is not a good day for planning marriages. The day is better for a little frivolity in relationships than for making long-term commitments.

15. THURSDAY. Good. It will be all systems go for Scorpio people. There will be no shortage of energy or enthusiasm to make a concerted push to reach your targets in employment and business matters. It will be up to you to make the effort. Don't hold back or let yourself be shoved aside. Your deep understanding of human nature will make it easier for you to deal effectively with awkward people. It shouldn't take too long for you to clear away any obstructions that others might put in your path. Scorpios who employ others should maintain firm control of threatening situations involving the work force. Any successes in commercial operations will add to your reputation.

16. FRIDAY. Important. Conditions will help you to climb out of any financial holes you have got yourself into. There will be opportunities to put economic prospects on a much firmer footing. You will be thankful in the future for the efforts you make now to strengthen your financial position. All important decisions in commerce and employment should be made keeping in mind the widest long-term perspective possible. Moves made now can have far-reaching effects and implications. This is a good day for attempting to collect money you are owed. You can count on some help and support from older people in financial affairs. Sensible investments can be made in antiques and stamps.

17. SATURDAY. Changeable. You should press ahead with any money-making projects initiated yesterday. There will be good chances of profitable dealings both in commerce and in the public arena. Your finances can receive a welcome boost from sources quite unrelated to personal efforts. Surprise gifts or inheritances are in the cards. But those involved in regular work today may be in for an exhausting time. You may be obliged to take on more than your usual duties or quotas. It may be a real sweat to get through all that you are set. The people you work with can be far from helpful and friendly. The complications caused by others at home can make relaxation more difficult.

18. SUNDAY. Fair. Friends will make pleasant companions today. But activities shared with them could cost you a bundle. If possible, you should try to steer them toward activities that cost little or nothing. It is also likely that a friend will be in financial difficulties and may come to you for help. There should be more harmony at home than you've experienced recently. It will be easier to discuss ideas concerning the home with family members. Plans for redecoration, building additions, or changes in homelife can be thrashed out in a friendly and cooperative atmosphere. Heartfelt desires can come closer to realization. But love affairs will not provide the happiness Scorpio people are seeking.

19. MONDAY. Disturbing. Scorpios may sail into choppy waters in financial affairs. They may need to batten down the hatches and lay low. It will be more difficult than usual to calculate just where you stand in money matters. It would be best not to take on any new financial responsibilities for the time being. With conditions so uncertain it would be foolish to try your luck in risky schemes or gambles. But in your present mood you are more than likely to ignore this advice and stick your neck out. Be prepared for heavy losses in this case. It is unlikely that commercial operations will run smoothly. It will also be more difficult to arrange loans and credits. Unforeseen bills must be paid without delay.

20. TUESDAY. Disconcerting. It will be to your advantage to conceal your activities and intentions now. It is from a background position that you can best further plans relating to home or family. Property deals will benefit from confidential arrangements. Today is good for handling transactions through nonofficial channels. Don't feel you have to deal through recognized sources as a matter of course. But it would be unwise to wholeheartedly trust information passed on by relatives. They are more likely to have got it wrong than right. At work, unease can build up and stay just beneath the surface. This will make working conditions infinitely more difficult. Don't take on more than you can sensibly handle.

21. WEDNESDAY. Fortunate. Things should be looking up where finances are concerned. But it can still be advantageous to draw a veil over your economic position. There may be opportunities for arranging a second income, but these should be kept strictly to yourself. You could also consider opening a secret savings account. You may be very thankful in the future for having made such a move. Consider trimming down expenses even though others know nothing about it. But you can count on the assistance of loved ones especially in serious matters. They are likely to rise to the occasion if the pressure is on. You may find yourself smitten by a quiet and unassuming person.

22. THURSDAY. Upsetting. Take what you are told by people in influential positions with a pinch of salt. Bosses and superiors cannot be trusted even when their intentions are good. They will probably let you down when it comes to the crunch. They can also be unwilling to grant small favors. This can leave you cliff-hanging where important plans and decisions are concerned. In fact, many dealings with others are likely to be unsatisfactory. People just will not be prepared to commit themselves. They can even stoop to dishonesty to avoid doing things they don't want to do. Family members can cause problems, especially in matters of health. It may be that they refuse to take precautions against catching flu.

23. FRIDAY. Disquieting. It is unlikely that the people closest to you will agree with your personal plans. You may have to compromise in order to keep peace at home. Family members will not be in the mood for having their environment changed around. It is best to leave the home just as it is for the time being. There will be more favorable times ahead for making improvements there. But Scorpios will be right on the ball in working matters. You will be able to turn your hand to practical problems with greater facility. And there will be no shortage of energy for carrying out physical tasks. Conditions are not supportive of property deals which are best postponed.

24. SATURDAY. Discouraging. This will be another unsettled day for financial affairs. It will be easier to make a disastrous wrong move now. It would be advisable to keep financial dealing and decision-making to an absolute minimum. Any business that cannot be avoided must be handled with kid gloves. Loved ones will not be in the most robust state healthwise. In fact, their condition can upset your pleasure plans and entail considerable expense. People in general can be more cold and distant now. The more you try to come close to them, the more they are likely to pull off. Others may feel need to protect themselves, making easygoing relationships impossible. Just try to play it by ear.

25. SUNDAY. Variable. The best time to attend to money matters is during the early part of the day. Later, conditions will become tricky for finances. Scorpio people may feel more like applying themselves to work than taking it easy. And this can be very healthy for your bank balance. Work you engage in now can earn higher wages than you realize. But you must keep a well-rounded approach to your life. Physical exercise is an essential part of keeping fit and well. You could consider joining yoga or other organized movement classes. You may become restricted if everything is all work and no play. Family members can have advice or direct assistance to give you in financial matters.

26. MONDAY. Tricky. Money can more easily become a bone of contention today. People you live or work with may hold widely differing views as to how assets should be spent. This can lead to unpleasant quarrels. Scorpio people should try to steer clear of disturbing situations and unpredictable folk. People may try to persuade you to put money into odd or unconventional projects. These are best avoided just now. Stick to the straight and narrow. Your own urges to splash out huge sums of money on unnecessary items must be curbed. You will attract undesirable consequences to yourself if you push your luck in speculative ventures. Avoid gambling in all forms.

27. TUESDAY. Fair. Although journeys connected with business or career affairs may appear worthwhile, they are unlikely to achieve much of consequence. Road travel, in particular, is more hazardous than usual. Far greater care must be taken while driving. Get all the rest and relaxation you can. Your health will be especially vulnerable to infection and overwork. Don't take on more than you can comfortably handle. Seek the cooperation of others. Avoid lifting heavy weights without help. Domestic pets will also be more vulnerable to accidents and illness. A little extra attention can save them much discomfort. But safe investments can be made in real estate holdings.

28. WEDNESDAY. Quiet. The absence of pressures and distractions will make mental concentration easier. Expect today to be good for attending to small matters and details. It will also be favorable for reading, writing, and study activities. Accounting and other operations which involve computations will present no problems. But on such an easygoing day there are unlikely to be any important developments. Shopping trips are likely to provide the only high spot of the day. A tour of stores and markets can reveal some excellent bargains. This lull in momentum will give you plenty of opportunity to attend to any unanswered letters. But major decisions should be left until you are more alert.

29. THURSDAY. Mixed. This is a good day for job changes and introducing new working methods. Conditions are encouraging for the launching of new commercial operations. Business ventures begun now have excellent chances of reaping lucrative profits in the future. Scorpio people will tend to settle down very quickly in new working situations. Decisions to leave old positions are likely to prove correct. It would be wisest to concentrate on far-reaching business propositions. Hopes of making a quick buck are doomed to failure. Neither can you afford to become involved in risky business deals. Losses rather than gains will be the order of the day. People are unlikely to back up their words with hard cash.

30. FRIDAY. Enjoyable. There will be good opportunities both for giving personal resources a boost and for cutting down on unnecessary expenses. Your financial situation should be in a much healthier state by the end of the day than it was at the beginning. You can count on the assistance of loved ones if economy measures have to be implemented. And it is improbable that you will meet any opposition from family members to your plans for domestic changes. There will be plenty of scope for putting family spending and household expenses on a more reasonable basis. Wining and dining friends and associates in your own home can be a great success. In fact, it will be good for all social gatherings.

31. SATURDAY. Positive. This is a stellar day for allowing the artist in you to come to the fore. Creative energies will be high and you should seek outlets for them. Devote whatever time you can to artistic and inventive activities. It will be easier to find original solutions to old and recurring problems. Don't opt for the most obvious course of action now. Plans and projects that are dear to you will benefit from some imaginative thought. Intuition will be a sounder guide than logic. Arrangements for recreation and entertainment should go as planned without the interference of people close to you. Others will be ready to have a good time though not entirely willing to help foot the bill.

FEBRUARY

1. SUNDAY. Variable. This day is good for continuing to push ahead with commercial operations that do not carry a high risk of loss. This applies to ones that are already well established. But it is inadvisable to take any gambles with new business or financial concerns. They will not get off to a good start in the current conditions. They could also quickly end in heavy losses. Your love life should be in good shape now. However, it is quite likely that you will have to spend a considerable sum on outings with loved ones. Today will be favorable for deals involving property and land and its products. And more than profit can come from home sales. A stroke of fortune may accompany any change of accommodation.

2. MONDAY. Deceptive. Conditions will be much to your liking at work. There will be opportunities to carry out work that favorably impresses those in authority. Any notice that you attract can be handsomely rewarded with increased earnings. Make sure you are thorough in all that you undertake, as unseen eyes may be on you. You may have need to call on employers for more flexible working hours, time off, or other special requests. They will be in a sympathetic mood and more ready to grant favors. It should be a good day for getting into better physical shape. It may be time to begin regular visits to your local swimming pool. Don't rush into important decisions. You would regret hasty actions.

3. TUESDAY. Good.   The day is most likely to be uneventful and even dull to begin with. But there will be plenty to get involved in as it goes along. There can be a surprising turn of events in working matters. Circumstances can change very much in your favor as a result. Be ready to change direction with very little or no warning. This is no time for rigid attitudes. It is possible that new jobs or positions can be offered to you that will both enhance your reputation and reflect favorably on your bank balance. Any worrying health symptoms can be quickly and cheaply dealt with. Conditions that have been bothering you for some time can suddenly clear up, probably as the result of medication.

4. WEDNESDAY. Fair.   This is a good day for pooling energy and enthusiasm with loved ones. The capabilities of partners are likely to match your own to perfection. And more than successful results can come from such joint efforts. Marriage partners or sweethearts will come much closer together after having completed work in tandem. The creative efforts of Scorpio people will be fired by inspiration. Scorpio writers in particular should have a field day. You will also have a greater command of the spoken word and a flair for conversation and entertaining people. It is almost certain that there will be obstacles to overcome in your working environment. Your perseverance should prevail.

5. THURSDAY. Disturbing.   People in influential positions can be erratic and awkward now. They can make life very difficult for the time being. Your plans for the day can be delayed or permission to go ahead with ideas denied you. This can be particularly bothersome if property deals or home planning or improvement are involved. Family members are likely to be at each other's throats. Scorpios can get caught in the middle, not knowing quite who is in the right or who to side with. Unpleasant disputes with spouses can result. Work or projects that rely on team efforts can be subject to hold-ups and complications. It will be more difficult to tie up the loose ends of long-standing affairs.

6. FRIDAY. Disquieting. It won't be easy to see eye-to-eye with others today. People are likely to take an independent line. This is especially true where discussions of mutual funds are concerned. Try as you may, joint owners of common resources will be very reluctant to accept your view of things or go along with your plans. If asked to take care of other people's homes, cars, or possessions, you would do well to decline. Things are likely go wrong from the start with breakages or losses almost a certainty. It is probable that exciting, though risky, commercial operations will appeal to you. You would do well to resist the temptation to get involved. You might get in over your head and face a penalty.

7. SATURDAY. Quiet. Not a lot will be happening today. While there won't be much excitement, neither will you be bothered by troublesome circumstances. Use this quiet time to take stock of your current situation. It could be that commercial enterprises shared with others need some reappraisal. From today's vantage point you should get a better idea of what must be done and what must be avoided. The pattern throughout the year is one of keeping a fairly tight rein on spending. Today is no exception even though it's a weekend day. It would be good for introducing new economy measures.

8. SUNDAY. Mixed. Scorpios can enjoy both leisure and romantic pursuits today. But if there is work or business to attend to you will probably want to put such pleasures to one side. You will prefer to devote yourself to whatever it is that has to be done. You must choose one or the other. And once you have made up your mind it will be foolish to waste time and energy wishing you were doing something else. But you shouldn't have too much difficulty knowing just what has to take priority now. Scorpios are not moderate people by nature. On the whole, you would do well to avoid all forms of extremes. Overeating and drinking are bound to have an unfortunate effect on your health.

9. MONDAY. Productive. Count today as good for making extended journeys. Trips closer to home are far less likely to achieve your desired ends. This may not be the best time to call on people you are fond of. Visits to friends and relatives can easily end unfortunately. Holidays or trips to faraway places, started today, have every chance of achieving resounding success. Overseas journeys will be interesting and productive. Today is good for pushing ahead with activities that depend on imaginative flair. Artists and designers will be in top form now, and what you achieve can bring lucrative rewards. But people you mix with today can be fairly slippery and even dishonest. Just don't let your guard down.

10. TUESDAY. Fortunate. People will be much easier to get on with now. They are likely to be in a cheerful and friendly mood. You should have no difficulty getting assistance and support for your undertakings. Others are more inclined to be generous with their time and energy. The personal lives of Scorpios are also likely to be more satisfactory. Things should be working out just as you had hoped in a love affair. Someone you have taken a fancy to may return your attentions now. Outings with loved ones will be a delight. Any problems relating to children will be much more easily contended with. You can meet helpful new people while traveling locally. Try to establish some rapport with them for the future.

11. WEDNESDAY. Satisfactory. The feelings of Scorpio people will be very finely tuned today. Close contacts with loved ones are likely to give rise to extremely intense and happy experiences. Your feelings of affection can be stronger than ever. But you may also be more emotionally vulnerable to adverse conditions and people. Spend as much time as possible with those you love and trust. New romantic attractions can spring up quite easily. You are likely to meet prospective new partners who match your own qualities and temperament perfectly. There will also probably be opportunities for fun and flirtation. People in faraway places can give your hopes and dreams a boost.

12. THURSDAY. Demanding. Scorpio people are likely to dig their heels firmly into the ground if confronted by business associates. Certain ones always insist on having their own way. Power struggles are in the cards. These, of course, can be highly disruptive to business activities. However, you are advised to take another look. Try to determine where you can back down or how you can meet others halfway. Some concessions may save the day. In the long run, nothing will come from a rigid and inflexible attitude. Loosen up. Don't take these things as personal affronts. But it seems you won't get much joy from your personal life either. Obstacles may be placed in the way of carrying out your plans.

13. FRIDAY. Mixed. There will be good opportunities for furthering business interests. But there is also the possibility that Scorpio people will blow their chances by overreacting to situations or losing their temper. Try to be as much the master of your volatile nature as possible. The loss of goodwill with business associates will only foul up current commercial operations. It may also jeopardize future possibilities. People close to you may try your patience. Family members can be in a wayward mood today. They will have little time for your views and plans for domestic changes. But Scorpios should put their shoulders to the wheel now. If they do, they will win the favorable attention of bosses.

14. SATURDAY. Enjoyable. Friends will make happy companions and activities shared with them will be fun. They may also have useful contacts and information to send your way. They should certainly help you put your plans into effective operation. Today is good for devoting your energies to organized recreational and sporting activities. Scorpios will enjoy being among people who are involved in pastimes and interests similar to their own. But if you are so inclined, conditions favor efforts made in employment matters. Your grasp of future trends will put you in a strong position to plan future financial killings.

15. SUNDAY. Tricky. If you have already made plans to meet with friends you may be in for a difficult day. If no such arrangements have been made you would do well to avoid your pals. They are likely to be in a disagreeable and provocative mood. And they may be saddled with problems that would involve you in many kinds of extra expense. Scorpios may find it hard to be as tolerant and diplomatic as these circumstances demand. Differences could develop into heated arguments. Those aftereffects might take ages to blow away. Any urge to work can be favorably channeled into home decorating and improving your property. Experienced people may have useful advice to offer in relation to new jobs.

16. MONDAY. Quiet. The week gets off to a fairly frustratingly slow start. There may not be the openings that allow you to get essential jobs and business underway or completed. With little to keep them occupied immediately, Scorpios are likely to retire into their shells. Being alone in quiet surroundings can seem extremely attractive to you. There will be plenty of opportunity for self-reflection. And it is possible that once you are on your own, you will find the energy and enthusiasm to be industrious. Work you complete under these circumstances will give you a feeling of satisfaction and help restore any lost confidence. The day will be good for getting irritating little jobs out of the way.

17. TUESDAY. Sensitive. Keep all activities and arrangements out in the open. Undercover operations will have a tendency to backfire. Don't pass on facts about your personal life or any other confidential information. It could become common knowledge or be used against you. Loved ones may be undependable. Or their erratic and uncharacteristic behavior may give you cause for worry. Try to be understanding and tolerant with them. Your lovelife may contain some adventures. This is a good time for popping the question. Marriages planned now have every chance of becoming very happy unions. Single Scorpios may indulge in a little frivolous romance.

18. WEDNESDAY. Difficult.   Scorpios can be highly charged up today. They may tend to have a browbeating effect on others. You may even adopt bulldozer techniques easily in order to get your own way. But this can be highly counterproductive in the long run. Hidden resentments are almost certain to build up under such circumstances. They will have a tendency to spill over when you are least prepared for them. Or people you offend will do all they can to impede your progress behind your back. In financial affairs it can pay to be a little secretive in your actions and intentions. Property deals can also benefit from hidden or confidential actions. Don't give away more than is strictly necessary.

19. THURSDAY. Fair.   Your personal drive is again likely to upset others. Too much determination and single-mindedness can bring about head-on collisions with people around you. This can cause disruptions, particularly in the personal sphere of your life. A heavy-handed approach will breed resistance when you should, in fact, be going all-out to win the cooperation of others. Tone down your ambitious urges. You must show more consideration for the need and desires of others, especially if you are hoping for their help. But outings with loved ones will be enjoyable. Imaginative changes made to homes and other property will reflect favorably in potential selling prices.

20. FRIDAY. Positive.   Give all the time you can to artistic and imaginative projects. Surprisingly lucrative rewards can come from creative work. Don't hold back. Take the products of your handiwork around to prospective buyers or display firms. Be prepared to be assertive and stick your neck out; luck is with you. Valuable opportunities can be missed if time is frittered away. Any offers of work or business projects that come your way will be worth taking seriously. You are likely to be given a chance on a winner now. On such a fortunate day calculated risks and gambles will be worth the taking. The chances of coming out on top are high. Any time spent with loved ones will be pleasurable.

21. SATURDAY. Disquieting. It will be far too easy to overspend on materials and tools required for creative work. In fact, expenses on artistic and inventive projects can begin to seriously undermine any profits you were hoping for. Trim down such expenses where possible. Local journeys will not achieve their ends. All driving is more hazardous today than usual. Damage to vehicles can prove costly and extremely inconvenient. Take extra care. Cars can also suffer mechanical breakdowns. People you have arranged to meet can forget appointments or be held up. Your schedules may be badly disrupted. This, in turn, can interfere with entertainment plans. Children can be quite a handful.

22. SUNDAY. Difficult. Money matters can give rise to headaches. Your budgets are likely to get thoroughly out of line through no fault of your own. The people close to you can behave irresponsibly. This can involve you in heavy extra expense. They may indulge extravagant whims. The additional strains imposed on your resources may have you wondering where your next dime is coming from. It would be foolish to add to your financial responsibilities while funds are at such a low ebb. You should also limit your duties to those that are already part of your routine. This is not the time to expand your circle of action. Old people can be cantankerous and you don't need that burden.

23. MONDAY. Deceptive. Loved ones and recreational activities will make a happy mixture. Scorpios will enjoy living it up a little now. But sweethearts and spouses may not be as honest or direct as you would like. It is possible that they have something to hide. They can also change direction erratically. Unfortunately, they cannot be taken at their word. Scorpio people may have to do some digging to get to the bottom of any mysteries. There can be some tension until problems are brought out into the open. Keep on your toes when dealing with matters related to family members. Things may not be what they seem at first sight. On the other hand, financial risks can pay off.

24. TUESDAY. Rewarding. It will be much easier today to get along with the people close to you. The time is good for asking relatives and neighbors for their cooperation. You should get all the help and support you require. Today is also favorable for social contact with such people. You can pass very pleasant hours in their company. You can establish helpful contacts now that will stand you in good stead in years to come. Local journeys can be productive. It will be easier to get on the same wavelength as other people in discussions and transactions. Favorable terms can be agreed upon. Intellectual interests can be turned into money earners. Something that arrives in the mail can lift your spirits.

25. WEDNESDAY. Disturbing. The people whose cooperation you need in order to carry out your plans will more than likely raise objections. Lending their support will not appeal to them. The people close to you will have their own ideas as to how things should be done. In particular, matters relating to the home and family can be a bone of contention between marriage partners. But it would make more sense for Scorpio people to play down such differences. If you insist on taking a stand on issues of a domestic nature major disturbances can result. This is a time for tolerance and, if necessary, for backing down. Serious arguments can get so far out of hand that long-established relationships are threatened. This is the last thing you want to have happen.

26. THURSDAY. Productive. Conditions are extremely favorable for property dealing. Profitable transactions can be made. Today is good for efforts to increase the value of homes and other property. A great deal can be accomplished in this regard through redecorating and modernization. Beneficial results can be obtained by pooling energy and resources with other family members. Solo efforts will be less productive than teamwork. This will be true especially with people with whom you have an affectionate bond. It will be easier to see eye-to-eye with people in important positions. Influential persons are more likely either to back you up or go along with your ideas and suggestions.

27. FRIDAY. Challenging. Scorpio individuals' characteristic sureness of purpose makes them eligible for taking a leadership role. And there should be opportunities waiting for you today. Take command of situations and show others the way. Your initiative is likely to be well rewarded by influential people. Your ability to guide people will not go unnoticed. You may also be brimming over with original ideas. These can be put into operation both effectively and profitably. A creative and imaginative approach can pay dividends. Don't be content with the known and tried ways now. This should be a good day for forming new romantic attachments that will play an important part in your life.

28. SATURDAY. Variable. Exciting but risky commercial propositions can come your way. You will find these hard to resist. Scorpio people are more likely to take an overoptimistic view of shaky business ventures. These, when put to the test, will involve them in heavy losses. It would be wiser to avoid such deals if you want to preserve your bank balance in any sort of respectable state. Romantic plans can be thrown into disarray by health problems suffered by loved ones. Creative energies will be on tap if you can open the right channels. Concentrate on artistic work, hobbies, and favorite pastimes. These can, in fact, be made into additional sources of income. Short trips will be productive.

MARCH

1. SUNDAY. Manageable. You may feel like forgetting employment affairs for the time being. You would do well, however, to keep your wits about you and your ear to the ground. New job offers may come your way even while you're making regular Sunday visits or engaging in other typical Sunday activities. Don't miss any opportunities if you are ready for a change. There should be happy experiences for Scorpios involved in love affairs or in newly formed romantic attachments. But your plans may be thrown for a loss by the disabilities of relatives. Loved ones will appreciate honesty and frankness now. By all means don't hold back if you have something important to get off your chest. Everyone concerned will be glad to have matters brought out in the open.

2. MONDAY. Good. This is a good day for career affairs whether you are self-employed or salary earning. It will be worth your while to put in extra efforts now. The returns on your industry will be very satisfactory. You will be in a good position to gauge both future employment trends and your own needs. Strategies can be better planned accordingly. But this is not a day for living or working for the moment. Take a long-term view. And it will be entirely up to you to make the attempt. It is your personal drive and hardworking ability that will reap handsome rewards. Any ailments that have been bothering you should clear up now. The health problems of older people should also diminish. That in itself will be good news for you.

3. TUESDAY. Rewarding. You should push yourself to the fore at work today. This is no time to be timid or hide your light under a bushel. Show your superiors just what you can do. Draw attention to the special skills and abilities you possess. People in authority may have vacant positions to fill. Scorpio people should make themselves eligible for possible promotion and pay raises. Affairs of the heart are likely to take a turn for the better, in spite of the meddling of family members. Even though some doubts are shown by the interference of others, you should keep a positive outlook on romance. Today is good for making journeys in the company of loved ones. You can meet helpful people while on the move and you might be able to make a business deal.

4. WEDNESDAY. Sensitive. Scorpio people are advised to put themselves second today. The needs of partners or spouses should be at the top of your list. They will not take kindly to being left out in the cold. Any neglect of loved ones or domestic responsibilities will bring you nothing but trouble. You would do better to sacrifice some of your personal plans and desires than to lose the goodwill of those you depend on. Conditions continue to favor all affairs of the heart. In fact, some adventure could accompany romance. Scorpio lovers should be floating on air. People close to you can come up with inventive suggestions and practical ideas to aid your creative projects. Try to implement these.

5. THURSDAY. Easygoing. Today you can expect a much more relaxed day. It should make it easier to calm any troubled waters resulting from recent tensions in close relationships. With less pressure and more time on your hands you will find plenty of opportunity to prove to loved ones that you care. You do truly have their best interests at heart. But the whole world will seem to be crawling along at a snail's pace. People will definitely be in a friendly mood. But it will still be difficult to make constructive use of any offers of help that come your way. During this lull in regular momentum single Scorpios may feel the pinch of loneliness more acutely. They may remedy this by finding a permanent partner.

6. FRIDAY. Upsetting. Loved ones can be headstrong today. They will want to go off on their own or organize things in their own particular way. This attitude is likely to cut across the plans and hopes of Scorpios. That will ensure rearrangements or compromises becoming necessary. But you must beware of overreactions or violent responses if things do not go your way. Close relationships can be in a highly inflammable state. It might take only a small spark of impatience to set them in flames. This can result in the ending of long partnerships. It would be better to give loved ones the freedom they require rather than risk destructive confrontations. Others will tend to misread your intentions.

7. SATURDAY. Disturbing. It won't be easy today to find common ground with people whose support is essential to your financial plans. They are more likely to withdraw from discussions or joint ventures, leaving you in the lurch. You are advised to be extra cautious where activities involving a high-risk factor are concerned. Gambles will tend to backfire. The less money that flows through your accounts now the better. Mutual funds, in particular, can suffer from mismanagement. You may well overspend on outings with loved ones. Even so, you are unlikely to find the happiness or satisfaction you are seeking through romance. Scorpio people may find it difficult to look on the bright side today.

8. SUNDAY. Mixed. People who live in faraway places, or those who have come long distances, can give you valuable assistance and advice today. This would relate to projects that are breaking new ground. These people can serve as catalysts to creative and original enterprises. But it would be wise to seek expert opinion if you are faced with formidable problems. This is no time to rely on your own limited knowledge or ill-informed sources. It is better if employment affairs stay just as they are for the time being. Attractive offers that involve job changes should be given deep thought before being accepted. Moderation is essential to maintaining a healthy state. Not only moderation is essential, however. A good diet, exercise, and rest are equally important.

9. MONDAY. Satisfactory. Scorpio people should receive both support and encouragement from loved ones or business partners. These will help them make a success of future employment or commercial plans. This is no time for beating about the bush with mates or spouses. Come straight to the point and lay your cards on the table. Don't bottle up problems, anxieties, or frustrations. Let others know how you feel or what is bothering you. Mental powers will be more acute. This is a favorable time for taking up new studies, education courses, and training programs. You will probably have to expend a good deal of extra work on what you undertake now. However, the results will be most satisfactory.

10. TUESDAY. Uneventful. Not much will be happening today. Pressures and demands will be greatly reduced for the time being. With fewer distractions, Scorpios will have plenty of time for contemplation and making plans and arrangements for the future. The day is good for activities that require unbroken concentration. You should be able to catch up with any unanswered letters and any reading or factfinding you wish to do. If you are planning journeys or trips abroad, travel agents are useful. They can supply essential information that makes travel less complicated and more enjoyable. But important decisions regarding business matters should be left for another time.

11. WEDNESDAY. Difficult. Money or lack of it can be a troublemaker today. All spending must be accompanied by restraint. Once you start to make unnecessary or extravagant purchases, it will be difficult to stop. You will soon get a taste for throwing money around, having taken the first step. Restrict spending to essentials. Your judgment on domestic or property issues can prove unsound. You may concoct imaginative ideas for improving the home only to find they are a flop once they have been executed. It will be easy to upset loved ones today. Any romantic outings will doubtless end in disappointment. The erratic behavior of family members can force a change of plan on you.

12. THURSDAY. Discouraging. Money is again likely to be the cause of your headaches. People upon whom you depend for support and backing in commercial undertakings may suddenly leave you in the lurch or reject your plans. It may be very difficult to go it alone now. The withdrawal of others may ultimately lead to the loss of money and valuable opportunities. It will be quite easy to fall in with dubious characters whose reputation can reflect badly on your own. Be more selective than usual when choosing friends or business associates. You cannot afford to weaken your position or show yourself up in a bad light right now. Money lent to others may never be seen again. Money borrowed may be extremely difficult to pay back; don't either lend it or borrow it.

13. FRIDAY. Disconcerting. It is still necessary to handle all financial affairs with extreme caution. This is not the time to stick your neck out with risky schemes or gamble money away. Play it safe. Stick to regular and dependable means of earning your living. Speculation can bring disastrous results. It may be hard not to get involved in the financial projects proposed by friends. But you would be well advised to steer wholly clear of them, even at the risk of upsetting your pals. Sentiment is a bad motive for losing money. This is not a day for committing yourself to anything in writing. You may have to spend more than anticipated on the needs of children.

14. SATURDAY. Rewarding. The results of business operations can be especially lucrative now. But you will doubtless need the help of people close to you. Only then can you make the most of whatever opportunities are at hand. Loved ones and business associates are quite likely to be in a cooperative mood. With their backing, the chances are excellent that you will realize the potential. While organized recreational activities may leave you feeling exhausted you will not regret the time and energy you devote to them. It will be possible to meet new and compatible people through them. If marriage partners share club or group activities marital tensions can be reduced.

15. SUNDAY. Disturbing. It will be fairly easy today to have disagreements with your friends. Arguments with close acquaintances can necessitate changes in plans and arrangements. But even if you manage to preserve the peace with your pals, activities shared with them can cost you far more than you can afford. Keep a close watch on your personal budget. Don't overspend in an effort to keep up with others. You would do well to steer clear of any financial proposals suggested by people you have only recently met. Wait until you get to know others better before putting your trust in them. Avoid financial risks and gambling. Losses can be enormous. Sparks may fly in a love affair. Feelings can be both intense and volatile, almost at a flash point.

16. MONDAY. Deceptive. People and situations are unlikely to be quite what they seem at first glance. Nothing should be taken for granted. Keep on your toes. But with the ground under your feet feeling so uncertain this is not the best time for making important or irrevocable decisions. It will be too easy to back the losers now. Don't rush into new financial or business offers. Look before you leap. Some background investigation of commercial propositions is essential before you commit yourself. Scorpio people will not make the best workmates and business partners now. Your thinking is likely to be so scatterbrained and erratic that others won't know quite where they stand.

17. TUESDAY. Sensitive. Scorpio people can work quite happily and efficiently in the shadows or in hidden surroundings. Your ability to handle background maneuvers will work to your advantage now, with beneficial results. Your financial resources are likely to get a boost, either now or in the near future. Today is good for attempts to gauge future trends. It will also be good for making arrangements and then planning strategies accordingly. You would do better to restrict your leisure pursuits to simple and inexpensive activities. Any seeking of excitement or adventure can end in loss of both money and confidence. Attempts to live the high life can have disturbing consequences. Romance is bumpy.

18. WEDNESDAY. Mixed. Scorpio people will be more inclined to dig their heels in today and adopt a rigid attitude. But the more you can counter this tendency with a flexible approach the better will be your chances of carrying out your plans. In fact, you should swim with the tide. Make an effort to fit in with other people's needs and you can probably realize many personal desires. You will have the ability to find fresh and effective solutions to problems. Great satisfaction can be gained from practicing new procedures and methods. Don't opt for the traditional ways when there is room for creativity. Scorpios have a fluent command of the spoken and written word so that ideas are easier to convey.

19. THURSDAY. Upsetting. It will be almost impossible to maintain harmony in close relationships. Tensions are likely to build up to the point where they could explode violently. This can lead to broken partnerships and unions. But Scorpio people should refuse to take the bait. If they avoid angry responses, emotional upheavals can be minimized. It will be up to you to exert a pacifying influence. If you succeed, people will be won over to your side. You can then count on their help and support. But family members are likely to be headstrong and self-willed and can throw a monkey wrench in the works where your plans are concerned. Loved ones may need extra affection and understanding.

20. FRIDAY. Useful. Scorpios may experience some conflicts between work and pleasure. But you would be wrong to settle for an easy time at the expense of employment and business opportunities. The call of the good life should be put firmly behind you. That assumes you want to make the most of the excellent chances available through work and commerce. The financial rewards from such activities can be extraordinarily good now. Wages and profits can be improved on a permanent basis. This is also a good time for seeking more interesting and better-paid jobs. But your creative ideas may be unacceptable to others. Short trips and visits can lead to upsets. Don't take any chances now.

21. SATURDAY. Productive. Financial affairs should be looking a little brighter now. But you should not spoil any change in fortune, however small, by overspending. Don't start indulging extravagant whims and fancies again. Guard your resources. Do what you can to assist your noticeably improved financial conditions by sensible economic management. Good returns can come from real estate investments. Time and money put into home improvement will be well spent. The market value of property can be favorably increased through redecoration and modernization. Today is good for wining and dining friends and associates in your own home. Conditions will be quiet rather than stimulating.

22. SUNDAY. Satisfactory. If problems have to be confronted, or important decisions made, the morning is the best time for doing so. But this is not a favorable time for contemplating job changes. Give yourself more time before deciding that present positions are unsatisfactory and new ones might be better. It would be all too easy to jump out of the frying pan and into the fire. Scorpios who have to work today may come in for more than their fair share of difficulties and obstructions. Co-workers can be in a bad mood and unhelpful. Awkward situations can arise. Local journeys will be productive. Relatives will be in a cheerful and cooperative state. Your love life should supply all you ask of it.

23. MONDAY. Tricky. Scorpio people must be more prepared themselves to toe the line. An overly headstrong and self-willed attitude will put you on the wrong side of employers and superiors. Hard-earned employment positions must be protected by practicing more patience and flexibility. Friction is likely with colleagues and fellow workers. Arguments must not be allowed to interfere with your duties. Know your own physical and mental limitations. Don't push yourself too far. Try to keep your intolerance and criticism of others within bounds. You are more likely to fly off the handle at the smallest provocation today. Speedy and reckless driving will lead to the inevitable consequences.

24. TUESDAY. Challenging. A much brighter, though short period is in store for Scorpio people. And in the longer term today can mark the ending of an old phase in employment affairs and the beginning of a new one. Both employed and self-employed Scorpio workers will be affected by the changing conditions. There are good chances of offers of new jobs or new positions in existing employment situations. People in authority can have welcome suggestions and proposals to make. Good fortune can come through people in prominent positions. The day is good for expanding any interests or dealings in property affairs. Recent health problems should subside now so that your activities are no longer hampered.

25. WEDNESDAY. Fortunate. Scorpios' run of good luck and favorable conditions continues unabated. But you may have maneuvered yourself into a tight corner financially. Or you may need additional cash to secure property or accommodations. If so, relatives are more likely to come forward with the necessary assistance. Don't hesitate to ask family members for loans. Loved ones will greatly appreciate gestures of affection in the form of presents, outings, clothes, or flowers. Money will also be well spent on new furniture and cooking facilities. Anything that contributes to the smoother running of the home will be worthwhile. Don't take a short-term view when making financial decisions.

26. THURSDAY. Successful. Scorpios will be particularly good at entertaining friends and associates in the home. Parties and social gatherings in your own territory will go over smoothly. All involved should have a lively and enjoyable time. You may have to turn to loved ones for some financial assistance. But they are likely to be in a generous mood and willing to help you out. Lucrative gains can come through the buying or selling of property and land. This will also hold true for transactions involving farm and garden produce. You may be delighted with a present you receive now, but you will also thoroughly enjoy giving presents to others. The day is favorable for asking bankers for loans.

27. FRIDAY. Enjoyable. A more easygoing and relaxed day is in store for Scorpios. There will be no difficult people or situations to contend with. There will be plenty of time to give to hobbies, subjects of interest, and artistic or imaginative projects. Give all the energy you can to activities that absorb or fascinate you. Employment affairs will go very much according to plan or expectation. You will be left to concentrate on your own work at your own pace. The day will be good for giving guidance and instruction to children. It will be easier to resolve any problems bothering youngsters now. There will be no exciting or dramatic developments in love affairs. Nevertheless, time spent with loved ones will be more than usually happy.

28. SATURDAY. Mixed. Scorpios should get practical help and advice with inventive and artistic ventures. If they need it, it should come from the people close to them. But any financial moves must be preceded by measured thought and consideration. This is no time to rush into transactions or economic decisions. Unforeseen situations that result in additional financial burdens are likely to occur. You should also leave some margin for contingencies where romance is concerned. People may change their minds or act in irregular ways. Your plans could thus be turned upside down. Glamorous descriptions of new jobs can conceal arduous working conditions and other, similar unfavorable factors.

29. SUNDAY. Demanding. Scorpio people will want to concentrate on employment affairs or business matters. But you are likely to meet obstructions that prevent you from making the headway you would wish. There will also be plenty to attend to around the house or garden. But again, circumstances may so work against you that very little is completed by the end of the day. Health can take a downward turn now. It may also be a factor that interferes annoyingly with your plans and desires. Fortunately, as the day goes on, you will probably meet with less and less resistance. Before conditions improve, however, Scorpios may have to cope with a weak-willed person. Don't let it upset you.

30. MONDAY. Buoyant. Conditions will be much to your liking at work today. You should get through your allotted tasks and duties with ease and efficiency. Any extra efforts you make are likely to win the favorable notice of employers or superiors. Scorpio people have the ability to know what they want and to make right judgments. This will also be backed up by some original thinking. This combination of talents can reflect very favorably on your bank balance. You will quickly have the advantage in any financial dealings. Your resources can be further boosted by totally unexpected sums of money. Worrying physical symptoms should quickly clear up.

31. TUESDAY. Mixed. This is not the time for banging your head against a wall by adopting a rigid and uncompromising stance. You will only lose the goodwill and assistance of the people around you by adopting an inflexible attitude. You should, instead, be going all-out to win cooperation. Head-on confrontations and stormy scenes can develop if you dig your heels in. But with a little give-and-take, peace can be preserved. Quiet conditions will allow you to devote time and concentration to writing, reading, and study activities. Mental energies will be strong, so take advantage of them. Consider today good for drawing up contracts and other important documents.

APRIL

1. WEDNESDAY. Quiet. Scorpio people should carry on with any mental pursuits, letter writing, or accounting that they had begun yesterday. The day is good also for maintaining a flexible and conciliatory approach. This should serve to keep loved ones in good humor. Don't follow any tendencies to take unnecessary or idealistic stands on issues. The people close to you will be in an easygoing and affectionate mood. This will ensure that domestic harmony will prevail. In romance, you can expect warm responses from sweethearts. You should be able to cope with most household or employment tasks without help. Assistance will be easier to find than usual if it is needed.

2. THURSDAY. Sensitive. This is another day when recreational and leisure pursuits should be put aside. You should concentrate totally on employment and business affairs. There will be excellent chances now of increasing business profits and boosting earnings. Affairs of the heart may not turn out as well as you had hoped. Quarrels with loved ones are in the cards. As a result, outings or other arrangements may be postponed or ruined. But things should be looking up where mutual funds are concerned. A good-luck factor is likely to assist projects involving pooled resources. But joint savings must not be employed to finance commercial operations that carry a high risk of loss. Taking chances with your own money is not really wise.

3. FRIDAY. Mixed. Today should be approached much as yesterday. Pleasure pursuits must give way to efforts to get personal finances in a healthier state. It will be easier to find more prestigious jobs that pay better wages. Keep your ear to the ground and search through the job columns if you desire an employment change. Today is good for requesting time off from work, or more flexible working hours. Employers will be in a sympathetic mood. Conditions are more supportive of business and other ventures that are funded by pooled resources. It will be a good day for ascertaining just where you stand with regard to tax and insurance matters. You may find additional ways of saving money.

4. SATURDAY. Sensitive. The less money that passes through your hands now the better. It will be easier to make drastic mistakes and miscalculations if large sums are handled. Put off important purchases for the time being. Keep spending down to essentials. But romance should be in a much healthier state than before. It can bring all the pleasure and affection you are seeking. Loved ones will be happy to go along with your plans. This is a good day for turning hobbies, creative pastimes, and subjects of interest into money earners. Both satisfaction and financial reward can come from thinking big where such activities are concerned. It will be easier to let others know how you are feeling.

5. SUNDAY. Manageable. Long-distance phone calls or letters can provide useful information. This can help you to better organize personal plans or romantic arrangements. It should be a good day for rejoining loved ones after long periods of separation. Or chance meetings can lead to happy reunions. Lengthy journeys may provide opportunities for meeting new romantic partners and sharing adventures with them. But Scorpios must keep their feet on the ground. It will be easier than ever to be taken in by superficial appearances. You will puzzle other people if you are erratic and jumpy in your behavior. Duties must be attended to, no matter what other distractions there are.

6. MONDAY. Challenging. It may be easier today to put original ideas and innovative schemes into practice. This is the result of experience and information gained by travel to distant places. Love affairs, on the other hand, can benefit from journeys of shorter duration. A trip may certainly help to overcome romantic difficulties or bring lovers closer together. However, Scorpios are likely to incur unforeseen expenses en route. Mental energy and long spans of concentration will be available to you today. These will make study and intellectual pursuits easier and more stimulating. Scorpios could be attracted to people much older or younger than themselves.

7. TUESDAY. Challenging. This is a good day for Scorpios to utilize their rich reserves of determination and willpower. You should be putting your full weight behind projects funded by joint resources. It is the pooled cash and the coordinated efforts that will pay dividends now. Your deep understanding of human nature will give you a great advantage when dealing with difficult people. And they are very likely to be on the scene today. There won't be much that can stand in your way. Nor will anything prevent you from reaching your goals now. You will have both feet firmly on the ground. People will respect your sound judgment and common sense. When others see your energy and drive in operation they may seek to employ your talents.

8. WEDNESDAY. Successful. Conditions for both employed and self-employed Scorpio people will be especially advantageous. For the former, there will be prestige, promotion, and pay raises in the cards. For the latter, more business outlets will be found and more profitable headway made. The time is right for making job changes. But Scorpios must ensure that they do not undersell themselves. Don't be backward in demanding the rate of pay you know you deserve. You will get more help than you anticipated from people in prominent positions. Difficult jobs or absent employees may make it impossible to delegate work normally handled by others. But you can handle such tasks more efficiently in all probability. So, for the present, no harm will be done.

9. THURSDAY. Productive. Conditions are highly favorable for business operations. You should definitely keep plugging away with regular commercial enterprises. The gains and profits are likely to come from unexpected quarters. This is not the time to adhere only to known and tried ways. Imaginative and unconventional approaches can succeed where traditional methods fail. Or at least they will achieve only limited success. The opinion of people close to you regarding financial matters should not be ignored. Your own economic judgments may need to be leavened by a broader perspective. But money and friends are likely to make a volatile mixture. Arguments can develop over who pays the bill.

10. FRIDAY. Special. The extravagant side of the Scorpio nature should be held in check. Your desires for pleasure and good things can override your economic common sense. It will be easier to make hasty purchases that, on later reflection, you realize are really unnecessary. All financial moves need measured consideration. Scorpios will be mentally agile today. This will make accounting, study, and reading and writing easier to handle and far more satisfying. Dramatic and even dangerous situations can show Scorpio people in a very good light. You are likely to remain cool and in full control when under pressure. Other people's safety and well-being can benefit from your quick thinking and firmness.

11. SATURDAY. Disturbing. Business finances can take a distinctly downward turn now. It may be difficult to summon up the energy and willpower to steer commercial enterprises through to the bitter end. A lot of hard work may be necessary with very little reward to show for it. Some depression may set in. This will make problems seem much larger than they are in reality. Try to maintain an undistorted picture. There may be a cry for help from a friend. Problems you thought over and done with can crop up again. The unreliability of others can throw your plans and schedules into disarray. Any neighborhood activities in which you get involved can turn out to be a letdown.

12. SUNDAY. Disconcerting. People close to you can be full of whims and fancies today. Frequent changes of mind and direction are likely on their part. It will be difficult to involve them in your plans with any certainty. Or the health of loved ones can force a change of plan. Neither should you be overly casual in matters that can affect your own health. Take food, drink, and pleasure in moderation. Don't burn the midnight oil. Even though you are powerless to do much about it anxiety over employment matters may play on your mind. It may be in the interests of others to pull the wool over your eyes. Information that would be to your advantage could be withheld. Find out who is responsible and why.

13. MONDAY. Difficult. It can be more beneficial to keep financial moves and intentions confidential now. It is by working quietly and unobtrusively that you can make the most headway in money matters. The day is good for utilizing unofficial channels. But the atmosphere at work is likely to get you down. Someone may be harboring hidden resentment for you. But it is expressed only in covert ways. You may get edgy without quite knowing why. There is also a chance that Scorpio workers will have to shoulder more than their fair share of the work. Even then, though they work their fingers to the bone, they may still not meet the expectations of employers. Angry reactions are possible.

14. TUESDAY. Pleasant. Scorpio people should have less trouble in getting things their own way now. The demands of others and similar external pressures will not crowd you out so much. This will leave you more freedom of choice and action. Conditions are particularly good for study and researching. The reason for this is that you will have the ability to absorb facts and information to a far greater extent than usual. It is by keeping on the move that you can meet up with people who offer assistance and service. This will be particularly true of your local neighborhood. Family members may have access to valuable information which they can pass on to you. There will be a good chance to catch up with your mail.

15. WEDNESDAY. Rewarding. Scorpio people today will seem extremely attractive to others and exert a strong pull on them. New love affairs are likely to spring up as a result. If single Scorpios are looking for partners, they should frequent places and gatherings where their innate magnetism can go to work. Creative energies will be high now. You will thus have a greater command of expressive forms. Writers, artists, designers, and all those whose work depends on imaginative flair should have a field day. You will have a good eye for buying new clothes. Paying a little more attention to appearance will enhance your chances of meeting new partners.

16. THURSDAY. Positive. Both self-employed Scorpios and those employed by others can give personal resources a boost with the efforts they make now. It will be up to you to improve the situation you are in so that you can gain more from it. Higher pay or higher profits are there for the taking. This is provided you put in the requisite drive and brain work. You will be backed up in your efforts by people in positions of influence and authority. They are more likely to give credit where credit is due. Sums of money can come out of the blue. Or long-awaited inheritances or legacies can finally be paid. It will be easier to throw off any health problems. Physical energy will be high and you should be proud of this fact.

17. FRIDAY. Disquieting. It will be impossible to rely on colleagues and regular contacts in the way you would like. They can behave erratically or even cause trouble. This could easily interfere with working patterns and procedures. Targets and quotas may not be achieved as a result. Scorpio people may have to stay late at work to catch up. Be extra cautious in choosing someone in whom to entrust confidences. Don't expect others to be as dependable or honorable as yourself. You may find yourself in a tight corner financially. Approaches to older people for temporary help are likely to be turned down. In fact, the affairs of elders are quite likely to cause you additional expense.

18. SATURDAY. Productive. This can be a most advantageous day providing Scorpios employ a steady and measured approach. Rushed jobs and hasty decisions will not give satisfactory results. They can, in fact, leave a trail of complications in their wake. But there will be opportunities to improve employment positions and pay. Follow up any new jobs that have caught your eye or your imagination. Or if you are still looking for a change the job columns are likely to contain something that suits you down to the ground. Don't hesitate to state your past record and achievements when applying. Those and any special abilities should be brought to the notice of prominent people or prospective employers.

19. SUNDAY. Disturbing. It is the most familiar or workaday people and situations that are likely to cause you problems today.

Routine tasks and chores can contain irritating complications. Regular contacts can be awkward and contrary. When faced with difficult choices Scorpio people will probably want to remain sitting on the fence. It will not be at all easy to come to definite decisions. Confidence may be lacking or thinking be muddled. But you may have to cast your vote one way or the other before the end of the day. Your system will be more vulnerable to infection, tiredness, and various minor other ailments. Take more care of your health. Time spent with loved ones can include upsets.

20. MONDAY. Harmonious. Thinking will be clearer now and mental agility greater. You will find it easier to concentrate for long spans of time. This, in turn, will make study and other intellectual pursuits less trouble to complete and more enjoyable in the doing. It will be easier for you to express ideas and feelings. This will allow you to give full vent to your creative impulses. There should be no shortage of original and lively ideas on which to base new enterprises. Recent disruptions in romance should have blown over by now. Time spent with sweethearts will be happy. Exciting but short-lived attachments are in the cards.

21. TUESDAY. Productive. It is probable that your hopes of better working conditions, pay, or position may not come about quite as you had expected. But there are still good chances that welcome improvements will take place. A lot will be up to you. If you are prepared to put your shoulder to the wheel, you can pave the way to increased earnings. The proverbial Scorpio drive should come to your aid now. This can ensure that you hit the targets you have set your sights on. It will be worth sticking your neck out as luck is with you. Your actions will be guided by a beneficial influence. Family members can be cooperative where money is concerned. But your plans may meet with some resistance.

22. WEDNESDAY. Successful. Today is particularly favorable for bringing plans and projects to the attention of people in prominent positions. You are more likely to receive encouragement and support from influential quarters. It will be good for applying for planning permission and for official go-aheads. The way should open up for you now to switch into top gear. Any inclination to team up with others in business ventures should be followed through. There is everything to gain by forming new partnerships now. There will also be happy results from new romantic attachments. You may suddenly be presented with a solution to a money problem that has been bothering you.

23. THURSDAY. Uncertain. Listen to what neighbors and family members have to say today. Their advice or whatever information is in their possession can be of great benefit to putting original and innovative ideas into practice. But they may also have some cautionary remarks to make regarding risky investments. And as speculative activities are a bad bet at the moment you would do well to take their advice to heart. It will be particularly dangerous to involve mutual funds in commercial operations that carry a high-risk factor. Money can be a bone of contention between marriage partners. But recent efforts put forth by Scorpios will probably reap some personal benefit and success.

24. FRIDAY. Successful. Your own judgment and grasp of financial matters will be more trustworthy than outside advice. No doubt others may put pressure on you to spend your money in certain ways. But you would do well to reject such influences. Your best bet is to save every penny you can. You must lay up reserves for holidays and household expenses that will surely come in the near future. But you should follow any impulses to give others a helping hand. Scorpios can be particularly successful in investing others' money for them. Some good fortune can come your way from rendering service to others. Your astute and sensible thinking will be much valued. This is a tribute to your integrity.

25. SATURDAY. Deceptive. A protective influence will be shading Scorpio people from harm and bad feeling now. This is just as well. The people you work with may not be in the friendliest or most cooperative mood. In fact, they can be devious and thoroughly irresponsible. This could certainly make mistakes and accidents more likely. They would be happpier if it weren't for the above-mentioned good-luck factor. But even so Scorpio people should keep on their toes. People and situations may not be what they seem at first sight. Appearances can be deceptive. With the conditions so uncertain, important decisions are best left to a more appropriate time.

26. SUNDAY. Rewarding. Financial burdens and pressures may ease up a bit now. This will be due to the making of new economic arrangements. If you are unhappy with the way your finances are organized, it will be up to you to initiate the necessary changes. Or you could at least start the discussions that could lead to change. You may be relieved of regular payments in support of relatives or acquaintances. Circumstances in the lives of family members can change. This would also result in your spending less. Visits to street markets can be both fun and productive. The day is also good for turning to older and wiser folk for advice and guidance. Their experience could be very useful to you.

27. MONDAY. Sensitive. Scorpio people will be more sensitive than usual to the rejection of their ideas and views by others. But you must learn not to take yourself so seriously and avoid any angry responses. Others must be allowed their own outlooks and ways of doing things. This is not something you are going to change single-handedly. It will be a good day for cultivating intellectual interests. Reading, writing, and study activities taken up now will give rewarding and satisfying results. But there may be a tendency for Scorpios to withdraw from others and create a corner for themselves. This can be interpreted badly by people close to you. The more you share interests and activities the better.

28. TUESDAY. Encouraging. The day will no doubt proceed at an easy pace. Scorpios will have plenty of energy and enthusiasm for mental interests. Any intellectual pursuits begun yesterday can be continued with success today. This will apply especially if loved ones are able to share in or contribute to your activities. The emphasis should be pooling efforts now. Much more can be achieved through teamwork than solo efforts. You will also be happier in the company of others than in spending the day alone. It will be good for seeking the backing or encouragement of people in prominent positions. Superiors will be in a sympathetic mood. You will find it easier to express feelings and ideas.

29. WEDNESDAY. Sensitive. There will be much less happening today than yesterday. But it continues to be to your advantage to pool energy and resources with others. Be more prepared to go along with the plans and projects proposed by others. Don't expect to have things all your own way. People will appreciate your attempts to meet them halfway. Conditions will not be supportive of the launching of new beginnings. You would do well to concentrate on regular and well-established activities. It is good for clearing the decks in preparation for busier times ahead. It will be easier to heal any rifts with loved ones. Maintaining harmony, once peace is restored, will be up to you.

30. THURSDAY. Manageable. Unexpected sums of money are likely to come your way now. Or Scorpios may somehow be let off the hook where financial pressures are concerned. But it will be all too easy to throw away the advantages that such occurrences bring. Once you are given a little financial leeway you may tend to throw money around on extravagant tastes and nonessential purchases. But this will only put you in a worse position than you were in formerly. Hasty actions can lead to carelessness. Be more patient and deal with everything in a thorough way. Do not overlook details. It should be good for taking on extra responsibilities at work. It is quite likely that your pay envelope will get a boost.

MAY

1. FRIDAY. Disturbing. This is not a good day for parting with large sums of money no matter what you are exchanging it for. The less money that passes through your account now the better. Avoid new financial investments and commitments. It will be difficult for new projects to get off the ground. They are more likely to fizzle out before they have had time to get established. Schemes that are funded by joint capital are even more risky. Money may be spent on cars and expensive household goods. But even they can fail to give satisfaction. Your judgment of the best items to buy can be impaired. Older people may need more help or support. Their needs can prove extremely expensive.

2. SATURDAY. Useful. It will be very easy to back the wrong horse now. You are likely to base your judgments on faulty or misleading information. You may attribute quality to people and situations that do not merit it. Scorpio people can lay false trails for themselves. Some healthy skepticism can save you a lot of trouble. Put your own motives and perceptions to the test. Ask the opinion of people you trust if there is any doubt. But you can find some relief from current problems by making arrangements for holidays. Distant people can be extra helpful in this respect. Your spouse's relatives are likely to be in a friendly and cooperative mood. Today is good for forming new associations.

3. SUNDAY. Mixed. It will be easier for Scorpio people to push themselves past their limits. Restrict journeys to those that are really necessary. You can do a lot of running around to no avail if you're not careful. Try to conserve your energy wherever possible. Leave whatever chores and tasks you can until you feel more energetic. You are likely to meet people who are experts in their particular field. It will happen while you are on Sunday visits or outings. And it is likely that you will get involved in quarrels with them. You may have to rearrange your schedule to make room for loved ones. But activities shared with mates or partners will be enjoyable as long as you choose low-key things to do.

4. MONDAY. Untroubled. The week gets off to something of a sluggish start. Conditions will be slow and other people can be lethargic. But Scorpio people will have the alertness necessary to pursue mental interests and activities. All work connected with study, training, and education will go well. The day will be good for research and delving into books. Make use of this lull in the regular helter-skelter. Look ahead and make plans that will benefit your business and career prospects. You could contemplate signing up for refresher courses or retraining programs. It is a good time for getting new skills under your belt. Your spouse's relatives will be in a cooperative mood.

5. TUESDAY. Mixed. This can be an advantageous day both for Scorpio workers and for those who employ others. Productivity will be high and profits can be increased. This can mean more money all around so that there is a good chance of pay raises. But later, fellow workers can become awkward and uncooperative. Superiors may have so much on their minds that they have little time to give to you. Or their thoughts may be constantly turned to other things. Sweethearts and marital partners will be in an agreeable and affectionate mood. Time spent with them can be very pleasant. Love affairs can include some adventure. But you should certainly find all the love and reassurance you are seeking.

6. WEDNESDAY. Challenging. Today is good for activities that involve large numbers of people or the public in general. Scorpio people who have set their targets high have excellent chances of attaining their ambitions. It will be worth pushing yourself hard to realize your aims. Conditions will support your extra efforts. This is no time for halfway measures. Swing into action. Your name may go up in bright lights now. Scorpios who have worked hard and maneuvered themselves into important positions can win fame and reputation. It should be good for pooling finances with others. Joint projects can be extremely profitable. Don't live for the moment; take a long-term view.

7. THURSDAY. Important. Friends may give you introductions to people you desire to meet. Or they could help your personal plans along in other ways. Visits to social gatherings and parties can be both enjoyable and productive. You are likely to meet people who are on your wavelength in business matters. This may occur during social events organized by friends. New financial arrangements can be made under informal conditions. Funding for new commercial enterprises may be promised or planned. It is good for creative thinking and adopting new methods and techniques. All intellectual pursuits can benefit from an imaginative approach. Scorpios will find it easier to convey ideas to people.

8. FRIDAY. Mixed.   Keep friends and money well apart. Their advice on business finances can be disastrous. Friends can get into difficulties with their own business or personal finances and make requests for assistance. And you may have no choice but to give whatever temporary help you can. But it would be an idea to get written guarantees for any money that you part with in their direction. This is not a good time to take on new commercial propositions. This is especially true if returns will be some time in coming to you. But enjoyable times can be spent with friends and loved ones. This presumes that money is left out of the reckoning. Opt for activities that cost nothing.

9. SATURDAY. Happy.   This is not the time to take a frivolous attitude to romance and close relationships. You should instead be seeking to deepen trust and affection in marital unions and love affairs. It will be easier now to start romantic attachments that have good long-term prospects. It is also good for showing others just how much you care. Go out of your way to make gestures of kindness. Partners and spouses will be congenial and time spent with them will be pleasant. But don't expect too much adventure or excitement. It is possible that loved ones will be in a position to give you financial help. The rewards for Saturday workers can be especially good, though some people will prefer free time.

10. SUNDAY. Upsetting.   People in obscure or lowly positions are likely to throw a monkey wrench in the works insofar as your career plans and ambitions are concerned. Be on your guard. Background people may have been harboring hidden resentments. Only now do these come to expression. You may even be misrepresented behind your back. Your case may be unfairly treated due to the intervention of revengeful people. Disappointments are likely to affect you badly. Try to avoid emotional disturbances. Too much inner upheaval can produce some health symptoms. Promises should be made only if you are certain you can keep them. Others may not hold to their word.

11. MONDAY. Lucky.   This will be an excellent day for going all-out to put your financial position on a more secure footing. Any moves in economic matters you make now are likely to put your mind at rest. And don't worry if things do not go according to plan or expectation for some time to come. Unexpected happenings can bring you good luck in their wake. Keep on your toes in order to take full advantage of sudden changes. Don't draw unnecessary attention to your activities. Keep in the shadows. Concealed moves can bring the greatest advantage. You are also likely to receive help and support from background people. Consider the day good for digging and delving and getting to the bottom of things.

12. TUESDAY. Fair. Scorpio people will probably want to break out of the mold of routine and familiar patterns. You will be looking for new horizons, fresh faces, and excitement. But there is a danger that you will go too far and land in trouble. Some restrictions may have to be placed on your buccaneering spirit. But it will also be necessary to keep mobile and flexible. Use energy constructively. Avoid digging your heels in. The day can be wasted in power struggles if you are too idealistic or rigid. Visits to local libraries, museums, or educational institutions can further your intellectual or academic interests. Useful information can be collected. But if you collect it, find a way to make it accessible.

13. WEDNESDAY. Disturbing. It won't be so easy to put your personal plans into operation now. Loved ones are likely to have their own ideas as to how you should be spending your time. Compromises may be necessary to preserve the peace. People who could give you support and encouragement are unlikely to do so. Your proposals may be turned down for fairly frivolous reasons. It won't be easy to see eye-to-eye with others on most topics. Transactions can end in stalemate. The terms of contracts may not be to your liking. People who live close to you or under the same roof can spread a net of complications. Others may seem to stand in your way out of spite.

14. THURSDAY. Upsetting. This is not a time for feeling overconfident. You may think you have firm hold on the rudder, especially where finances are concerned. But money matters can have a way of not conforming to expectations. They can get out of hand in the twinkling of an eye. You will be better placed to deal with problems if you half expect them. But if you go sailing along thinking that everything is in its right place you will probably get clobbered by fate. Projects involving mutual funds are particularly vulnerable to miscalculations. Loved ones can draw heavily on shared resources. They will doubtless spend the proceeds irresponsibly. They won't have much time for economy measures.

15. FRIDAY. Mixed. Don't give in to extravagant tastes or whims. Stick to moderate spending. There is more chance of making bad mistakes where mutual funds or projects backed by pooled resources are concerned. All decisions in such ventures should be given careful consideration. You cannot afford hasty moves. Money is likely to be a bone of contention between you and loved ones. In fact, fierce quarrels are in the cards over cash. You may have to cover more ground than is really necessary at work. This will be due to the carelessness of others. But Scorpio people are unlikely to be held up by obstructions for long. They will find ways of winning pay increases or more favorable positions.

16. SATURDAY. Deceptive. This is no time to allow the heart to rule the head. Logic and clear reasoning must be the order of the day. There may be some important decisions to make and these must be preceeded by measured consideration. Hasty moves or choices made on the basis of emotion can prove disastrous. Adopting a wrong direction now can adversely influence your circumstances for some time to come. Scorpios will more easily be taken in by attractive propositions or so-called window dressing without first checking to see that the proposal merits their trust. You must cast a critical eye over your own motives now. You may be pulling the wool over your own eyes. Self-honesty is essential.

17. SUNDAY. Buoyant. This is a favorable time for serious talks and discussions with loved ones. Any problems of an emotional or economic nature should be faced up to. It will be easier to iron out the wrinkles in marital affairs. New understandings can be reached. The wheels of domesticity can be made to run more smoothly. Don't brush difficulties under the carpet. You have everything to gain by bringing them out into the open. It can be of benefit to check over recent correspondence. You may have overlooked some useful information. Letters sent off today can solicit welcome and helpful replies. Journeys made in the company of family members can be enjoyable. Everything today seems to have gone in your favor which should make you feel pleased.

18. MONDAY. Changeable. Dealing in property can result in profitable returns. Money spent on improving homes and other property will not be wasted. Market prices will be favorably increased. Decorating or modernizing your home will put you in a strong bargaining position in any future decision to sell it. Don't make solo moves where mutual funds are concerned. The advice and experience of other joint owners of resources should be sought. This is mandatory if new investment plans are on your mind. It is probable that the suggestions of your business partners will improve future financial prospects. Scorpio people must be more prepared to move with the times and swim with the tide.

19. TUESDAY. Mixed. Family members are more likely to be cooperative if you see fit to introduce economy measures. Loved ones should do all they can to strengthen family finances. But it will be up to Scorpio people to keep a weather eye on future family or personal security. And there should be opportunities now to establish your economic base more firmly. Be prepared to break away from the herd. Adopt unconventional or untried methods. Originality can pay dividends now. Traditional means and approaches can leave you simply running in place. The more you can rely on your own initiative the better. People who could offer you help may be unwilling to do so. Try to find out their reasons.

20. WEDNESDAY. Important. Scorpio people should thoroughly enjoy this relaxed and pleasant day. While there won't be a lot happening neither will you be plagued by new pressures or distractions. You will find plenty of time to devote to favorite pastimes, hobbies, and creative work. It should be a good day for experimenting and exploring new avenues. You can draw on your funds of imagination and innovation. You should be able to muster all the help and support you will need. It will be a pleasure to be in the company of loved ones who will be both warm and encouraging. You should find all the affection and reassurance you need from sweethearts. Good news can come in the mail.

21. THURSDAY. Disturbing. Conditions are not supportive of financial risk-taking or gambles. In fact, all money matters should be handled with kid gloves. Restrict your spending to absolute necessities. Don't stick your neck out with new investments. Old difficulties you had thought were dealt with and out of the way can come back to bother you again. These will be a source of added expense. Affairs of the heart can take a downward turn. A romantic attachment can turn sour for you. Loved ones can leave you in the lurch because of a sudden change of mood or feeling. The unexpected actions of others can cause deep disappointment. A change of plan may be necessitated by health problems.

22. FRIDAY. Fortunate. Your financial situation should be looking brighter. Affairs relating to mutual funds or projects financed by pooled resources are favored by the prevailing conditions. People in prominent and official positions can be surprisingly helpful. You may find that you are much better off than you had realized. You may be informed of property or money that has been left to you. Unexpected assets can come to light. If you have been waiting for payment on an insurance claim it will very probably come either today or in the near future. Tax rebates may be paid. You may also receive planning permission on home or property alterations. You have been waiting for these a long time.

23. SATURDAY. Successful. There are good things in the pipeline for both Scorpio managers and workers. Business owners are likely to increase their profit margins and enlarge their share of the market. It is an especially favorable day for Scorpios who are ready for a change of job. There is a good chance that you will find another position. It will doubtless be one that suits you down to the ground. People who are impressed with your past record and talents can come forward with offers of new jobs. Loved ones will be in an affectionate and cooperative mood. They will be more than ready to go along with your plans and proposals. Worrying health symptoms should begin to clear up.

24. SUNDAY. Rewarding. Scorpio people may be more in the mood for work than for rest and relaxation. And all efforts given to employment or business affairs can pay handsome rewards. There will be plenty of energy so that you should reach whatever targets you set for yourself. In fact, you will probably need working activities to absorb the abundance of vitality that will be pent up inside you. Put your shoulder to the wheel and you will accomplish much. Come straight to the point when discussing financial matters with owners of joint resources. This is no time for beating about the bush if you have plans for the future in mind. It's a good time for getting into better physical shape through exercise.

25. MONDAY. Happy. Scorpio lovers should be on cloud nine today. Love affairs are likely to be in tip-top form. Loved ones will be very appreciative of expressions and gestures of care and affection. Show spouses and sweethearts just how much you feel for them. Close relationships can be put on a much firmer basis. New understandings forged now will make domestic harmony easier to maintain in times ahead. Loved ones will be more than ready to go along with your plans. They will be in a warm and happy mood. The day is good for starting new romantic attachments. It will also be favorable for planning marriages and becoming engaged. It will be easier to win over any people who are standing against you.

26. TUESDAY. Disquieting. It will be a good day for shopping. However, this is provided you have the time and patience to

pick out useful purchases and bargains. Don't get caught up in a
mad rush. It will be easier than ever to buy a string of unnecessary
items. It can happen to you if you once give in to the urge to spend
for the sake of spending. Take your time and buy wisely. There
will be no shortage of erratic and contrary people to deal with. In
fact, they are likely to cause complications and extra expense.
Don't rely on others when you can possibly go it alone. Where de-
pendency is unavoidable there is a chance that you will be let
down. This is not a good time for pooling resources with others.

27. WEDNESDAY. Encouraging. Past efforts can come to fruition now. If you had previously pooled money with others to fund
projects these are likely to start showing excellent returns. This
presumes that there is a well-established base to work from. If that
is true, new branches of existing businesses or new phases of old
programs can be initiated. But there is not much point in attempting to launch new ventures from scratch. These are likely to
fizzle out before they have picked up sufficient momentum. Wait
for more supportive conditions to get new projects off the ground.
Far and away the best results will come where there has already
been an investment of time, energy, and planning.

28. THURSDAY. Productive. There may be some hassles with
joint financial partners over who is to foot the bill. How much
money is advisable to spend could become a source of controversy.
But on the other hand they are likely to put forward excellent
plans and suggestions. These would cover making investments or
joint assets more valuable. A streak of good fortune is running for
them now. It would thus be wise for Scorpio people to listen to
what they have to say. This is a good time for applying for pay
raises. Your resources can get a boost now from both past and
present efforts. Keep your ear to the ground for news of more lucrative jobs. Even though these can involve heavier responsibilities the additional pay can make them worthwhile.

29. FRIDAY. Changeable. This will be a good day for agreeing
to economy measures with the people with whom you share resources. Financial partners will be more than ready to go along
with your ideas for reinvestment of funds. Nor will they contest
other financial changes you wish to introduce. But such dealings
and discussions should be restricted to the early part of the day.
Any contracts or other important documents that have to be attended to should also be handled in the morning hours. Business
plans and long-term commitments should be made early on, too. It

won't be so easy to see eye-to-eye with business associates or financial partners as the day proceeds.

30. SATURDAY. Challenging. Contacts with people in faraway places can give your spirits a lift. It is likely that suggestions and plans will be made for holidays and trips. You will probably have an exciting journey to look forward to. Distant people may have other ideas that affect your personal plans favorably. Harmony should prevail on the domestic scene. Loved ones will be in a more cooperative and congenial mood. Love affairs that start now are likely to result in happy marriages. Scorpios will enjoy time given to intellectual pursuits, study, and training programs. It should be good for efforts to broaden the mind and investigate new subjects of interest. Perhaps you should enroll in a class.

31. SUNDAY. Quiet. The complete absence of pressures and disturbances will make this a most pleasant day for Scorpios. You will be left much to your own devices. There will be plenty of time for rest and relaxation. It will be good for devoting yourself to leisure pursuits and favorite pastimes. You can probably be as active or as lazy as you like. Nothing is likely to come along to distract you or interfere with your plans. Events that concern you in distant areas will fall into place. The result is that any worries concerning them should fall away. Today is good for plotting future business and financial strategies. All study and research activities will go well; useful information can be found in encyclopedias.

JUNE

1. MONDAY. Mixed. Your personal plans may be somewhat at odds with business interests today. Colleagues or financial partners may be critical of the time you give to leisure pursuits or outside relationships. But neither the criticism nor time given elsewhere will hamper the advances that Scorpio people can make on the commercial scene. You can take significant strides forward with relatively little expenditure of energy and effort. But don't allow any successes to go to your head. Guard against overconfidence. It is just when you think you are king of the castle that things can start to go wrong. This is a good time for pooling resources with others to fund new schemes.

2. TUESDAY. Changeable. People close to you can have their own ideas as to how you should be spending your time and money.

In fact, they can be purposely obstructive so that opportunities for business advances are lost. All outside activities can be jeopardized by people who are jealous of your company or attention. But these disappointments can be partly offset by a measure of good luck that is likely to come your way. Conditions in regular employment activities can be extremely favorable. There may be good chances of increased earnings. Future security should be looking more reassuring. Lend an ear to what older and wiser people have to say. The fruits of experience will tell.

3. WEDNESDAY. Good. Now there is an excellent opportunity for expanding any overseas business interests. Commercial dealings with other countries can be especially lucrative. Long journeys can be made to combine pleasure and profit. Your personal presence in distant business transactions can mean a lot. Try to handle important negotiations yourself. You are likely to meet compatible new companions through travel. Your spouse's relatives can provide welcome help and support. All attempts at study and learning will receive great assistance from people who are experts in their field or from professional educators. Don't rely on your own limited experience.

4. THURSDAY. Disturbing. Hang on to your savings at all costs. It would be crazy to tie up your resources in new commercial projects. It is likely that unforeseen circumstances will place a heavy demand on your funds. Keep at your immediate disposal all the ready cash you have. All joint finances must be treated with great caution. It would be unwise, at least for the time being, to speculate further with mutual funds that are already committed. Business finances are unlikely to work out quite as you had hoped. You may have to work hard to get out of a tight corner. A cry for monetary help can come from a friend. The financial ideas of friends and companions won't hold much water.

5. FRIDAY. Encouraging. In contrast to yesterday the suggestions or financial assistance of friends can be crucial to the successful outcome of commercial projects. And it may not be just the long-established friendships that come to your aid. Recently made friends can also play their part. Returns are likely to be significantly increased through the intervention of close acquaintances. Matters can take a very pleasing turn in love affairs. It could be time for tried and tested relationships to become marriages. Organized recreational activities can be most enjoyable.

Don't be encouraged by free-spending friends into throwing your own hard-earned cash about. You worked long and hard for it.

6. SATURDAY. Deceptive. People may refuse to go along with your plans or disagree with your ideas. But it would be very foolish to try to batter them into agreement. You must keep a firm rein on your emotions. Erratic actions and behavior will do nothing to further your own cause. Angry responses and harbored resentment will only make life more difficult for you. Be more tolerant of the outlook and needs of others. Don't make hasty or impulsive choices. Important decisions need careful and measured consideration. People and situations can be other than they seem on first acquaintance. Reserve your judgment, for better or for worse, until you are more familiar with the circumstances.

7. SUNDAY. Tranquil. Health will be more vulnerable to infection and overstrain. Look after yourself. Get plenty of sleep. Don't overindulge in food, drink, or smoking. Ensure you have a balanced and nutritious diet. Avoid crowds if possible. It should be good for working behind the scenes to improve your finances. Don't draw unnecessary attention to your financial moves and intentions. Keep others in the dark where your financial position is concerned. The day may be spiced up by some surprising events. People who make cheerful companions can turn up quite unexpectedly. But Scorpios will be just happy to be left on their own. A peaceful and tranquil day will help you find your footing.

8. MONDAY. Fair. It will be easier to realize heartfelt desires and ambitions. You should meet little or no opposition to your personal plans. Arrangements you have been looking forward to for some time can work out to perfection. Tolerance and flexibility are essential. Power struggles are likely if you dig your heels in. It is best not to take a stand on issues now. Much energy can be consumed in thrashing matters out. Local journeys can be productive. Family members can provide introductions to influential people. Long separations from friends and loved ones can end now. Events in distant places that concern you can take a turn for the better. So take advantage of the good conditions now.

9. TUESDAY. Upsetting. Commercial dealings can be disrupted by people taking a totally different approach from yours. Associates can adopt a quite different and opposing viewpoint to yours. Friction can soon develop into heated arguments. It may be impossible to do business with such people for a while in consequence. Financial conditions are likely to be in flux. It would be unwise to invest large sums of money as situations can suddenly go into reverse. What looked like a winner can suddenly become a certain failure. All outside interests are more sensitive and need careful handling. Past difficulties can reemerge and give Scorpios more to worry about. Try to get these straightened out.

10. WEDNESDAY. Disquieting. Although there won't be a lot happening today there can still be plenty of opportunity for heavy financial losses. The less money that flows through your account the better. Defer important financial decisions and activities for the time being. Wait until you are more sure of your ground. You will be inviting disaster if mutual funds are used to finance commercial operations that involve a high risk factor. It would be best to avoid all speculation in so uncertain a climate. Money can be the cause of unpleasant domestic quarrels. Loved ones may want to indulge extravagant urges and will resent being chided. Show them a graphic example of income versus spending.

11. THURSDAY. Variable. Although money can come with less effort it will also be easier to throw away any financial advantages. Once you start on spending sprees it can be difficult to stop. The buying bug will soon get to you. Then you will be left with a lot of nonessential items on your hands. Any financial gains should be safely deposited. Don't draw on savings or joint resources unless strictly necessary. It can be more tempting than ever to utilize mutual funds in unproductive ways. Keep future security in mind. Bosses are likely to review the past records of Scorpio employees and reward achievements. Luck can come in the form of prizes or legacies, neither of which you had been expecting.

12. FRIDAY. Tricky. Family members or neighbors are likely to come to your aid if you are in a tight corner. Don't hesitate to call on such people if it looks as though your personal plans are going awry. They can also be very understanding in matters relating to the home. Letters of inquiry dispatched can now solicit informative replies. Peruse today's mail carefully as useful facts can turn up. But in general, conditions are uncertain. It would be foolish to rush into hasty decisions. Give plenty of time and consideration to important moves and choices. Ensure that you are not being misled. Scorpios can get excited about the wrong things now. Put things in perspective before you make a final decision.

13. SATURDAY. Disturbing. Scorpio people may suffer disappointments in working matters. Recent hopes of increased pay and benefits are unlikely to be realized. It does not matter how hard you have worked. Don't put too much trust in others now. It would be wiser to anticipate unreliability than to breeze along thinking everything is going to be all right. The trouble is that people can go back on their word or simply forget promises they have made. This can throw plans and schedules into disarray. Journeys carry a greater likelihood of complications or accidents. But if due care is exercised, trouble should be avoided. Differences with distant people or foreigners can develop into heated arguments.

14. SUNDAY. Enjoyable. Strangely enough, it will be by foregoing their own plans and wishes that Scorpios will most enjoy this day. You will do better to fall in with the plans and needs of loved ones than follow your own inclinations. Happiness can come from togetherness with partners or spouses. Family members will be in a cheerful and cooperative mood. It is a good day for discussions about joint finances. This is a good moment to institute economic changes if old arrangements are proving unsatisfactory. Parties and gatherings held in your own home will be most successful. It will be easier to form new romantic attachments. Existing love affairs can go from strength to strength.

15. MONDAY. Rewarding. Personal finances are likely to receive a boost today. Routine employment affairs can offer bonuses or pay raises. Any property dealing that involves you can prove extremely lucrative. The sound judgment and clear-sightedness of Scorpio people will stand them in good stead. Your grasp of future trends can place you in a most advantageous position. You will know just what plans to make to get the most benefit from future opportunities. Successful strategies can be laid now. It will be easier to persuade wealthy or influential people to pool resources with you and back commercial schemes. The day will be good for digging and delving and getting to the bottom of things.

16. TUESDAY. Mixed. Don't get on your high horse with people in authority or in official positions. It would be better to employ all the diplomacy you can muster in such contacts. There may be long delays with official business, but patience and tolerance are the watchwords. Anger and irritability will only make matters worse. Unexpected bills which eat into mutual savings can come in. Financial targets can be missed as a result. It will be necessary to conserve as much cash as possible. Neither you nor your spouse or partner can afford to splurge on extravagant or unnecessary purchases. Outings with sweethearts will be delightful. Loved ones will make affectionate companions.

17. WEDNESDAY. Changeable. It can be easier for Scorpios to find outlets for their pleasure-loving urges now. But although leisure pursuits will provide plenty of fun and enjoyment, you may have to reach deep into your pocket when it is time to foot the bill. Romantic adventures are in the cards. Single Scorpios have a better chance of finding compatible partners. It's a good time for taking stock of your present position. Weigh the possibilities of future moves in business and employment affairs. Holidays and trips abroad planned now have every chance of being successful. Events in faraway places will be looking brighter. Distant contacts are likely to get in touch; these could be long-time friends.

18. THURSDAY. Easygoing. Scorpio workers will be able to proceed at their own pace today. You will not be expected to take on more than your fair share. Neither will time pressures be imposed upon you. This means jobs can be done thoroughly and may be more enjoyable because of it. Conditions in general will be less rushed and more easygoing than usual. This can make for better chances of taking time off from regular employment. If there are pressing matters of a personal nature to attend to, now would be an opportune time. Health problems, in particular, can merit permission for time off work. Fellow workers will be in a cheerful and cooperative mood, but don't look for extra rewards.

19. FRIDAY. Variable. There may not be the job satisfaction or promotion hopes you would expect from regular employment affairs. But this is not the best time to consider job changes. You have more to gain by sticking with it, for the time being. Keep your nose to the grindstone. Rewards for arduous and tedious work can be surprisingly good. Even if alternative positions are offered to you, you should think long and hard before accepting them. Jobs that involve traveling long distances are likely to be a particularly bad bet. Let more time elapse before changing working patterns. It should be a good time for efforts to improve health and fitness. It will pay you to maintain both at a high level.

20. SATURDAY. Important. Excellent opportunities can be laid in the laps of Scorpios who are prepared to work hard. Be sure to put loyalty to employers before other considerations. Keep on your toes. Don't miss the chances when they come. Be prepared to abandon personal plans in order to follow up promising offers. But whatever arrangements are made today, it is unlikely that they will work out according to plan. Unexpected events can intervene and turn your expectations upside down. But don't panic or get disheartened. Alterations that seem problematic at first can soon be seen in a more positive light. People in prominent positions will be more cooperative. They may even offer to help you.

21. SUNDAY. Fair. This will be another day when some self-sacrifices can be to your advantage in the long run. It may be difficult to see it ahead of time. Scorpio people will be happier if they go along with the arrangements made by loved ones or close acquaintances. If they follow their own devices, the day will be dull. You will get pleasure from the happiness of others. But Scorpios who do not have to consider the needs of others will probably have plenty of energy to devote to work. You can have industrious inclinations now. Utilize any innovations that come to mind. Don't fall back on traditional and overused methods and ideas whenever there is room for invention.

22. MONDAY. Productive. Loved ones or close friends may be prepared to make long journeys that you are unable to make. Or they may have suggestions and insights that allow distant events to run more smoothly. One way or another, affairs that concern you in faraway places can be assisted by people who are close to you. If your mind is on holidays and trips overseas, it can be both fun and productive to scan through brochures collected from travel agents. Journeys begun today have a good chance of success. Mental and physical resources will be high. This will enable you to attend efficiently to most tasks. This week will be good for all activities relating to education and research. You may be taking courses and have to dig up material for a paper.

23. TUESDAY. Uneventful. This can be a rather sluggish day. There are unlikely to be any important developments. But neither will added pressures or demands be placed upon you. This will give both the right conditions and the time to attend to intricate jobs. Accounting and expense sheets should be brought fully up to date. It is good for getting paperwork concerning mutual funds into order. Visits to accountants to sort out taxation matters can be productive. It will also be favorable for checking that all insurance policies and payments are not overdue. Problems relating to rents and tax rates can be more easily sorted out. But conditions are not supportive enough to attempt the launching of new projects.

24. WEDNESDAY. Disquieting. Time spent with sweethearts or spouses is unlikely to give the pleasure and happiness you would hope for. But this will not be because of moody or hard-to-please partners. The circumstances you find yourself in will not be conducive to happiness. Unsought problems can catch up with you. Money can become a bone of contention between lovers. Heated arguments can develop over the best way to utilize assets. Try to minimize differences by looking at the other person's point of view. This is not the time to adopt hard-line tactics. Difficulties encountered by older people can involve you in additional expense. Projects backed by pooled resources are unlikely to run smoothly.

25. THURSDAY. Slow. Not much will be happening today. People and events will plod along at a distinctly slow pace. But at least there should be no new problems to confront. It is good for a tour of shops, stores, and markets. Keen-eyed Scorpio shoppers can pick up bargain buys. Conditions will be regulated and predictable so that you know just where you stand. No surprises are likely to overtake you. Pleasure trips can be fun, but journeys of any consequence will tend to attract complications. Leave important visits till a more encouraging day. This should be a good time for resuming studies and attempts at self-improvement. Books can open new horizons for you.

26. FRIDAY. Rewarding. Scorpio thinking will be sharp and to the point. Your grasp of events and trends will put you in a strong position to plan future moves relating to business and employment. You can fully trust your judgments now. Not much of importance will escape your notice. Your reading of situations is likely to be dead on target. Your aims and ambitions will assume a much clearer outline. This will help you to mobilize your forces so that targets can be reached in the most economical way. Plans can be laid that avoid unnecessary expenditure of energy and capital. You should be able to please yourself during leisure hours. Useful information can be collected on short journeys.

27. SATURDAY. Disturbing. Slow down now. Do a thorough rather than a fast job. It will be a case of more haste less speed today. You can get caught up in a whirl of activity and achieve very little. A patient and steady approach is more likely to help you reach your targets. With too much force or heavy-handedness you can easily overshoot your mark. You will probably be needing the assistance of other people, so make sure you do nothing to lose their sympathy. Be more tolerant and willing to help others. Don't lose sight of people's needs because you are too wrapped up in your own interests. Time given to work can be counterproductive. In your present state you will probably take on too much.

28. SUNDAY. Deceptive. Bad feelings can develop between you and contacts in faraway places. Or meetings with people who have traveled long distances can provide emotional flash points. The feelings of Scorpio people will be more volatile so that you are more easily irritated or angered. People you live with or are close to may try your patience to the limit. Next-door neighbors may be looking for trouble. You are advised to give your motives close inspection before any important moves or decisions are made. Your values and judgments can be a bit askew now. Or you may be looking on the optimistic side in matters that need a hardheaded or impartial approach.

29. MONDAY. Variable. Recent successes can make you a little too sure of yourself. You may think you have a better grasp of future trends than is, in fact, the case. Look before you leap. An overly buoyant mood can lead to mistakes and wrong decisions. Balance optimism with some thorough background research. Don't throw away advantages through recklessness. Pay due attention to the small print in any contracts or important documents you handle. Attend to details in all undertakings. But conditions in the world of commerce will be much to your liking. Very favorable terms can be agreed upon in business negotiations. Prominent people will back your causes.

30. TUESDAY. Mixed. Conditions are very encouraging for an active involvement in external affairs. The day is good for activities involving large numbers of people. You can make substantial advances in business. The opportunities for gain will be there if you can take advantage of them. This can be a lucky day for Scorpio employees. Hard work and loyalty can be rewarded with increased pay. The offer of more interesting work or more responsible positions may be made. Someone else's misfortune can work in your favor. Unexpected changes can come about. But with finances in a sensitive state it would be advisable to draw the purse strings tight. Only essential purchases should be made.

JULY

1. WEDNESDAY. Good. Distant events will take a turn for the better. Money can come from sources in faraway places and can be plowed into business ventures. Overseas commercial interests can show excellent returns on invested capital. Scorpio people will cut through problems and complications like a hot knife through butter. You will not stand unnecessary delays and obstructions for long. It will be good for getting expert advice and opinions if you are planning future strategies. Don't rely on your own limited knowledge when wider experience is available. Your spouse's relatives will be in a cooperative mood. Journeys can be productive although holdups may be encountered.

2. THURSDAY. Upsetting. This is not the time to commit your funds to new commercial operations. It is possible that the minute your cash is tied up in a project you will need it to deal with an emergency. Keep financial resources where you can get at them quickly. Bills can come in all at once. Joint monies need more protection. It will be easier to misuse them. Losses can be so large that Scorpio people may have to draw on independent funds. They will have to make good the losses to joint capital. Don't expect much help from loved ones in financial matters. They will probably turn up their noses at attempts to introduce economy measures. They can be more intent on spending sprees.

3. FRIDAY. Misleading. Much good can come today from contacts with people in faraway places. But it will be necessary to express yourself very clearly and directly. It will be easier for others to misunderstand what you have to say. Leave no room for mistakes. Check that your instructions, as well as any information that has to be passed on, are not misinterpreted. Journeys can take much longer than anticipated. Give yourself plenty of leeway for delays or missed connections. You must not allow your heart to rule your head. Scorpios can take an overly optimistic point of view and ignore the plain facts. Keep on your toes, as others may try to mislead you. They may have discovered you are gullible.

4. SATURDAY. Productive. It is people in the background who are more likely to provide helpful suggestions and assistance. This will pertain particularly where money is concerned. Don't for the moment put your faith in people who occupy prominent positions. Don't underestimate the usefulness of secrecy now. Avoid drawing unnecessary attention to your affairs. Visits to places of education or healing can be productive. Sick people will much appreciate a visit. Libraries and museums can provide interest and stimulation. Scorpios could be exposed to provoking situations. It would be better to allow trouble to pass over their heads than to engage in counterattacks. These prove nothing, anyhow.

5. SUNDAY. Mixed.　People and situations from the past are likely to turn up again and cause you a few headaches. Difficulties you thought you had dealt with once and for all may need yet more attention. Health problems suffered by friends or relatives in distant places can bring added worries your way. This is not a day for being too generous or openhanded. People are more likely to be suspicious of your motives than thankful for any help you attempt to give. You may even have to put up with harsh words from people you try to assist. But love affairs will be in fine fettle. It should be a good period for secret romances. Also, it will be favorable for starting savings accounts only you and loved ones know of.

6. MONDAY. Fortunate.　Business interests in distant places can come on apace now. The returns on investments of time and capital will fully reward your efforts. Business agents and contacts are more likely to do all they can to advance your affairs. You can count on first-class service in your absence. If you are saddled with insoluble emotional or marital problems it may be time to seek professional advice. There is no point in soldiering on against the odds if you have done all in your power to come to terms with difficult situations. The expertise and experience of others can suggest the solution you are seeking. Don't leave important letters unanswered. You could stand to lose an important contract.

7. TUESDAY. Active.　You should shift into top gear now. Pull out all the stops. Conditions will be so supportive of your efforts that you can achieve much more with the same amount of energy. With extra efforts, therefore, you can make tremendous advances. Now is the time to fully express and utilize your drive and enthusiasm. You won't get a better chance to realize your aims and ambitions. It will be easier to bypass obstructive people and situations that have been holding up your personal plans. Today is good for meetings with friends whom you haven't seen for some time. Events that concern you in distant places will be looking brighter. You should find the day favorable for study and research.

8. WEDNESDAY. Upsetting.　The day is likely to get off to a good start. Then conditions will become less favorable as it goes on. Take advantage of the early hours to attend to financial matters. There will be less risk of mistakes and bad judgment then. But complications can develop later which involve higher expenses. You may have to undertake journeys or activities that could cost you dearly. People may call on you for loans or advances. You will probably have cause to regret recent extravagances. Pleasures previously enjoyed must have to be paid for soon. Past mistakes can result in heavier bills. It will be more difficult for Scorpio people to keep their spirits up.

9. THURSDAY. Manageable. Financial affairs can take a decided turn for the better now. Once you get wind of brighter prospects, you may even derive some fun and enjoyment from financial activities. Sums of money can come out of the blue. Surprise happenings can lead to increased pay or profits. There may be better opportunities for Scorpio workers to impress superiors and win bonuses. Scorpios who employ others can learn a great deal. They can perhaps avoid trouble by listening to what members of the work force have to say. Their suggestions can help to streamline working procedures. Breakthroughs can come by convincing yourself and others that money problems are short-lived.

10. FRIDAY. Disturbing. Scorpio people will be more easily provoked. But no matter how much your patience is tried you will not do yourself any favors by giving in to anger and violent responses. It is likely to be people living with you, or nearby, who annoy you most. Neighbors can encroach on your time and your territory. Relations with people living in or coming from distant places can be far from harmonious. It is unlikely that you will see eye-to-eye with overseas contacts. It would be best not to have any secrets from loved ones. They will probably get to the bottom of things sooner or later. Close relationships can be terminated or loved ones may have to travel away. But you could keep in touch.

11. SATURDAY. Difficult. It will be quite easy for Scorpio people to spoil what can be a very favorable day for romance. Avoid heavy-handedness and a willful attitude. Pay more attention to the needs and wishes of loved ones. It can be better to leave certain things unsaid. Restrict travel to essential journeys. Unnecessary trips can absorb much time and expense and leave you with a feeling of dissatisfaction. Take extra care on the roads. Other drivers can be a menace. Neighbors may still be indulging irritating behavior. Casual acquaintances can be a source of trouble. Rifts with loved ones can be overcome. Relationships can be put on a firmer basis, perhaps because of recent difficulties.

12. SUNDAY. Good. There can be an upturn in financial affairs now. Future economic prospects may be looking brighter. The intervention of relatives can release you from an awkward financial situation. Or family members may do all they can to make economy drives successful. You will have better luck in trying to raise loans for work on your home or to buy property. Friends and relatives will be more willing to give you a hand with decorating and home improvements. Older people can be more sympathetic to your plans. Parents can give welcome support. Matters that should have been wound up ages ago can now be brought to a successful conclusion.

13. MONDAY. Lucky. There can be fortunate contacts with wealthy people or bankers. Loans or financial gifts can be forthcoming. Today is good for presenting projects to people who are in a position to invest capital in commercial ventures. It should be favorable for expanding any interests you have in property and property dealing. Profits from real estate can be increased. Don't be backward in bringing your special skills and talents to the attention of superiors. You can benefit from a little self-advertising now. There may be vacant positions to be filled at work. Your record for hard work can make you eligible to take on more responsibilities. Any suggestions for innovations can win you favor.

14. TUESDAY. Manageable. This is a good day for giving time to artistic and imaginative projects. They are likely to be both satisfying and remunerative. Ideas and feelings are easier to express. Scorpios will have a greater command of the written and spoken word and indeed of all means of communication. You are likely to fall for someone in a big way. Well-established relationships can be made even more trusting and affectionate. But outings with loved ones can be accompanied by rather big bills. Leisure pursuits and entertainments can be more expensive than you had anticipated. You can lose ground you have painstakingly achieved through stringent economy measures.

15. WEDNESDAY. Productive. Do nothing that is likely to alienate people in prominent or official positions. You are likely to be in great need of their assistance, particularly where distant events and people are concerned. Instead, you should do everything to win their cooperation. This should be a good day for applying for visas to visit foreign lands. This is a time when the horizons of Scorpio people can be widened. Important changes of direction and attitudes to life can result from contact with spiritual teachers or professional educators. It will also be good for conferring with people who are experts in their field. Take quick advantage of any opportunity to improve your public image.

16. THURSDAY. Mixed. This is another day when Scorpio people will find it more satisfactory to concentrate on work and earning money. Having merely a good time will not appeal. You should do everything possible to strengthen your finances rather than deplete them through frivolous or nonessential spending. Any particularly hard work you have put in at your place of employment recently is likely to be well rewarded now. Consistency and diligence can win better positions. But complications in affairs that concern you in distant places can be a source of worry. You are likely to get on the wrong side of people while traveling long distances or on arrival at distant destinations.

17. FRIDAY. Mixed. Scorpio people can earn extra money by taking on overtime or additional work. Loyalty and incentive will be well rewarded by employers. If you have suggestions for ways of making working procedures run more smoothly or efficiently you should take them to the top. Your initiative can win you more interesting work, better pay, and more responsible positions. This is another day when unexpected sums of money can come in with little or no effort on your part. Fortune will be with you and can bring prize money, legacies, or gifts. But it will be easier to fall out with contacts in distant places. This will also be true of people who have traveled long distances to see you. Try to determine quickly if the fault lies with you and do all you can to resolve the issue.

18. SATURDAY. Sensitive. It is by putting yourself out for others that Scorpio people can, in an odd and indirect way, further their own interests. Your personal plans can work out as you would have hoped by falling in with the arrangements of others. But if you make a beeline for your own targets, complications are likely to arise. People can react violently if they see that looking after yourself is your first priority. Those whose goodwill you value will not take kindly to selfishness. And this is not the best time for you to enter into arguments or power struggles. You will probably lose out. Be as unobtrusive and as cheerful as possible. But do the best possible job you can and you will be noticed.

19. SUNDAY. Happy. It won't be necessary to compromise or make sacrifices to gain any of the help or support you need today. Others are unlikely to raise objections to your plans and ambitions. On the contrary, you can get unexpected encouragement. Love affairs started now can be more important to your future than you might imagine. Happy and long-term relationships can develop from romantic attractions. Scorpios can meet prospective partners who are wealthy or own property. But rich or not, loved ones will have a beneficial influence on future prospects. Journeys can be fun and can lead to meetings with new companions. Such trips may be related to business, in which case time might be a negative factor. But if not, you might want to extend your journey.

20. MONDAY. Challenging. Plans agreed on yesterday toward arranging marriages can be furthered today. You will, of course, have the help and blessing of interested parties. Also the day will be good for continuing with business and creative projects recently initiated. It will be easier than usual to win the support and energetic help of those in influential positions. Prominent people can be in a sympathetic mood. Attempts to improve existing skills and knowledge of a certain subject can be most successful. Acquiring qualifications through training or further educational programs can also be rewarding. It should be a good time for exploring new outlets and broadening your mind.

21. TUESDAY. Mixed. Existing employment should only be abandoned if you are assured of an alternative line of work. You may find yourself in deep trouble if you leave your present job on impulse or in anger. New positions may not be too easy to find. Potential employers can be in an unsympathetic mood, unwilling to give you a chance. And the good offices of current employers cannot be depended upon. Don't push your luck. Travel can leave you feeling unwell and irritable. But this is a good time for pooling financial resources with others to fund commercial operations. However, first be certain that you are on pretty safe ground. Risky projects will tend to work out badly.

22. WEDNESDAY. Variable. Scorpio people may again find chances of improving incomes or earning more responsible positions at work. Your enthusiasm and diligence can win you special notice by superiors. Give as much as you can. Keep your nose to the grindstone. Money can come to you with very little effort on your part. You may receive inherited property or capital. Delays holding up the payment of legacies can finally be overcome. Family resources could get a further boost, as a pay raise for partners or spouses is in the cards. But good fortune may go to the heads of people close to you. They can run up debts by rushing out on a spending spree. You will have to curb their extravagance.

23. THURSDAY. Deceptive. It is possible that people you meet for the first time will try to pull the wool over your eyes. Keep on your toes. Watch out for dishonesty and deception. Casual romances can be a source of trouble. People's motives can be less straightforward than they make them out to be. All contracts and plans need extra thought and consideration now. Don't rush into new agreements. There may be problematic factors that emerge only after some investigation or logical thinking. But Scorpio people will be on the ball mentally. Long spans of attention will be available to you. These will make all research activities easier and more enjoyable. Help can come from faraway places.

24. FRIDAY. Positive. Strongly held opinions and attitudes can receive support and encouragement from others. This can do wonders for the confidence and self-assurance of Scorpio people. You will feel more firmly that the direction you have chosen is right. Your energy and enthusiasm to reach your goals can be increased. Any lingering doubts about heartfelt projects and hopes for success are likely to be laid to rest. Loved ones will be supportive and cooperative. Their intervention can mean the difference between failure and success in your undertakings. There will be a good opportunity for sharing outings and entertainment with associates. Those who traveled far will be welcome.

25. SATURDAY. Mixed. Conditions can be particularly tricky during the morning hours. Extra caution may help you to avoid trouble. But don't expect too much help from others. Your trust can be disappointed. People can be forgetful or act without consideration for the pains and efforts you have taken. Promises can be broken. This is a bad time to consider job changes. It would be better to weather the storm if things are not to your liking at work at the moment. Avoid overreactions. A casual attitude to health may have to be paid for by suffering illness or lack of vitality. Ensure that any symptoms receive medical attention. It should be good for getting new projects off the ground.

26. SUNDAY. Productive. Scorpio people will have tremendous energy and drive today. You can get a lot done particularly of a manual or practical nature. But the trouble is that you are likely to overdo it. Your will to achieve your ends may lead you to tread on other people's toes. You may even ignore their needs and wishes. The strength of your determination to succeed can baffle others and even frighten them a little. People you are close to may be feeling more like taking it easy. Your industry is likely to upset their peace. Arguments can result. But Scorpios would do well to channel their force into work or activities that can have lucrative results. The range of your choices will be broad and intriguing.

27. MONDAY. Rewarding. Your own financial interests can be advanced by people deciding to change their minds on important issues. Recent refusals of financial assistance can be revoked. It will be easier to raise loans or arrange advances. Bankers can be in a more sympathetic mood. Difficulties encountered in the course of business or external activities will not hold Scorpios up for long. You will know how to win over difficult people. You may be feeling that the world is your oyster. The likelihood of achieving your aims can seem even greater. Scorpio employees can win the favorable notice of superiors. Those who employ others can add to existing good reputations.

28. TUESDAY. Good. Family members or neighbors may have useful suggestions to make concerning business interests or potential commercial projects. They may know people who can give valuable assistance to money-making enterprises. Scorpios will have no shortage of original and creative ideas. Your breadth of mind can make studies, research, and other intellectual pursuits a pleasure. Writers will find it easier to express their ideas. You may be given a leadership role in any group or club activities that involve you. Others will be more willing to let you take the reins. You will also be very persuasive when it comes to convincing others of the soundness of your ideas.

29. WEDNESDAY. Manageable. You can put your mind at rest regarding future security, income, and profits. You can do this with extra exertions in business and money-making activities. Every little bit you give now can pay dividends. This is no time for halfway measures. Put your shoulder to the wheel. Give full vent to your forceful personality by channeling energy into profitable ideas. The longer the life of such projects, the better. You should be thinking as far ahead as possible. But financial schemes proposed by friends or people only recently met are unlikely to lead to success. In fact, losses are almost certain. A casual attitude to regular employment is very bad policy.

30. THURSDAY. Variable. Background people can supply welcome assistance. Their intervention in your affairs and undertakings can bring success considerably closer. Good fortune can come in unobtrusive ways. Undercover operations can be profitable or lead to the realization of a heartfelt desire. But you

will have to be very single-minded in business affairs. You are unlikely to win the trust and cooperation of business associates if they
see that your attention is divided between pleasure or private interests and work. Get your priorities straight. You can't have your
cake and eat it, too. While your generosity will be welcomed by
those who receive it, others will be resentful for being left out.

31. FRIDAY. Excellent. It is by utilizing concealed methods
that Scorpios can put finances on a firmer base. The foundations
you lay now can put your mind to rest regarding future security.
Steady incomes can be assured. Old and rare articles, stamps, and
paintings are excellent commodities to invest in. Prices are more
than likely to increase over the years so that profits are almost certain. Scorpios will be able to call on almost unlimited reserves of
physical energy. This will give you a great advantage over competitors in business, sports, and other activities. You can stay one step
ahead of rivals. Others will admire your achievements and your
reputation can thus be strengthened. The importance of that alone
in business affairs cannot be underestimated.

AUGUST

1. SATURDAY. Variable. This is no time to sit back and let
the world go by. Recent successes can convince you that you have
done more than enough for the time being. But complacency will
invite problems. You may feel that everything is under control,
but it is more likely that problems are building up. Or you just may
have overlooked unhappy circumstances. Background developments may only become known to you when it is too late unless
you stay on your toes. Relatives who depend on you can be affected adversely by situations that are avoidable. This means that
you must keep your wits about you. Or employers may be planning changes that will be disadvantageous to you.

2. SUNDAY. Sensitive. It will be a case of honey catching
more flies than vinegar today. Don't think you can force people
around to your way of thinking. Cooperation can only be won by
subtle means. Any attempts to pressure people into helping you
will only put their backs up. Support must be earned or won. Take
the needs and wishes of others into account. Don't put yourself
before others. In your enthusiasm to get ahead you may not realize
how much you are dominating others. The day will be more happily spent taking family members on outings and visits than in

pushing on with business activities. This is definitely not a good day to seek backing for your projects. Just relax and rest up.

3. MONDAY. Challenging. This is a good day for devoting time to intellectual pursuits and subjects of interest. Such activities can be most rewarding now. Your enjoyment will help you to cover more ground than would normally be expected. It should also be good for attempts to broaden the mind and explore new avenues of thought. Research can produce valuable information. Today is favorable for investigating such disciplines as yoga and meditation. While letters and phone calls to distant people can be effective, it is your personal presence that will carry the most weight. Travel to the spot wherever possible or necessary. Don't leave it to others to straighten out important issues.

4. TUESDAY. Important. People in prominent positions will be in a sympathetic mood. They will be more likely to answer your requests in the affirmative. Their timely intervention can save your money or indicate ways in which profits can be increased. Scorpios who set much store by their reputatons may be given opportunities to increase their standing in the eyes of others. High praise and honor can come your way. The success or public projects can win you fame. Invitations to social gatherings should be accepted. Even though you are not in a party mood, you will find yourself glad to join a happy group. The chances of conducting serious business in informal surroundings are high.

5. WEDNESDAY. Fair. Yesterday's advances in business affairs can continue today. Unscheduled profits may come in. Surprise gains are in the cards. But you should be as self-sufficient in financial matters as possible. If you are overextended to the point of having to rely on others you could find yourself in deep water. Others can go back on their word and leave you in the lurch. Loans can be refused at the last moment. It would be better to come straight to the point with business associates who have been less than cooperative of late. Open channels can be reestablished by letting others know just how you feel and what you expect of them. It doesn't make sense to expect people to read your mind.

6. THURSDAY. Disappointing. Situations are unlikely to work out as you had hoped or expected. It will be easier to misjudge people and events. Keep a close eye on all developments. Be prepared to change your direction or arrangements at short notice. People who have promised you help can just as easily go back on their word as stick to it. Disappointments are possible. Try to be self-sufficient. Don't act on first impressions. Wait until you are familiar with new people or situations before committing yourself. Conditions at work may get you down. There won't be much cooperation or friendliness. But you would be unwise to consider resignation at this point.

7. FRIDAY. Fortunate. Scorpio people should get all the help and encouragement they require from business associates. Your ideas on financial strategies will have great appeal for colleagues. The confidence shown in your planning can give you the freedom to initiate new moves. This factor will have important future consequences. And the further ahead your thinking extends the better. You should be planning your personal long-range security. Provision should be made for the future well-being of dependents and loved ones. It should be good time for starting new pension plans. Taking out long-term insurance policies is a wise move. Prominent people can bring your name before the public.

8. SATURDAY. Upsetting. There could be some mudslinging today. Do nothing that will give ammunition to scandalmongers. Be especially choosy about anyone to whom you divulge any secrets. Even people you trust can be less than discreet. Damaging rumors can be spread about your love life. Your reputation could be in the balance. Play it safe. Take no chances. Avoid people of dubious character. Remember that you are known by the friends you keep. Companions must be chosen with additional care now. It would be better to give business activities a miss today. Conditions are not favorable for commercial operations. This is not a day for signing contracts.

9. SUNDAY. Disturbing. There will be no improvement in the conditions affecting business and public activities. You would do better to turn your back on professional interests and concentrate on family and domestic affairs. Loved ones will not take kindly to being left out in the cold. They will be hoping for your full attention. It would be wise to stick to regular Sunday patterns. Put personal desires second. Attend to the needs and wishes of others. Close associates are likely to be in a sensitive mood. It will be easier to hurt their feelings with a sharp word or ill-considered action. Quarrels are in the cards if you push people too far. It will be up to you to preserve the peace. Avoid controversial topics.

10. MONDAY. Useful. This will be a good day for drawing on your wells of imagination and invention. It is in artistic and intellectual fields that you can make the most progress now. You will gain much satisfaction from experimenting with new approaches. Monetary rewards can spring from originalilty. Don't be content with using traditional methods and ideas if there is room for innovation. The more flair and gusto you can bring to creative activities the better. Don't hold back. Go for it and go all-out. Express yourself to the full. The unsettled trend in business affairs continues. Don't give associates the cold shoulder. There is not much chance of earning profits in property dealings.

11. TUESDAY. Mixed. This is not a day for expecting financial gains in risky ventures. Gambles are not worth the risk. Play it safe. Avoid nonessential purchases and extravagance. Expenses must be moderated. Outings with loved ones can cost a great deal and still not give the required enjoyment. Romance may not come up to expectations no matter how much money is spent. Leisure pursuits can be a letdown. But conditions on the commercial scene should take a turn for the better. Scorpios can meet with more success in business dealings. Your resources can get a boost from collected debts. Original ideas and proposals are again likely to be the most profitable for you. Keep them coming.

12. WEDNESDAY. Tricky. People at work will not be at their most reliable or steady. This can cause delays, complications, and perhaps heavier work loads for Scorpio workers. Try to rely on your own strengths. It would be unwise to give up existing jobs on the basis of attractive new offers. First, you should have fully satisfied yourself as to the reliability of new job descriptions. It will be easier to be taken in by reports that on further investigation do not fulfill their early promise. Do not commit yourself until you know what you are letting yourself in for. A visit to the doctor may be required to identify unfamiliar health symptoms. It is always better to take precautions than to wait for illness to develop.

13. THURSDAY. Challenging. There should be plenty of scope for Scorpio employees to exercise their ambitious urges. Your diligence and industry will allow you to cover much ground now. Employers will not fail to notice your efforts or to reward your achievements. Further, your ability to take command in situations that need a leader can win you promotion and pay raises. Demonstrate your ability to bring order into confused situations. Now is a good time for involvement in neighborhood and community activities. Such ventures stand to gain from social gatherings. It should be good for discussing lines of action in informal surroundings. Scorpio magnetism can turn events to their advantage.

14. FRIDAY. Important. During the morning Scorpio workers should again go all-out to win pay raises and promotions. Your efforts will not go unnoticed. Efforts once made are almost certain to be well rewarded. Opportunities can open up that convince you that this is the time to spread your wings. You are eager to move on up the ladder of success and responsibility. Don't opt for security and safety if new horizons become available. Take the bull by the horns. Your drive and energy will see you through. Such opportunities are unlikely to be repeated. Later on it will be advisable to play second fiddle to the needs and wishes of loved ones. Personal desires are best given up for the time being.

15. SATURDAY. Worrisome. It won't be easy to maintain harmony in relationships now. Loved ones may drive you to distraction with their demands and lack of consideration. At risk of causing heated arguments Scorpios may have to take a firm line with close associates. They appear to be excessively self-centered. But it could also be that partners are more easily touched to the quick by remarks or inconsiderate actions. Again, these can lead to quarrels. Don't further inflame marital relations by giving too much attention to outside interests. And if you feel that loved ones are neglecting their home responsibilities for other activities you must make it plain. Speaking out is fairer than holding a grudge.

16. SUNDAY. Mixed. Domestic disturbances are again likely to dominate the day. But it will be up to Scorpio people to minimize upsets and make efforts to restore peace. Don't rise to the bait of provocative words or actions. Do all you can to pacify angry or disgruntled mates. If you give in to angry impulses the situation is bound to get even more uncomfortable. Keep a tight rein on your own reactions. Patience is a key word for today. But the more favorable trend in business affairs continues. It will be easier to win the backing of prominent people. However, be careful not to mix with people whose reputation can cast a smear on your own, even if you work with them in business deals.

17. MONDAY. Sensitive. Scorpios can get worked up into an unnecessary frenzy over financial problems. Take it easy. The picture is unlikely to be as gloomy as it appears at first. Your own imagination can inflate problems to a size they do not warrant. Keep things in perspective. Don't invent difficulties. But money can become a bone of contention with partners or spouses. Heated arguments can result. You would do well to stick to your guns if you feel that loved ones should adopt less extravagant habits. But

Scorpio business people can pull off lucrative deals today. Your personality can play a big part in winning favorable terms. But don't overplay your part.

18. TUESDAY. Mixed.   Scorpio people are likely to meet with success for either of two reasons. If they are investing joint capital or if handling commercial operations funded by pooled resources, things will go well. But don't allow any good luck or economic gains to go to your head. This is no time for overconfidence. Once you let yourself get overexcited you can make hasty and unwise moves in money matters. Maintain a steady and measured approach. Business activities will continue their upward run. Goods and services are likely to be in greater demand. Markets may be increased. Advertising campaigns could pay dividends. Beneficial contacts can be arranged while you are enjoying yourself.

19. WEDNESDAY. Deceptive.   This is not the time to delegate any business relating to distant places to others. The personal presence of Scorpio people can mean the difference between success and failure. If distant situations can be handled by phone well and good. But it is quite likely that you will have to travel to the spot. Conditions are favorable for journeys. But any important decisions should be slept on before they are implemented. When considering issues of some consequence it will be easier for Scorpios to overlook crucial factors. Judgments should be reassessed tomorrow. Family members or neighbors may act from motives other than those that they give.

20. THURSDAY. Quiet.   You can enjor an easygoing day with few if any important developments. Events in distant places will take a turn for the better. But it would be better to allow them to develop at their own pace. Do not initiate any new moves for the time being. Conditions are not supportive enough for making fresh starts. Wait for past efforts to come to fruition. The absence of pressures and distractions makes this a good day for attending to study and other mental activities. Scorpios will have a good grasp of facts and figures and can pick up knowledge quite readily. It should be a favorable time for conferring with people who are experts in their chosen field.

21. FRIDAY. Unsettled.   Scorpios may again have anxieties over developments in distant places. Business or work interests can become complicated and unpredictable. People you rely on in faraway places are likely to let you down. Promises can be broken. The budget you have allowed for distant interests and activities can be far exceeded by necessity. Although chances for improvement exist it will be very difficult to take advantage of these. More frustration is likely on this account. But closer to home there will be opportunities in regular employment affairs that can be snapped up. Positions can be improved. Fellow workers will remember help you have given previously and will reciprocate.

22. SATURDAY. Fair. Those Scorpio people who have an eye on improving their reputations may see their names go up in lights. Fame and recognition can be won by those working in the public arena. Past efforts can come to fruition. It is a good time for building on existing firm foundations. New job opportunities can come your way. A new line of work or a new career may be offered to you. But it will be largely up to your own strenuous efforts when it comes to enhancing your standing in the eyes of others. Credit will be given where it is due. But you will have to be the initiator of any action designed to draw favorable attention. Luck is with you but don't be overbearing with others.

23. SUNDAY. Important. This looks as though it is a very happy day for Scorpios. A tour around Sunday markets and shops can reveal some excellent bargains. Shopping trips can be both productive and enjoyable. Useful business contacts can be made while you are out and about. New financial partnerships can be formed. It may be good for discussing business affairs in informal surroundings. This would be especially true in the comfort of your own home. Associates will enjoy Scorpio hospitality. Important deals can be clinched over food and wine. People you mix with today are likely to be in a cheery mood. Loved ones, too, will be happy and will give their support in any home entertaining.

24. MONDAY. Sensitive. It will be easier for Scorpio people to tread on others' toes. Your drive and determination can make you blind to the needs and rights of people around you. But associates are unlikely to put up with such treatment for long. You will only leave a trail of resentment which will soon turn to obstruction unless you show more consideration. Much time and energy will be consumed in bitter arguments unless you go about your business with more tact. But providing you can maintain peaceful conditions around you, you can cover much ground in intellectual pursuits. Study and research can be rewarding. Friends will make happy companions. Since you get along well, stay with them.

25. TUESDAY. Changeable. Friends can have good advice and assistance to give in the personal sphere of your life. But you would be unwise to give much credence to their money-making ideas. Their financial projects are likely to entail more losses than gains. In fact, it is more than likely that they will be coming to you for financial advice or loans to tide them over. Some prominent people can be somewhat cold and formal. But there is a good chance that they will give any help they can. However, you must keep your wits about you while in their presence. You will meet with success in club and group affairs providing you proceed at a measured and steady pace.

26. WEDNESDAY. Uneventful.   This day will jog along at an easier pace. There are unlikely to be any new pressures or problems to deal with. Time is best spent in gently pushing ahead with anything that was started yesterday. It is the projects that are already partly established that can be constructively attended to. But there will not be sufficient energy to give new ideas a strong send-off. Wait until conditions are more supportive for initiating fresh starts. Friends will be in a cooperative mood. They can be called on for help if required. You should find time for recreational pursuits through clubs and groups. Meetings can involve a lot of talk and little action; avoid them when you can.

27. THURSDAY. Important.   Personal resources can get a boost as the result of some background maneuvers. Keep in the shadows. Don't draw unnecessary attention to plans and intentions. Avoid obvious approaches and methods. The day is good for making confidential agreements with older people, perhaps parents. Such pacts will have an important bearing on the future. New savings funds can be started that have children's education or future security in mind. Love affairs should be happy and fulfilling. Accept any invitations to social gatherings. It is more than likely that you will meet new romantic partners, if this is your desire. It should be good for planning marriages.

28. FRIDAY. Sensitive.   People can be unreliable and go back on their word. At first, such changes may seem to ruin your plans. But it is quite likely that you will be better off in the long run. Happy endings can come from bad beginnings. People you have helped in the past will remember your generosity. They may well come forward with help now. Money you are owed can be unexpectedly repaid. It won't be easy to see eye-to-eye with friends now. Your different points of view can lead to heated arguments. Pushy associates can think they know better than you how your life should be run. Scorpios may have to put interfering people firmly in their place. With a little tact, you can do so kindly.

29. SATURDAY. Manageable. This is not the best time to engage in head-on confrontations. Be prepared to step aside and let others have their say. If Scorpios dig their heels in, violent disturbances are likely. It will be necessary to adopt a more conciliatory approach if you are in need of cooperation. People won't take kindly to attempts to bludgeon them into thinking or acting along lines that you propose. But more subtle methods can win people over. Family members can supply welcome information or contacts. There is a good chance now for sharing activities with friends who can make cheerful companions. It is likely that your friends can put you in touch with prominent people.

30. SUNDAY. Positive. You will enjoy getting on the move as early as possible with friends. Don't waste valuable time. Trips to beauty spots and places of interest will be stimulating and refreshing. Avoid the crowds by making an early start. Get out of the rut. Today is good for taking in new experiences and breaking old patterns. Organized recreational activities can be enjoyed through clubs and societies. Others will recognize the authority and leadership abilities that Scorpio people have at their disposal. You may be asked to take command of situations or bring some order out of chaos. It could be good for reaching agreements with family members and neighbors through friendly discussions.

31. MONDAY. Sensitive. It may take a degree of skill to maintain harmony in friendships now. It will be easier to rub your friends the wrong way. They can be particularly touchy on the subject of money. They need to be handled with great gentleness if upheavals are to be avoided. Avoid being overadamant in your own views and desires. Give others more room for maneuvers. You will have to find a tactful way of refusing any offers to become involved in money-making schemes initiated by friends. These can have disastrous results. Both friendships and finances can be put in jeopardy. But people who are well placed to help you can further your personal plans.

SEPTEMBER

1. TUESDAY. Disturbing. Your finances are unlikely to get the boosts you have been hoping for. Expectations of pay raises can be disappointed. Promises of debt repayments will probably be broken. You may even start feeling a little desperate where money matters are concerned. But it would be unwise to listen to the financial advice of friends or people only recently met. You would do better to rely on your own judgment. But give yourself time to mull over the possibilities. Don't make hasty moves or decisions under stress. Be especially careful if you are driving in your own neighborhood. The behavior of people close to you can be highly unpredictable, and a change of plan might be necessary.

2. WEDNESDAY. Variable. Recent disappointments and setbacks at work can be put to rights now. Scorpios should be given opportunities to prove their worth. As a consequence you can win pay raises and promotion. Use your own initiative. Extra efforts and enterprise will be well rewarded. Difficult situations or people may have to be dealt with at work. But if you can keep your cool and handle them effectively you can do a lot for your own personal cause. The favorable notice of employers can be won. Luck will be with you so the chances of your making good are high. But don't allow the sweet smell of success to make you overly imaginative and too optimistic. Keep your feet on the ground, and take your head out of the clouds.

3. THURSDAY. Good. You can make a truly favorable impression on business associates. Try taking them out on the town or wining and dining them at home. Today will be good for discussing business under informal circumstances. Favorable agreements that bring about an increase in profits can be reached. Love affairs can benefit from short journeys. A visit can help to overcome a lovers' tiff. This is a good time for marriage proposals. Friends can act as go-betweens to arrange important issues. Heartfelt desires can come closer to realization through the intervention of a pal. Not much will stand in the way of the determined Scorpio. Personal targets can be reached.

4. FRIDAY. Disconcerting. This can be an unsettled time for close relationships. Long partnerships can come to sudden ends. Or loved ones may have to travel away on business or other affairs. Well-established patterns can be disrupted. Your health can be more vulnerable to infection or strain. Plans may have to be

dropped or rearranged as a result. Workmates can be uncooperative and argumentative. This can make it difficult to get through
work loads and schedules on time. Scorpios may have to take on
more than their fair share of labor. But at the same time you must
remember the condition of your health. You must not push yourself too far.

5. SATURDAY. Rewarding.   Useful economic agreements can
be made today. Scorpios can gain a strong position in financial negotiations. You are likely to see the ending of old patterns and the
beginning of new ones. Scorpios can start out on a new course of
life from today. Don't cling to the old in preference to the unfamiliar. Take up the challenge of exploring new ways and directions.
Conditions favor discussions with family members. Talk over future financial prospects and ways of safeguarding income and security. The buying and selling of property and land and its products
can be profitable. The market price of homes can be improved
through redecoration and modernization.

6. SUNDAY. Enjoyable.   Any plans or moves made yesterday
to get homes and property into better shape should be continued
today. Home improvements can give you a psychological lift as
well as making good economic sense. Money spent on decorating
or on building extensions will be reflected favorably in potential
selling prices. Family members are unlikely to raise any objections
to your domestic plans. In fact, you should get all the cooperation
and encouragement you require. But don't devote the whole day
to work and effort. Take some time out to enjoy yourself. Outings
or entertainment in the evening can round off an industrious day
most pleasantly. It should be good for creative energies.

7. MONDAY. Difficult.   It will be more difficult to win important people over to your point of view. This can make it harder to
raise backing for programs or go-aheads for projects. Financial
risks and gambles should be left completely out of the picture.
Attractive-looking speculation is more likely to end in heavy
losses. If you indulge any extravagant urges you will probably be
left with nagging feelings that you have been irresponsible. Restrict spending to essentials. Unnecessary outlays will catch up
with you in embarrassing ways in the near future. Friends can
make argumentative companions. Love affairs can end in tears
and disappointment.

8. TUESDAY. Disquieting.   If you have business or financial
links with friends these can prove to be a hot bed of disagree-

ments. It is unlikely that you will see eye-to-eye with close associates over the best way to proceed with commercial operations. This can hold up developments. Then important opportunities may be lost. The less money that passes through your hands now the better. Any dealings that carry a high risk of loss should be avoided like the plague. You may be inspired to push ahead with projects that require imaginative flair. Such work can involve heavy monetary outlays. People you work with may be concealing something from you to their own advantage.

9. WEDNESDAY. Satisfactory. It will be to your advantage to set yourself definite goals in employment affairs. Then do everything in your power to work toward them. This can involve stepping back to see just what is attainable. Next, determine what is the best way to go about attaining it. But hasty changes of jobs are not advisable. Employment moves need careful consideration. Even though present positions are proving unsatisfactory, it would be easy to jump out of the frying pan and into the fire. There are likely to be opportunities for making current jobs more remunerative and the work more varied. You may need to avail yourself of the fruits of the long lives and experience of others.

10. THURSDAY. Sensitive. Scorpio people must keep strictly to the straight and narrow. There may be a temptation to get involved in activities that are less than honest, but doing this would be folly. Keep out of the shadows. Make sure you have nothing to hide. You may, on the other hand, be blinkered by high ideals. These could prevent you from seeing the plain facts. Take your head out of the clouds. Keep things in sensible perspective. You can make situations and people appear worse than they are. It will be easier to delude yourself or for others to pull the wool over your eyes. But you can make strong positions at work even more secure by winning a better-paid job.

11. FRIDAY. Mixed. The day could work out to your advantage. But you must be prepared to give up some personal plans and desires. Lend what support you can to loved ones. Put your own wants second to the needs and wishes of partners and spouses. The pay off, in terms of greater affection and understanding between partners, can be enormous. Domestic relations can be put on much firmer foundations, as a result. But there are those whose marital problems cannot be cleared up by giving more help and consideration. An outing in the company of mutual friends can do wonders for patching up rifts and reducing tension. Friends can go out of their way to give assistance.

12. SATURDAY. Good. This will be an especially favorable day for home entertaining. It could be equally good for attending parties and social gatherings elsewhere. Accept any invitations you receive to festive occasions, especially if friends are to be host and hostess. Romance is in the air now and it is likely that new romantic partners will be found through social activities. And it is unlikely to be merely a passing flirtation that you get involved in if you do take a fancy to someone. New attractions are likely to develop into serious relationships and happy marriages. You can come closer to realizing secret desires. You can end the day in a more acceptable position and you will be happier.

13. SUNDAY. Favorable. You are experiencing a favorable time for putting savings or mutual funds to work. Don't allow resources to remain dormant. They could be earning increased interest or be used to finance profitable commercial operations. Family members can be energetically helpful and encouraging. They can prove reliable helpers if assistance is needed. It would be advisable to keep your affairs and intentions to yourself now. Secrecy can mean the difference between success and failure. It will be good for undercover operations and for confidential meetings. Some unobtrusive digging around can help you to get to the bottom of things. A visit to a sick person will brighten the day for both.

14. MONDAY. Disturbing. In constrast to yesterday conditions do not favor pooling resources with others. Making new investments or backing new business prospects is not advisable. Neither should personal funds be used to finance commercial operations. Others may try to persuade you to share in new business ventures. But their advice, particularly if they are friends, should not be heeded. Trust to your own judgment rather than that of your pals. You will be protecting your own interests by restricting spending and buying to essentials. Expensive items bought on the spur of the moment can prove to be faulty. They may even have to be returned to the place of purchase.

15. TUESDAY. Sensitive. Scorpio people will now be much happier in giving their time and energy to employment and business activities. Searching for enjoyment and sensation will simply not appeal to them. You will gain more satisfaction from knowing that you are keeping the dollars rolling in, however dull some jobs may seem. Keep your nose to the grindstone. Time spent with friends can be unsettled. You are unlikely to see eye-to-eye with them now and heated words are more than likely. Someone may be envious of your position or of a relationship that is dear to you.

Be sure you do nothing that will give scandalmongers something to get their teeth into. Events in distant places can become worse.

16. WEDNESDAY. Tricky. Keep close tabs on any business interests you have in foreign parts. There may be developments that need a speedy response. Long-distance phone calls and letters can provide valuable facts and figures relating to business finances. But this is not a day for being overadventurous with money. You should do all you can to husband your resources. The money-making schemes of friends or people only recently met should be avoided. Such proposals can take more than they make. It is advisable to keep all your dealings open and aboveboard. Confidential arrangements can lead to unforeseen complications. Other parties can take unfair advantage of secret affairs.

17. THURSDAY. Fair. You may be finding your regular job or routine business affairs dull and dreary at the moment. But it would be unwise to make any hasty moves. Do not hand in your resignation or seek another position without careful planning. Place the emphasis on the positive aspects of your present situation. Stick to your guns. There will be opportunities for improving your lot in the near future. Don't throw away all the past efforts and hard work you have put in because you feel a need for more excitement. Long journeys can lead to meetings with people who become lifelong friends. Overseas business interests should hit a high note now. This is a good time for the book trade.

18. FRIDAY. Difficult. Scorpio business people may have to put up with a lot of flak. They should be prepared for skirmishes with associates. Your plans are likely to meet with much opposition. In all probability, you won't get your way by taking a stand. The best policy would be to listen carefully to the objections of others. Then try to incorporate their ideas into your own. Success can come by taking the middle road. If you stay out on a limb you can become more and more isolated. Join forces with others when possible. Adopt a soft line with the people you work with. An overly forceful or rigid attitude will only multiply your difficulties.

19. SATURDAY. Rewarding. Stick to your present course in business affairs with all the drive you can muster. Don't be deflected by difficulties and obstructions. Current efforts will be rewarded by greatly increased profits. Your resources can get an immediate and unexpected boost. It will be the surprise repayment of money you are owed. You may have cause to be deeply thankful for foundations you have laid in the past and for previous thoroughness. Great advantages can be won as a result. Scorpio people are likely to receive presents. It should be good for throwing parties on the spur of the moment. If you find yourself in a tight corner financially older people can offer help. They may be relatives or old family friends.

20. SUNDAY. Harmonious. You may have been looking forward to a day of rest. But some unexpected favorable business opportunities may be offered during the morning. It would be a shame to miss out on them. Scorpios will be in an efficient and energetic mood early on. Your business activities will be accompanied by a good-luck factor. Not only can financial gains be won but reputations can be favorably added to. During the afternoon and evening, friends will make happy companions. It will be a good time for sharing activities with them. Family visits are in the cards. Relatives will enjoy trips to places of beauty or interest. Scorpios will have no shortage of original ideas.

21. MONDAY. Discouraging. Business finances can go into reverse for the time being. There will be more difficulty to maintain any recent advantages you have won or to push ahead any further. Misjudgments and mistakes will be more easily made. It would be wisest to slow all dealings down at least for the immediate future. Don't get tangled up in the financial plans of friends. They will prove to be argumentative and unreliable business partners. Older people may be beset with problems and call on you for assistance and moral support. This can be irritating but unavoidable. Scorpio shoppers can run into difficulties but providing they keep their wits about them bargains can be found. Take your time.

22. TUESDAY. Variable. Friends and money will again make a bad mix. The financial opinions of your friends are best ignored. Their advice is likely to lead you widely astray. Stick to your own judgments or else the advice of people who are really in the know. People are likely to be more unreliable than usual. This can disrupt your schedules and cause you extra expense. Moves made in haste and without due consideration can bring more trouble down on your head than you might anticipate. Impulsive decisions will not produce desired results. But today is good for undercover operations. Secret moves can lead to advantages. Scorpio thinking will be lively and creative.

23. WEDNESDAY. Deceptive. It is possible that sweethearts or spouses are concealing something from you. Emotional partners can lead Scorpios a merry dance now. It would be better for you to repress strong feelings for another, rather than letting them gush forth. Ideally, you should try to maintain a poised and detached air. Others may be playing with your sentiments. Hang on to your secrets. Confidential facts can become common knowledge if they are revealed to the wrong person. And it will be more difficult to know just who you can trust. The high hopes of other people can be bitterly disappointed. Your sleep may be disturbed by nightmares and strange images. Avoid erratic people.

24. THURSDAY. Good. It is background people who can give you the best financial help and advice now. Money matters are best handled in confidence. Don't draw undue attention to your financial operations or intentions. Competitors will attempt to steal a march on you once they know what you are up to. Play your cards close to our chest. Secret discussions can lead to favorable agreements. Scorpios can win the advantage in any transactions that take place behind closed doors. You are more likely to win the cooperation of others through back-room conversations than through official channels. Scorpios may have a strong urge to help those who are deprived or down on their luck.

25. FRIDAY. Manageable. Scorpio people can be their own worst enemies today. It is only your rigid attitudes that will prevent you from achieving your aims. Loosen up. Your arrangements are more likely to work out if you swim with the tide. Overly forceful measures will be counterproductive. Adopt a gentle approach in all your dealings. Tact will be more effective than brash methods. You will gain absolutely nothing from power struggles. You will be placing more obstacles in your path by being obstinate. You can ill afford the bad will and resentment of others. But pleasant times can be spent in the company of family members. There will time to devote to intelllectual pursuits.

26. SATURDAY. Disquieting. It can be more difficult to make sound appraisals of people and situations. The grounds on which you base decisions can be faulty. Your grasp of events and future trends can be unreliable. Scorpios are likely to put their trust in people who do not merit it. You can be let down by people you rely on. Even those you know well and who are usually reliable may be prevented from keeping their side of bargains or arrangements. Factors that are outside their control could be the cause of this unusual lapse. The personal lives of associates can interfere with their outside commitments. Keep your intake of food and drink to moderate proportions. Put off visits to hospitals.

27. SUNDAY. Mixed. Confidential contacts with influential people can be beneficial to your financial prospects. Useful economic agreements can be drawn up in secret. But in spite of any strengthening of your financial position you should still adopt a cautious and conservative approach to spending. The emphasis should be on building up resources not depleting them. Avoid extravagant tastes and purchases. Don't leave money or valuables in places where they can be easily stolen. If thieves are given the opportunity to steal they will quite naturally do so. Wallets and purses must be safeguarded as a matter of course. Time spent with friends can be unsettled and expensive.

28. MONDAY. Changeable. It is those people holding background positions and demanding little attention or recognition who can bring advantages to Scorpios. Older people, in particular, can steer some good luck your way. Sweethearts and spouses will be in a warm and loving mood. Loved ones will be happy to join in with your plans. Outings with those you are fond of can give great pleasure. But don't be too ready to reveal your plans to others. Keep as much to yourself as possible. People may attempt to stand in the way of your desires once they know your intentions. A number of heavy bills are likely to come in all at once in the near future, so keep your cash reserves in safe accounts. Check out minimum balances and interest rates, and get the best available.

29. TUESDAY. Variable. Be prepared to listen to the points of view of friends and recently met people. Friction will develop if you are too full of your own opinions. Don't try to foist them off on others. New friendships can be quickly terminated if you are too heavy-handed. Even well-established friendships can be threatened by arguments stemming from your overbearing manner. Be more tolerant and flexible. Luck will be on your side in attempts to win more interesting work or a better paid position. Love affairs will be in tip-top form. Secret romances can give especial pleasure. You may have to turn to an older person if you are in a financial fix.

30. WEDNESDAY. Important. You can pick up valuable informaton today. This should be of help to you in planning your personal future. More immediate personal affairs can benefit from what you learn now. The day is good for all study and self-improvement attempts. The minds of Scorpio people will be agile and will find it easy to absorb knowledge. Learning will not only be enjoyable but can have profitable future consequences. It will be easier to get on the same wavelength as associates so that favorable terms can be agreed upon. Transactions can be terminated on a highly satisfactory basis. Local journeys with family members or neighbors can be productive.

OCTOBER

1. THURSDAY. Variable. This should be a good time for getting written agreements and contracts from others. Attempts to get go-aheads or planning permission from influential people or bodies can meet with success. Scorpio people can take a vigorous part in negotiations and discussions. Don't wait for others to make the moves in business activities. It will be far more advantageous to take the initiative yourself. Don't take a backseat. Put your point of view forward in no uncertain terms. But the health of Scorpio people will be more vulnerable. You cannot afford to push yourself to the limit. Take it easy. But it can be essential to tackle dull and dreary tasks.

2. FRIDAY. Satisfactory. You should get from well-placed people the help you need to tie up the loose ends of long-drawn-out projects. Then you can get new ventures on the road. Today can see the ending of one phase of activity and the beginning of a new. But do not turn your back on past experiences before you have wrung them dry of all useful lessons. You should be able to avoid future pitfalls by examining past mistakes. Capitalize on past successes. Make the most of previous ups and downs. Conditions are likely to become increasingly advantageous for property dealing as the day goes on. But Scorpios can be in a rather serious and concentrated mood that others can find hard to take. Try to unwind somewhat and communicate with others.

3. SATURDAY. Good. The early part of the day is good for making secret arrangements to meet loved ones. It will be easier to set up romantic liaisons that you want nobody else to know about. But it seems that for certain Scorpios the time has come to break off existing attachments. Again the morning is the best time to let those concerned know that it is all off. It will be worth getting into top gear for those Scorpios who have to work today. The more work you get done, the higher can be the rewards. If you can beat deadlines by taking work home and completing it over the weekend, well and good. Your efforts will not go unnoticed. The agility of your mind today will make all mental activities quicker.

4. SUNDAY. Challenging. Scorpios have a happy day to look forward to. Leisure and pleasure pursuits can give you all the relaxation and enjoyment you are seeking. Time given to hobbies and favorite pastimes will be most rewarding. Creative energies will be high and should be challenged into imaginative activities. Scorpio sports people will be in good form and can gain both satisfaction and success in their sporting endeavors. In fact, you can be favorably surprised by your own performance. Scorpios who are looking for romantic partners can be presented with opportunities for meeting such people. But once the opportunity becomes available it will be up to you to make the approach.

5. MONDAY. Sensitive. There can be unexpected bills to meet now. The affairs and needs of children can cost more than you had anticipated. Outings and entertainments can become very unexpectedly expensive. You may also have to spend more then you can afford to keep loved ones happy. Contacts helpful to financial plans can be made through social situations. Scorpios can use their charm to win over influential people. Let others know if you are impressed with their achievements. They will be more willing to help you in consequence. Friends can spoil romantic occasions by getting more interested in your sweetheart than you like. Keep personal arrangements to yourself. Then if things do not work out well, you won't have to explain.

6. TUESDAY. Deceptive. Scorpio workers may have to shoulder extra work loads due to the absence of colleagues. And this is not the best day for you to have to cope with additional responsibilities. You could find yourself in a rather dreamy state. You will probably prefer to sit staring into space rather than knuckling down to hard work. But it is important that you snap out of it and apply yourself diligently. Employers will not take kindly to your wasting time and idle chatter. They will want to see you earning your money. Don't rely too much on the help and support of people in prominent positions. It may be impossible to make contact with them when they are most needed.

7. WEDNESDAY. Productive. Recent or current efforts at work can win unexpected rewards and notice. This can give your self-confidence and self-esteem a great boost. Scorpios should make every effort to fulfill the trust employers put in them by giving them extra responsibilities. Your newfound assurance will help you to adapt to new situations. Try to live up fully to the expectations others have of you. These developments should put you on top of the world. You are likely to be in a cheerful and efficient mood. There won't be many situations that you find difficult to handle. But underneath your gaiety there may be a slight feeling of sadness that is difficult to pinpoint.

8. THURSDAY. Mixed. Imaginative and original projects are likely to receive both encouragement and practical help from loved ones or the people you work with. Business and emotional partners will be in a most cooperative mood. They can make all the difference to the success or failure of your projects. They can have excellent suggestions and insights to offer if you are planning advertising campaigns or publicity stunts. They will have a keen sense of just what is likely to draw the greatest attention. There will be stronger bonds of affection and support between Scorpios and their sweethearts or spouses. But Scorpios may have to keep their forceful natures in check. You have a tendency to be overbearing and to expect to get your way.

9. FRIDAY. Disquieting. You will again get far more done and to greater advantage by working along with others. Go all-out to recruit the cooperation of others. Lend a hand where you can. Solo attempts will provide disappointing results. There is no point in trying to strike out on your own. Put purely personal goals aside for the time being. But it may be difficult to ascertain where you stand with certain people. And others will more easily misinterpret what you are saying or what your intentions are. You can bypass a lot of trouble by speaking and communicating more distinctly. Making your position absolutely clear would also help to clear the air of any misinterpretations.

10. SATURDAY. Successful. Legal disputes are best handled through unofficial channels. Settle disagreements out of court whenever possible. Everyone concerned stands to gain by amicable arrangements. It should be possible to avoid heavy lawyer's bills by direct contact with other parties. If others have asked you to take care of their finances or to handle their investments, don't draw undue attention to the fact. Proceed with such affairs as unobtrusively as possible. It is by working in the background that you can gain the greatest advantage for the interests of others. It may be best to invite influential people out for dinner if you have important business to discuss with them. Support will be more readily forthcoming under informal circumstances.

11. SUNDAY. Satisfactory. Avoid touchy issues when speaking to loved ones. They will quickly take the bait if you bring up contentious subjects. Minor money matters can assume gigantic proportions if you attempt to thrash them out now. Such topics are best avoided as nothing whatever will be settled. But this is not to say that Scorpios should avoid going over family accounts in private. Get a good, solid picture of your resources. Then you can discuss the situation with loved ones at a more harmonious opportunity. You will be well equipped to deal with any mental activities later on. Important people will be happy to see the results of any research you undertake.

12. MONDAY. Mixed. The mail can bring news that causes some anxiety. Events in distant places may not be going to plan. Tax problems are likely to occur. You may get notification of higher tax bites than you had anticipated. It would be well to review insurance policies to ensure that they still cover all your needs and possessions. But don't make hasty changes in this department. Get professional advice if necessary. Neither should you introduce new banking arrangements in a hurry. It could be that a pay raise is in the pipeline for your spouse so that family resources would get a welcome boost. Your own job prospects can seem more optimistic. These should come first and foremost on your agenda.

13. TUESDAY. Manageable. It would be unwise to put your trust in people in faraway places. Nor should you trust those who come in from overseas. Such folk are unlikely to stick to their word or stick to arrangements. They will be more easily distracted by personal affairs. It would be safer to deliver messages and packages by hand, wherever possible. Some people may impart wrong information so that packages can go astray in the mail or be incorrectly delivered. Don't hold to a narrow point of view now. Step back and take the widest perspective possible. You should be well placed to ascertain possible future trends. Don't lose sight of long-term objectives because of immediate minor problems.

14. WEDNESDAY. Disturbing. Writers and advertisers may have problems to contend with today. The people who make decisions in the publishing field will have their own and not your interests at heart. Hopes can be dashed as a result. The plans of Scorpios can meet resistance from employers. But even though you are forced to set new objectives for yourself and new ways of achieving them, the opposition you have met may come from selfish motives. Superiors may be purposely leading you up the garden path. Despite that, exciting plans and possibilities for the future are filling your mind. However, you must not allow them to make you neglect current responsibilities.

15. THURSDAY. Productive. You would do much better to drive straight to the heart of the matter than dither about on the fringes. The time has come to make clear decisions and to act on them. You cannot afford to put things off any longer. It will be up to you to supply the initiative and drive to get employment matters or business affairs on the move. Don't wait for others to wave the magic wand. Working conditions are likely to get more and more dreary if you leave it to circumstances to bring about change. You will have to make some extra effort to alter the trend. You may meet old faces and friends from the past who can do you a good turn. Scorpios are attractive to the opposite sex.

16. FRIDAY. Mixed. It will be easier for Scorpio people to make blunders today that could lose them the respect of business associates. You will need to employ all the subtlety and tact you can muster to avoid making mistakes. You may be saying all the wrong things, and generally putting others off. It would be a mistake to attempt to impose strongly held opinions on others. People will only see such crusades as intrusions. Keep your ideas to yourself, at least until someone shows a genuine interest in hearing what you have to say. Commercial operations that have taken an age to establish themselves can at last begin to show signs of returns on invested time and capital.

17. SATURDAY. Lucky. Today should be good for meeting prominent people under informal circumstances. Influential friends can be made during social events. Such acquaintances can stand you in very good stead in your business and employment affairs. The backing of newly formed friends can help swing decisions and events your way. Financial assistance may be forthcoming through them. Self-employed Scorpio workers or business people will have excellent opportunities for increasing their earnings and profits. And those Scorpios who are employed by others can also be offered many chances for increasing their income. But people you see only now and again can be difficult to track down.

18. SUNDAY. Enjoyable. Scorpios will enjoy making the social rounds today. You will be in your element among large numbers of people or family and social gatherings. Friends can make lively companions. Activities shared with them can become adventures. And some Scorpios may be looking for romantic partners. The introductions friends may arrange could put them in touch with compatible new people. Serious love affairs can be the result. In fact, for Scorpios who do not want to commit themselves at this stage, new attractions may have too many strings attached. Partners can have greater expectations of romance than you. You may have to reveal that you are only interested in a casual affair.

19. MONDAY. Disappointing. Bad news can come by phone or letter. This will be akin to letting the fox into the chicken coop where business finances are concerned. Disappointments and reverses are likely in commercial operations. But Scorpio business people must keep their heads. The situation can only worsen if you act impulsively or give way to panic. But you may be able to contain the problem if you keep cool and act sensibly. You may come close to realizing heartfelt desires. Failure could occur through not having sufficient funds available. High hopes can be thwarted at the last moment. Friends and acquaintances may request loans.

20. TUESDAY. Deceptive. Scorpios may feel they are going around in circles today. Things are unlikely to go according to plan. People and situations can turn out to be very different from your first impression of them. You can be led up blind alleys and down dead ends. Undercover operations can backfire. Secret dealings are best avoided. Others may take unfair advantage of the hidden nature of such activities. Transactions should be conducted in the full light of day. People can arrive at very wrong conclusions where your generosity or willingness to help is concerned. Wrong motives can be attributed to you. Feelings can become very volatile later on. You will have to try to keep the lid on tempers.

21. WEDNESDAY. Good. Today will be favorable for attending to details and tying up loose ends. It is by clearing the decks of minor matters that you can pave the way to bigger things. This should be a good time for balancing the books. You should make every attempt to collect monies you are owed. It is a day for keeping your prejudices in the right perspective. You can lose valuable opportunities because of bigoted attitudes. The point is that useful offers or propositions can come from strange sources. If you can keep an open mind you may be on to a winner. Suggestions from such quarters can have very profitable consequences. A tour of shops and stores could reveal useful items at reasonable prices.

22. THURSDAY. Important. Although there won't be much happening today the time can be used to great advantage. Don't be lulled into laziness or inactivity by the unusually slow conditions. The absence of pressures and demands make this a perfect day for getting your affairs in order. Clear away any backlogs of letters, paperwork, and accounting. Make preparations to swing into action when the momentum gets going again. This will be a good opportunity for streamlining procedures and introducing new methods. All overdue projects should be rounded off now. It would be a good idea to look back over recent weeks and months to see where you could have made more progress.

23. FRIDAY. Challenging. Scorpio people won't have much trouble in pushing ahead with their personal plans and goals today. In fact, by pulling out all the stops you can accomplish more than you thought possible. An inventive streak should prevail in your thinking. You will have both the inspiration and the enthusiasm to launch new ventures. And just as important, you will have the determination to see them through to a fruitful conclusion. Get your brainwaves into action. Don't opt for the old and familiar ways where there is room for expansion and invention. But Scorpios can easily ruin their chances by using unnecessarily harsh words. Needless to say, other people are put off by such criticism.

24. SATURDAY. Rewarding. Today offers a favorable and unexpected turn of events in employment matters. This can bring advantages and financial gain to Scorpio workers. Keep on your toes so that you can make the most of any opportunities that come your way. The satisfaction afforded by regular work can make this an enjoyable day. Contrary to expectations, routine employment activities are unlikely to be dull and dreary. But other people will more than likely fall in with the wishes and wants of Scorpio people. So there is a good chance that you will want to sit back and take it easy. You would be better advised to remain alert and active. Health should be in tip-top form. Keep it that way.

25. SUNDAY. Exciting. Scorpios can be particularly adroit in handling background maneuvers and manipulating events from behind the scenes. Keep in the shadows now. Don't draw undue attention to your activities. Cultivate contact with those of your acquaintances who have inside information. Such sources can provide valuable knowledge. If this is acted upon, it will give extra impetus to your money-making schemes. Scorpios can fulfill their humanitarian urges by collecting money for worthy causes. But with mental energies in a particularly sharp state, some Scorpios may feel like retiring into seclusion. They may want to pursue intellectual and other interests that require full concentration.

26. MONDAY. Manageable. Financial conditions are likely to be in a state of flux. There can be rapid ups and downs and shifts of position. With so much change it will be difficult to make certain judgments and assessments. It would be wiser to wait for more stable times before committing large sums of money or making important financial decisions. But consider the other side of the coin of change. It also means that it will be much easier to introduce new methods and procedures into working practices. Seek ways to minimize drudgery and monotony. Workers will be quick to adapt to new approaches. And if Scorpio employers want to introduce new pay arrangements, this would be the time to do it.

27. TUESDAY. Misleading. The day should be good for making contacts by phone, letter, or short trips. Communications can be an avenue to success. But all news and information must be passed on with care. People will quite easily misinterpret the information and get it all wrong. Ensure that you do not leave room for such misunderstanding. Messages of extreme importance should be double-checked. Take pains to express yourself clearly. But others may also use garbled words or make unclear or misleading statements. It should be unwise to act on what they try to tell you. At least withhold action until you are sure that they have got it right. Scorpios should draw on their rich funds of imagination.

28. WEDNESDAY. Sensitive. Loved ones will be in a congenial and cooperative mood. It will be easier to discuss important topics with them or lay plans for the future. Journeys or visits to interesting places in their company will give great pleasure. But if you are separated from sweethearts by long distances, a love letter or phone call will bring you closer together. Scorpios will find it easier to express their thoughts and feelings in words. It may be difficult to keep your mind on regular employment activities. Don't hesitate to approach superiors if you have a favor to ask. They will be in a sympathetic mood, and will more than likely to grant your requests. But don't try to manipulate them.

29. THURSDAY. Mixed. Scorpios may have to face a difficult choice. It will be between catering to their own desires and preferences or attending to their home and family responsibilities. But you would be well advised to sacrifice personal wishes. Give family members the help and support they need. You may not even have domestic duties to handle. But the need to complete jobs or projects already in progress can prevent you from giving time to preferred activities. You have succeeded in obtaining planning permission or other official go-aheads on property matters. But even so, real estate transactions are unlikely to fulfill their early promise. Writers of fiction can win publishing success. But it won't be a snap. Competition will be fierce.

30. FRIDAY. Manageable. You may well have extra time in which to work. Even so, it can be to your financial advantage to get jobs finished at the earliest possible moment. It is by beating schedules that you are likely to win the favorable notice of employers. You should do your utmost to pay off old financial debts or any others. It could be that feelings of obligation to others are slowing you down without your fully realizing it. But with a clean slate you will probably feel much lighter and freer. If you are bothered by health symptoms this is a good time to seek the services of medical doctors or specialists. Problems can often be nipped in the bud through timely and expert advice.

31. SATURDAY. Fortunate. Scorpios can luxuriate in some easygoing conditions today. There will be plenty of time for rest and relaxation. Or you can do the things that most interest you. The day is especially good for recreational activities. These could include outings to places of interest or cinemas and theatres. Imagination will be lively, making artistic and inventive work more satisfying. There should be no shortage of original ideas. Deep-felt hopes and wishes of romantic Scorpios can come to realization today. Compatible partners can walk into your life. Love affairs can reach new peaks of fulfillment. You may receive the encouragement and financial backing of influential people for risky ventures.

NOVEMBER

1. SUNDAY. Disturbing. Once you start heavy spending for extravagances and entertainments expenses can begin to soar. You will have to keep a tight rein on nonessential spending or you will soon go into the red. Conditions do not favor speculation. Those gamblers who cannot resist trying their luck should restrict the sums they play with to very small amounts. Big bets will take you for a real ride. It will be a downward spiral if you take risks with large amounts of cash. No matter how attractive the odds are, your chances are almost nil. Scorpios may be full of lively and original ideas. These may, however, be impossible to put into operation for lack of financial backing.

2. MONDAY. Deceptive. There may be wolves in sheeps clothing about today. Workmates, in particular, can be wearing one face but showing a different and not very pleasant one behind your back. Secret resentments may have built up against you that people express in surreptitious ways. It would be best to take nothing for granted. Keep on your toes and you may anticipate any evil intentions before they take effect. You may not be doing yourself any favors by winning the support of influential people for your personal plans. You could be sticking your neck out further than you realize. There is a chance that you are overstretching your resources. Try to step back mentally and review your finances.

3. TUESDAY. Variable.   Your mainspring can get coiled up to the snapping point before you have realized it. Nervous tension can develop through contacts with difficult people and conditions. Keep tabs on your inner state. Take every opportunity you can to relax. Let off steam in ways that do not harm your reputation. Your health will be more vulnerable to infection. Avoid people with coughs and sneezes. Attempts to make money through get-rich-quick methods are doomed to failure. Your best bet to keep money flowing into the coffers is through regular employment activities. Play it safe for the time being. Take any overtime opportunities. Employers should make more contacts with employees.

4. WEDNESDAY. Mixed.   This is not the best day for seeking new jobs or positions. The morning hours, in particular, can be bad for interviews with prospective employers or existing superiors. You are unlikely to make a favorable impression at the moment. Nor will you feel at ease with the people you work with. It would be best to keep going by yourself as much as possible without making others feel that you are shunning them. But the evening can provide a pleasant contrast to a difficult working day. Time spent in the company of sweethearts or spouses should wash your cares away. This would be a good opportunity for giving special treats to loved ones. A gourmet dinner will be much appreciated.

5. THURSDAY. Disconcerting.   Scorpios can be rather heavy-handed with people who only want to help them or draw closer to them. Be more sensitive to those who have the best of intentions toward you. You can do with all the friendship and cooperation you can muster. Beware of making enemies of people who began by liking you. The trouble is that your own inner force and drive can blind you to the positive qualities in others. You frequently try to railroad people into accepting your ideas and ways of doing things. By doing so, you may be throwing away valuable partnership possibilities. Let others have their say. Sound out the opinions of loved ones in career affairs.

6. FRIDAY. Quiet. Be ready for a very slow and uneventful day. But at least there should be no new problems and pressures to contend with. Put business and employment activities aside as early as possible. By doing so, more time can be spent with sweethearts or spouses. This is a day for showing loved ones just how much you care. It's a good chance for making practical as well as more intimate gestures of affection. Help to lighten the load of loved ones if they have jobs or chores to attend to by giving them a hand. A little gift or treat will put a smile on their faces. The wordly wisdom of Scorpios may come to the aid of collegues or workmates who have personal problems.

7. SATURDAY. Successful. Scorpio people's delight in digging and delving can be used to good purpose now. Conditions are extremely favorable for background research and solving mysteries. Valuable information can come to light as the result of concerted investigation. Don't be taken in by surface appearances. Get down to the nitty-gritty. The most profitable work can be done away from the public eye. This is a good time for background operations. Unobtrusive people can provide aid and support. This is not a day for associating with any sort of flashy types. But if you broadcast your intentions too soon others will jump on the bandwagon or steal your thunder. The day is favorable for fund-raising.

8. SUNDAY. Manageable. Family or other mutual funds do need some protection. But it would be a mistake for Scorpios to overreact. Putting too tight a control on the spending of financial partners or other joint owners of resources would be a mistake. Keep your thinking in perspective. Avoid extreme actions. Where money is concerned you can make mountains out of molehills. Don't exaggerate problems. If you bear down too heavily on those with whom you share capital, they are likely to react themselves. One way would be by going out on a spending spree. But conditions continue to favor background study and research. The day is good for establishing family history and family trees.

9. MONDAY. Tricky. Conditions can be extremely tricky where academic affairs are concerned. You may find it difficult to make important decisions while you are treading such unsure ground. And to add to the complications, people are likely to give you wrong information. It would be best to bide your time before committing yourself one way or the other. It is probably of no avail to turn to tutors or other academic staff such as advisors. They are unlikely to provide the guidance you are seeking. Neither should you place too much trust in people in faraway places. Distant events could work out contrary to expectations. There may be some secret plotting between your spouse's relatives.

10. TUESDAY. Sensitive. The best approach when trying to win over influential people is to adopt a positive and far-reaching outlook. Demonstrate that you can look on the bright side and make the best of things. It will also stand you in good stead to show others just how wide your range of interests and abilities are. Keep an open mind on what people in prominent positions have to say. They can pass on insights and experience that you can use to great advantage in furthering your own professional interests. But employers should not rush into changes of working patterns or methods. Employees may resent new procedures being forced on them. Don't allow criticism to weaken your resolve.

11. WEDNESDAY. Difficult. There may be some infighting in family circles. Your spouse's relatives may have some bad feeling about you but be unable to express it directly. This can lead to suspicions and the buildup of tension. Scorpios can be deeply irritated by stories they receive secondhand about themselves. Some straight talking will be necessary to clear the air. The health of Scorpios may not be in tip-top condition. You could therefore experience some depression or exhaustion. Emotional problems can get you down more than usual. It is important not to exert your forceful nature over others. You will save yourself trouble by using more tact. You should concentrate on improving this.

12. THURSDAY. Changeable. Scorpios can again spoil their chances in business and employment spheres. They do it constantly by employing overly brash and forceful methods. A diplomatic, and even gentle approach should be adopted whenever possible. Treat associates with more consideration. Listen to the points of view of others. Don't ram your ideas down people's throats. It is important that you maintain a cool head when dealing with business associates or the public. Once your volatile feelings get in on the act things will go from bad to worse. This is definitely a day for keeping the more abrasive side of your nature out of sight. Contracts and cooperation can be won by showing others just how affable you can be.

13. FRIDAY. Mixed. Scorpios can begin to reap the benefits of past efforts and planning. Business projects whose foundations were laid some time ago can now start to show handsome returns on invested cash and time. Scorpios may feel like patting themselves on the back for their foresight and earlier preparations.

Learn all the lessons available from such long-term operations. This is a pattern that can be adapted to similar projects again. But you may be left to rely totally on your own capabilities. While influential people will be in a cheery mood they are unlikely to be either practical or reliable. Extra efforts at work may not lead to immediate rewards. But they will stand you in good stead when the next round of promotions comes.

14. SATURDAY. Enjoyable. Friends can get themselves into all sorts of trouble and tight corners now. It may be up to Scorpios to help their pals out of dire straits. They may need a shoulder to cry on, a financial loan, or practical help. Whatever is required, Scorpios are likely to have what it takes to lift friends up out of the dumps. Give what encouragement and support you can. The day is good for cultivating contacts among designers and artists. Creative people will make stimulating company and may have professional advice to offer. Conditions are also favorable for Scorpios to put any unusual and imaginative projects into practice. Parties and social gatherings will be fun.

15. SUNDAY. Demanding. Activities shared with friends and outings with loved ones can prove more expensive than anticipated. You must strive to keep spending within reasonable bounds. Unless you put some constraints on your expenses, they will get completely out of hand. Don't overspend on sweethearts in an attempt to keep them happy. You should rely on your innate charm and loving nature for that. But it may be more difficult for everyone to keep their cool today. Tempers can flare at the slightest provocation. Old emotional wounds can open and lead to bitter arguments. But Scorpios should try to keep out of such contests and give others all the understanding possible.

16. MONDAY. Mixed. Business finances are likely to suffer reverses today. But Scorpios should be well equipped to deal with such situations, as a result of their previous experiences with these matters. You should know just what to do to minimize the bad effects of financial crises. It is by keeping cool, calm, and collected that you will be able to pick up the loose ends. And then you can get the show on the road again. But it is important that you do not devote the whole day to business and public affairs. You must find time to cater to your own needs and desires. A little solitude can have a healing effect and will help you to concentrate on problems. You may not have had an opportunity to attend to these yet.

17. TUESDAY. Important. Conditions will not be sufficiently supportive to launch new ventures successfully. But you can have great success with reshaping events and situations that have blown apart recently. It is a good time for bringing people together to effect reconciliations. It should also be good for coordinating the various strands of business operations to make a more effective whole. Pull things together wherever possible and concentrate your efforts. It would be a mistake to be lulled by the fairly easy conditions into spending a lazy and unproductive day. You can make particularly useful advances in any work requiring brain power. You should use imagination and sound judgment.

18. WEDNESDAY. Strenuous. It is possible that long-lost acquaintances will reemerge. They can bring certain benefits for Scorpio people with them. Reunions can lead to financial gain. It will be necessary for Scorpios to knuckle under in employment affairs. They cannot afford to let their minds wander in endless daydreams. Keep your mind on the job and your nose to the grindstone. This is no time to fall back on past achievements or reputation. Employers will want to see a good day's work for the money they pay. And any additional bonuses will only come on the basis of extra efforts made now. But Scorpios can also find time to give expression to humanitarian urges.

19. THURSDAY. Productive. This can be an enjoyable day for Scorpios. You may have to bide your time at first to see which way the wind blows. But it appears that the cards will fall in your favor. There should be plenty of leads to follow up before the day ends. Make the most of opportunities when they come. But at the same time, you must be careful not to tread on other people's toes while going after your goals. However, people will be more willing to forgive any inconsiderate behavior or actions on your part which crowd them out. This is a day to cultivate imaginative flair and creative talent that is lying dormant. The more you exercise that talent the better you will become.

20. FRIDAY. Disquieting. Scorpios will have the clarity of mind and grasp of events and future trends to make effective personal plans. However, conditions will not be conducive to putting such arrangements into operation yet. Build firm foundations, but delay building operations. But you can already be looking forward to Christmas. Start making shopping and gift lists and doing the first of the festive buying. Loved ones can be in an awkward mood and may behave like spoiled children. Nothing you do will seem to please them. Although there may be plenty of obstacles in your path now consistent efforts will eventually help you through to financial gain. You never quit in the face of obstacles.

21. SATURDAY. Encouraging. Some attention should be given to personal finances. You should go over your accounts to see just where you stand. But anything on the debit side will probably be offset by favorable news or developments regarding business or employment affairs. There should be sure signs of increased profits or of pay raises. Financial prospects will be looking up. You can lighten the load if you have dreary work to attend to by keeping your targets in mind. Hold the end result in front of you like a carrot before the donkey. You may have managed to turn hobbies or sidelines into additional money earners. Some extra efforts in this quarter can produce even better results.

22. SUNDAY. Variable. It looks as though financial affairs are again going to take a downward turn. It may be difficult to ward off anxieties and morbid thoughts concerning your financial outlook. New monetary demands can come up which tip the balance out of your favor. But Scorpios are likely to paint a gloomier picture than is really necessary. You must strive to keep an optimistic attitude. Past efforts, coupled with future prospects in career and business matters, should give you much hope. It is just a question of pushing through your current difficulties to more positive times ahead. Your love life can enter a volatile though enjoyable period. Concentrate on it to free your mind of gloom.

23. MONDAY. Deceptive. Scorpios may find themselves in a rather dreamy, even out-of-this-world state. You may be moved by strange and deep feelings. You will certainly be more inclined to let the heart rule the head. Your mind may be full of religious thoughts. You may also feel a particularly strong love for others. It is by following hunches and intuitions that you can give the greatest service and help to people. This is not the time to allow commonsense to prevent you from giving others a helping hand. Let feelings dictate your relationships. There may also be an urge to cast an examining eye over the way you relate to others. You can make some surprising self-discoveries now.

24. TUESDAY. Mixed. Don't get stuck in the armchair or office today. Get on the move. Short trips can be productive and enjoyable. It will be good for doing the rounds of business contacts. But you should also make sure you have not fallen behind with your letter writing. Scorpios will have a good command of language today so that correspondence can be handled well. You will also come across well on the telephone. Use of the phone can save much time and will achieve desired results. But time given to recreational pursuits or personal plans will be to the detriment of business and career interests. This is a day for single-minded efforts. There can be happy changes in your love life.

25. WEDNESDAY. Sensitive. Home and family affairs will need to be handled with a delicate touch. But this will not come easily to Scorpio people. You are more likely to jump in with two left feet and make a mess of things. Don't go at domestic affairs with a sledgehammer. Keep the feelings and needs of others in mind. Cultivate a more subtle approach. If there are important changes to be made around the home, consult the people whose lives will be affected. Don't go ahead under your own steam. And any household jobs must be done thoroughly. There may be a tendency to rush through things. But if you do, it will be a case of more haste and less speed. Also, the jobs will not be well done.

26. THURSDAY. Changeable. It will be easier than ever to whittle away the time in idle chatter. You must get yourself by the scruff of the neck and apply yourself to the work at hand. You will only get hopelessly behind schedule if you chin-wag half the day. You must find your usual, more responsible and hard-working self. Don't let others distract you with their anecdotes. But once you get involved with your work you can cover ground at a surprising rate. You may find that you easily finish ahead of time. This will be especially true if there are financial rewards for speedy work to spur you on. Any problems or tensions at home should blow over so that a more harmonious atmosphere prevails.

27. FRIDAY. Good. It is likely that processes and projects you have initiated in the past can come to fruition now. Scorpios can reap the rewards of previous efforts and preparations. Conditions at home continue to be happy and balanced. This will be all the more true if financial problems can be ironed out quickly. Loved ones will be in a cooperative and affectionate mood. Both creative energies and mental concentration are available to you right now. It would therefore be advisable to devote time to artistic and imaginative enterprises. Or you may prefer to pursue literary interests. In fact, you could get completely absorbed in such activities. This means that you have very little time left over for other things. But if you enjoy doing whatever interests you most, let the rest go.

28. SATURDAY. Disconcerting. Those Scorpios who do not have to work today will certainly be relieved to have reached the end of the working week. You will probably feel a sense of freedom and adventure. You may want to spread your wings and visit unusual and interesting places. But you must not allow your lighthearted mood to affect your attitude toward money. It is essential to remain levelheaded and responsible where funds are concerned. Any foolish usage of money will be followed by regrets. Conditions do not favor speculation. If you cannot resist playing the horses you are advised to restrict your stakes to small amounts. Larger sums will probably be lost.

29. SUNDAY. Disappointing. Plans for recreation or outings that you have been looking forward to all week may have to be called off at the eleventh hour. If they are not scrapped altogether substantial changes may have to be made in your arrangements. Children will not be easy to handle now. They can be grumpy or inclined to throw tantrums if they do not get their own way. Parents may have to exercise a firm hand. But it is essential to remain patient with difficult youngsters. Matters will only be made worse by loss of temper. Don't get carried away when spending on pleasure and entertainments. Keep your expenses moderate. Loved ones may want to drag you away from favorite pastimes.

30. MONDAY. Uneventful. You should take full advantage of this easy going day to get all the rest and relaxation you can. Those who have to work will find it is not too difficult to take things at a much slower pace. In fact, you can achieve good results at work with the minimum amount of effort. But the emphasis should be on refueling your energy and getting into better shape for busier times ahead. It will be a good opportunity for giving more attention to sensible and nutritious diets. Take a long walk in the fresh air. Loosen up your body with some exercise or fitness training. With less on your mind you should be taking the broadest possible view of the future. Determine that you will try to improve your health and minimize stress factors.

DECEMBER

1. TUESDAY. Good. Unexpected developments in employment affairs can bring benefits to Scorpios. Deadlocks in discussions on pay and conditions can suddenly be overcome. You are likely to be very happy with the outcome of any negotiations that affect your income. You must drum up a positive approach to dull and dreary tasks that have to be completed. Jobs will get done more quickly if you can handle them with a light heart. But any moaning and groaning will make them seem worse than they actually are. It may be that you are bothered with health symptoms. If so, you might get more relief from unconventional forms of treatment such as herbalism and faith-healing.

2. WEDNESDAY. Fair. This should be a good day for teaming up with another person if you have study and research activities to complete. Solo efforts in mental pursuits will tend to drag. It will be easier to get ahead by teaming up with other people, especially if you are working on the same projects. In fact, you can get into such a good rhythm with working partners that you will know what they are thinking before they express it. An excellent and intuitive rapport will also exist between marital partners and lovers. This should rule out the development of any tensions or misunderstandings. But if others do put a foot wrong Scorpios are advised not to come down on them like a ton of bricks.

3. THURSDAY. Sensitive. This will be a less eventful day than most of its predecessors. But Scorpios will have success in any legal business they have to attend to. Take advantage of the favorable conditions to confer with legal counsel on matters of concern. Give as much help and support as possible to mates and spouses. They will appreciate your assistance. But Scorpios may have to keep their wits about them in romantic affairs. People and situations may not be entirely what they first appear. It is better not to rush headlong and heedlessly into love affairs with a fast-beating heart. Some cool logic may save the day. But once your mind is at rest romance can take on a special quality.

4. FRIDAY. Mixed. It will be easier to make mistakes with facts and figures today. It would be advisable to recheck any accounting or other financial calculations you have to deal with. Large sums can be overlooked. It would be best to get professional help with tax and insurance matters. Any mistakes made in these areas can lead to dire legal consequences. Make sure that all insurance policies are fully up to date and still cover your needs. Don't risk taking a car out on the road that is not inspected, insured, and in compliance with all regulations. Requests for loans or other services from bankers can prove unfruitful.

5. SATURDAY. Difficult. You may not get official backing or the support of influential people in money matters. In fact, commercial operations may have to be called off. This can be the result of a lack of confidence shown by people who are crucial to the success of projects. Your financial prospects can take a downward turn. Plans to secure rock-solid incomes can come to nothing. Of course, any increase in the earnings of spouses can give family resources a boost. But it would be unlikely to offset the bills and debts that constantly accrue. Although the financial outlook is on the bleak side, it is essential to keep a cool mind. Anxiety will only cloud your thoughts and could easily lead to wrong decisions. You will be cutting off your nose to spite your face.

6. SUNDAY. Fortunate. The minds of Scorpio people will be particularly sharp-edged and agile today. You can derive deep satisfaction from mental pursuits and intellectual interests. Serious subjects can have great appeal for you. You may be drawn to philosophical and religious topics. It's a good time for looking into the background of exactly how things work. Scorpios should strive to get to the very bottom of matters that interest them. Having reached great depths, you will then be able to ascend to great heights. When you have gathered all the relevant facts and material you should allow your imagination to take over. Important relationships can develop from small beginnings. It may be just a casual exchange of little importance while traveling.

7. MONDAY. Changeable. The insights and broad perspective gained yesterday should enable you to adopt a very positive approach to life today. You have been able to see the deep significance of certain things. This will allow you to put details and minor irritations and frustrations in their proper place. You should have a better idea of what merits true importance and what does not. The study of profound subjects can put you in touch with deeper layers of knowledge. You may also have the urge to spread your wings and undertake long journeys. But this is not likely to meet with the approval of loved ones. High hopes of romantic plans can be disappointed.

8. TUESDAY. Quiet. This is a favorable day for contacting people in distant places. Overseas business associates may have a special need to get in touch with Scorpio business people. Foreigners will make happy companions and reliable partners. This applies both to the romantic and the commercial kind. It is good for poring over travel brochures and other information on faraway places. Scorpios may have a great urge to travel far afield. An absence of disturbances and distractions will make conditions excellent for study, research, and any work requiring long stretches of unbroken concentration. The day will be good for conferring with people who are experts in their chosen field. Take a long-term view in business operations.

9. WEDNESDAY. Mixed. New sources of finance can become available now. Scorpio business people may find new backers or raise substantial loans. Additional capital can be plowed into business projects making them more extensive and profitable. Scorpios can gain the upper hand in negotiations. Favorable new terms and working agreements can be arranged. But as the day wears on you can get more and more wound up. It continues until you come close to the breaking point. Don't push yourself too far. Take time off, if possible. You will only make blunders if you insist on continuing to work while in a tense state. Safety rules must be strictly adhered to when using tools and machinery.

10. THURSDAY. Good. The excellent past record of Scorpio employees is likely to stand them in good stead now. Positions can become vacant and superiors may well offer you promotion. Long-awaited permission is likely to arrive through official channels. It will allow you to get started on new commercial ventures. Influential people can show their confidence in your ideas by providing the necessary funding. The achievements of Scorpios are likely to increase their standing in the eyes of others. Improved reputations can be accompanied by wage increases. If you are disabled by serious illness you should go ahead with the best treatment available. The money for medical bills will be found more easily than you think.

11. FRIDAY. Disturbing. Long-held desires and hopes can come closer to fruition now. But don't expect any rapid developments. You are more likely to achieve your goals by working in a steady and measured way. Rush jobs may have to be done again. Don't look for shortcuts. Attend to everything with thoroughness. But it is still advisable to keep secret dreams to yourself until they are fully realized. It's a good day for attending parties and social gatherings in the company of friends. Your pals will make good partners in sporting activities. The feelings of Scorpios may be a little too sensitive today. The smallest remark can touch you to the quick, out of all proportion, and you may withdraw for a while.

12. SATURDAY. Fair.   Scorpios should follow up any urges they have to help underprivileged or needy people. Today is good for charitable acts and fund-raising activities. You can be highly effective in getting things changed for the better through neighborhood and community projects. It's a day for giving full vent to your idealism and desire to improve the world. While friends may be in need of a helping hand, they can also be in a position to give you some welcome assistance. But the money-making schemes of your friends should be avoided like the plague. Their financial advice will have you barking up the wrong tree. There should be some pleasing developments in employment affairs.

13. SUNDAY. Worrisome.   Your day or rest is likely to be rudely disturbed by worrying news concerning business finances. Unsettled conditions can affect commercial operations badly. Information about your business interests can come from unlikely sources. And just when you most need to confer with business associates they are likely to be available. They will probably be deeply involved in family or recreational activities. It may occur to you to turn to friends in an attempt to raise money to tide you over a difficult stretch. But they are unlikely to have the necessary cash. Your love life may contain disappointments due to the bad health of loved ones. You might have to work on behalf of others.

14. MONDAY. Disquieting.   Scorpios may experience some rumblings in their subconscious minds. It may make them restless and ill at ease. Personal anxieties may try to rise to the surface. It would be wisest not to suppress disturbing thoughts and feelings. You must put your problems in clear perspective now. The longer you hold them down the stronger they will become. At work it may appear that there is a planned conspiracy between people and circumstances to make things difficult for you. But it is more likely that Scorpios are making problems for themselves. There won't really be obstructions that you cannot shrug off fairly easily. You are inclined to get uptight very quickly.

15. TUESDAY. Variable.   A confidential approach can give the best results where personal finances are concerned. Meetings behind closed doors can bring about additional sources of income. New money-making schemes can be got off the ground. But Scorpios may have a tendency to cut off from loved ones. They, in turn, will naturally be disturbed by any lack of communication.

Keep your channels open. Officials and employers can take ages to come to decisions that affect your finances. While such delays are probably unnecessary, there is little that Scorpio people can do to speed things up. You will just have to resign yourself to a long wait. But things will work out favorably in the end.

16. WEDNESDAY. Rewarding. There will be no shortage of creative energies and imaginative powers today. Devote as much time as possible to inventive and artistic enterprises. This is a good day for using lively and original ideas in advertising schemes. Your products or services can be brought to a much wider public as a result. It is important that you keep fully alert during regular employment hours. Opportunities can arise that need to be seized immediately. Even though you feel in the pink from a health standpoint, this is a good time to have a standard medical checkup. Health problems might be nipped in the bud. Neighbors can go out of their way to give you a helping hand.

17. THURSDAY. Confusing. Scorpios can tend to be on the moody and irritable side. It won't be easy to predict just how you will be feeling even a short time from now. Your unstable emotional state can make routine work more difficult to handle. It will be almost impossible to stay on the beam. Gloomy feelings can color and distort your outlook. Then your problems will appear to be a hundred times worse than they really are. It may be difficult to face the world at certain times in the day, especialy early. But as the day wears on there may be an overadjustment in your mood, swinging it to the opposite extreme. You can become nervously energetic and highly strung. Try to maintain a balance between the two because either mood is far from ideal.

18. FRIDAY. Changeable. Try to give yourself something to look forward to. Make your weekend plans with loved ones during the early part of the day. Scorpios will find it much easier to get on with siblings and other family members now. Visits to relatives can indeed be very happy occasions. Old family differences can be patched up. Others will be more than ready to forgive and forget. If you are impatient for the repayment of money you are owed a phone call can galvanize people into action. But in general, money matters will require an extremely hardheaded approach. This is no time for pie-in-the-sky schemes. It is by looking at financial problems squarely in the eyes that you will find solutions.

19. SATURDAY. Productive. Try to put the morning to good use. If you can put in some overtime or find paying work to do, the rewards can be quite substantial. Do all you can to give personal finances a boost. A cautious approach is necessary if you are seeking financial help or advice from influential people. They can be in an up-and-down mood. But it is worth making the move, as Scorpios are likely to catch them at a good moment. You should be thinking ahead to Christmas week and making last-minute arrangements for shopping and holiday trips away from home. Check through your lists to make sure you haven't forgotten cards or presents for anyone. It is probably too late to mail cards.

20. SUNDAY. Variable. It seems that Scorpio people are up to their necks in money matters. It is probably difficult just now to concentrate on anything else. But you should try to take your mind off the subject. Give yourself a treat or a trip out. Get involved in physically energetic activities. Time spent with loved ones may help to take your mind off the specter of many bills coming to haunt you. There may be occasion to turn to older and wiser people for help and advice. They can provide useful insights and solutions. By talking things over with them you may be able to find your way out of a tight corner. You are likely to be blessed with inspiration while attending to mental activities.

21. MONDAY. Rewarding. Today should be good for visiting friends and acquaintances who share similar interests with you. Or perhaps they can give your personal plans a little encouragement. It is also a favorable time for sharing activities with people you like. But friends won't want you for a companion if you are in a gloomy and pessimistic mood. This is a time to show others just how energetic and positive you can be. Your drive and determination will appear as very attractive qualities to associates. If you are mixing with groups of people you would do well to turn on the friendliness and charm. Sales representatives can have a particularly productive day.

22. TUESDAY. Important. People will be in a congenial and cooperative mood. In fact, others are likely to lean over backward to help you out of any tight spots. It should be a good time for talking over problems with associates. The atmosphere is likely to remain reasonable whatever the topic. Long journeys can provide opportunities for meeting new romantic partners. Those Scorpios who are hoping to start a new love affair are more than likely to meet people they take a fancy to. And once a prospective partner is in your sights it shouldn't be too difficult to clinch a relationship. It could be a favorable moment in time for proposing and planning marriages. Be sure that you and your intended are compatible.

23. WEDNESDAY. Disquieting. It will be more difficult than usual to maintain harmony at home. Scorpios can be rather heavyhanded and do or say things that upset other family members. Don't pour cold water on the festive spirit. It is possible that you may not feel like joining in the fun in the buildup to Christmas. But there is no reason to prevent others from enjoying themselves. In fact, you would do better to counter any gloomy feelings within yourself. Do it by encouraging others to have a good time. Shake off the blues. Don't poison the atmosphere. At work it is best to do a straightforward and efficient day's work without any frills. This is not a good day for buying and selling real estate.

24. THURSDAY. Exciting. This is a day for tying up all the loose ends before the Christmas break. Don't put energy into getting anything new started. Clear the decks. You can win the favorable notice of bosses by bringing work to successful conclusions. There is likely to be a little bit extra in your end-of-year pay envelope by way of a Christmas bonus. The sooner you can wind things up the sooner you can begin to enjoy yourself. With work behind you, you can quickly get into the Christmas spirit. Enjoy yourself at the office party or in the company of friends. Set yourself totally free of work problems for a while. Now is the time to enjoy yourself. It could be a favorable time for short trips.

25. FRIDAY. Merry Christmas! Above all, this is the day for putting all your business, financial, and personal affairs behind you. Concentrate only on having a really good time. You will be all the fresher when returning to the world of work and business. Even a short period of pleasure and enjoyment can make a vast difference. Make the most of the company of friends and family. Youngsters can be especially delightful companions now. Scorpio parents will derive great pleasure from arranging a good time for their kids. A love affair can spring up in the midst of the festivities. It would be a good idea to share Christmas activities with sweethearts. The organizational talents of Scorpios can come to the fore in arranging parties and meals.

26. SATURDAY. Disturbing. Your Christmas cheer may get a slight shake-up if you let spending get out of hand today. Bills and expenses can mount at an alarming rate. If you had to cater to all your own whims and fancies or to those of your family and friends, you will be amazed at just how fast. You must keep expenditures moderate. It will be easy to get caught up in the helter-skelter of the festive season and forget that there is a limit to what you can afford. But you should just keep reminding yourself of the mess you will be in after the holiday if you go over the top spending. Scorpios may have to cancel journeys or vacations because money has run out. Sporting activities can suffer for the same reason.

27. SUNDAY. Variable. This is a good day for completing work at home or making household alterations and improvements. Loved ones will be in an understanding and cooperative mood. You may have some catching up to do with work or studies. If so, you are unlikely to encounter opposition from mates or spouses if you want to focus on it. They won't mind your retiring for a while so that you can concentrate on it. But you may find concentration more difficult than you had expected. Your mind is likely to wander hither and yon. Strong measures of self-discipline will be necessary if you are to make constructive progress. Don't indulge in fantasies or pie-in-the-sky pipe dreams.

28. MONDAY. Buoyant. Conditions at work and in business are likely to be very much as Scorpios would wish on their first day back. The break in routine should have prepared you well to swing back into action fully refreshed. You will find renewed vigor and enthusiasm. And there will be no shortage of opportunities to be taken advantage of. Personal finances can get a boost now. There may be promises of promotion in the New Year. Business profits will be in a healthy state. There should be scope for expanding your markets and adding clients to your books. News of excellent investment returns is likely. There should be good chances for settling accounts and repaying debts.

29. TUESDAY. Productive. Loved ones and people you trust can be in an especially sympathetic and receptive mood. It would be much better for Scorpios to unburden their minds to such people than to keep troubles and anxieties bottled up. You will feel much lighter for having shared problems with someone else. Acquaintances can also provide insights and solutions that you would never have come across yourself. If you have legal or other official documents to peruse or sign it is advisable to take extra care when reading them through. Don't gloss over details that you do not really understand. Make sure you are fully in the know before entering agreements. This is basic common sense.

30. WEDNESDAY. Quiet. A less eventful and cluttered day will give Scorpios more time for being with loved ones. This is the moment to patch up any differences in marital affairs. All partnerships can be put on a more understanding and affectionate basis now. It is advisable not to put self-interest before the needs and desires of others. Fall in with the wishes of loved ones. Give what help and support you can. Self-sacrifice can bring its own benefits in the long run. Scorpios would also do well to stand back and observe the ways in which they relate to spouses and partners. You may be surprised to see just how many covert demands you make of others. Ponder this and try to find ways to be less domineering.

31. THURSDAY. Disconcerting.   Today will be favorable for conferring with lawyers and sorting out any legal problems. This is not the best time to insist on making solo efforts or striking out on your own. You will achieve much better results by throwing in your lot with others. The supportive strengths of associates will make teamwork productive and enjoyable. But even joint efforts today are likely to make rather slow headway. A steady and consistent approach will achieve the desired results eventually, however. Scorpios would do well not to rise to any challenges offered by loved ones. Concentrate on the midnight festivities. Then 1988 will be at hand, another new beginning!

October—December 1986

OCTOBER

1. WEDNESDAY. Mixed. This is a day for playing it safe. Avoid risks and gambles. Don't tie up your earnings or resources in projects that contain any chance of loss. You cannot be too cautious now. Monetary advice or plans proposed by friends should not be considered. Their ideas are unlikely to be very practical. There may be requests for loans or support. Others may try to take advantage of the Scorpio's generous nature. You would do well to offer a firm but friendly refusal. The emphasis must be on conserving savings now. You could be the life of the party later on. Scorpios will be particularly attractive and entertaining. Love affairs will blossom.

2. THURSDAY. Good. Snap decisions and on-the-spot negotiating will pay off. Hesitations may lose you the advantage in commercial affairs. Be prepared to jump in feet first. Gambles will be worth a try. Grab the chances you are offered. Lucky breaks can pass you by if you are not on the alert. Be ready and waiting for the unexpected. Make use of any inside information that comes your way. Friends may be in a position to tip you off. Following up leads you are given can involve some running around, but the outcome is likely to be worthwhile. Opportunities will not be repeated. Make hay while the sun shines. Keep an eye open for reasonably priced items in the shops.

3. FRIDAY. Satisfactory. You will be left pretty much to your own devices today. No additional demands are likely to be placed on you by family members or associates. There will be plenty of time to take stock of your situation. You can learn much by going over past events connected with professional and private affairs. Take a candid look at occasions when you failed yourself or others. Try to see why targets you set for yourself were not attained. If you can find a trustworthy person to confide in, you may get some useful reflections of your performance or behavior. You can gain valuable insight and experience by contemplating your mistakes and successes. Future difficulties will be easier to avoid.

4. SATURDAY. Disquieting. You may have a strong urge to be by yourself. You will probably want to avoid the noise and fuss caused by others. Concentration will seem easier without the distractions and demands from outside. Retire into quietness by all means, but do not give people the impression that you are shunning them for personal reasons. Take pains to avoid unpleasantness and resentment. Concealed moves can cause suspicion or feelings of rejection. Let others know what you are doing and why. Unfortunately, you may have trouble in preserving the conditions of solitude you desire. Those close to you will have a tendency to barge in on your privacy.

5. SUNDAY. Disconcerting. There can be important developments in affairs that touch you deeply. Heartfelt desires and plans can run into obstacles. Your outlook may have been too optimistic. You seem to be asking too much of people and conditions, but all is not lost. Some reshaping and rescheduling is necessary. Your aims must be made more reasonable. No amount of determination will make impractical schemes work out. Trim your expectations. Do not stick rigidly to original targets. A sensitive and flexible approach will achieve most. Forceful measures will be counterproductive. Keep in rhythm with your surroundings. Be prepared to make alterations and changes of direction.

6. MONDAY. Happy. From the moment you wake up, you should know that this is going to be a happy day. Rarely does a week get off to such a pleasant start. You are likely to be on the crest of wave until you go to sleep again. A feeling of vitality and joy will be running in your veins. It will be surprising if anything affects you adversely, even if you run into difficult people or conditions. You may be able to shed a little sunshine in the world. There may be some yearnings in your heart for amorous adventures. If you have taken a fancy to someone, you can make a confident approach now. Your advances are unlikely to be rebuffed. Your needs or requests have an excellent chance of fulfillment.

7. TUESDAY. Disturbing. You couldn't expect to stay on yesterday's high for long. Today will seem rather disappointing. You may get overloaded with financial worries. Your economic burdens can seem endless and insupportable. You are likely to become despairing and depressed. If others come too close it may be impossible to avoid snapping at them. You may get increasingly irritable as the day goes on. Demands for bills and repayment of debts can pile up. Money that you loaned to others, which could alleviate the situation, will be difficult to collect. If you are at your wit's end, you had better turn to someone for advice. Call on the experience of older people who have probably once needed advice, too.

8. WEDNESDAY. Worrisome.   Yesterday's financial problems may be far from solved. You must conserve your resources as best you can. You may be tempted to overreact to economic burdens by going on a shopping spree. This clearly would be inadvisable. No relief will be provided, only more worry. Keep all spending to an absolute minimum. You are likely to receive some unsettling news from an unexpected source. The contents of letters can be depressing. Unforeseen difficulties can arise. You may be caught off guard. Steel yourself for an unpleasant shock. Beware of your reactions to bad tidings. Words, written or spoken in anger or unhappiness, may be deeply regretted.

9. THURSDAY. Mixed.   Conditions at work can be tricky. Colleagues may not be easy to get along with. You may not get the cooperation you need. Associates can be unfriendly and even vindictive. They may try to take advantage of your readiness to believe what you are told. Don't fall for tall stories or malicious gossip. Keep alert for dirty tricks. By writing letters and calling on people, you can sort out problems and put minds at rest. Don't wait for confusing situations to go away by themselves. They may linger indefinitely. Timely intervention can save a lot of bad feeling. You can win back confidence and sympathy that may have been lost through mistakes.

10. FRIDAY. Manageable.   Don't undermine your hard-earned position at work. Put in a full day's effort for your money. Don't take unnecessary time off. You may think you can get away with running out or having long talking sessions, but official eyes will probably be on you. Black marks will be chalked up. Slackness may be held against you in the future at a critical moment. Past diligence and efficiency will go to waste. Capitalize on your good record and don't spoil it now. Don't take too great an interest in new people. They can bring bad luck, or they may be a further source of distraction from your responsibilities. Sweethearts will appreciate phone calls, letters or visits.

11. SATURDAY. Sensitive.   There may be trouble brewing at home. Friction with loved ones is possible. Relatives will not be easy to please. They may be selfish and demanding. Don't expect much cooperation. Minor irritations can blow up into violent quarrels. You can get plenty done by working alone around the house. Unfinished jobs and maintenance can be attended to efficiently.

Large-scale changes will also be successful. Redecoration and modernizing homes will add significantly to their value. A change of accommodation could make sound financial sense. Family resources can be boosted by home moves. Scorpios are likely to be unsettled by family members today.

12. SUNDAY. Fair. This is a good time to tie up loose ends. It may not be apparent, but you stand to gain economically by bringing certain affairs to completion. Meetings with people in relaxed social situations can be to the advantage of domestic activities. Older people may have useful advice to give on house upkeep or decoration. People in the property business may give you inside information on house or apartment sales. Legal matters relating to property may be cleared up out of office hours. Your ideas for making money or for new investments are likely to get the go-ahead from influential figures. Love affaires may be overshadowed by commercial operations.

13. MONDAY. Variable. More will be gained by keeping on the move than by staying put. People you come in contact with will have useful knowledge and advice to give. Pamphlets and periodicals can be the source of stimulating ideas and technical shortcuts. You may be inspired to renew an interest in an old hobby. The artist in you is likely to be fired into action by pictures or methods you come across. Put inspiration for creative work, cooking or dressmaking into operation while the mood is on you. There could be a strong temptation later to take a financial gamble. Think twice, as losses are more likely than gains. Spending on pleasure should be kept within reasonable bounds.

14. TUESDAY. Fair. This is a starred day for being with children. You will find no problems in handling their affairs. They will be more responsive and affectionate. You can get on the wavelength of youngsters with ease now. Parents should meet no resistance when giving advice or guidance to their offspring. Outings to parks or museums will be enjoyable. Some good luck in money matters may bring problems in its wake. You may back a winner or find cash in your pocket unexpectedly. The use to which you put any gains should be carefully considered. You may find it necessary to draw on your reserves to back up an initial move or purchase. More money is likely to be lost than was gained.

15. WEDNESDAY. Tricky. Put your nose to the grindstone. Much can be gained by diligence and application. You will derive both satisfaction and financial rewards from increased efforts. You will get twice as much done as you normally do. You may even have some energy left over to help others out. Trouble could be waiting to surface at work. Neglect or carelessness on the part of a colleague can jeopardize your output and perhaps your safety. Try to monitor the actions of new or dubious work mates. School them in safety measures and working procedures if possible. Keep on the alert when using machines and equipment. Don't let your mind wander while you are driving.

16. THURSDAY. Tedious.   Very little happening today. Don't allow frustrations to get the better of you. Realize early on that slow conditions are making it difficult to achieve much. Trim your actions and output accordingly. Don't go knocking your head against a wall in an attempt to get things moving. You will tire yourself out to no avail. Pull back into yourself and take it easy. Use this lull to catch your breath. You must keep up with the regular and routine jobs. Don't allow work that seems boring and pointless to go undone. You will only build up a backlog that has to be sorted out in busier times. An orderly environment will make for more efficiency when conditions speed up.

17. FRIDAY. Troubling.   You must go by the book today. Stick to rules and regulations. Be punctual. Don't take time off from work. Keep everything open and aboveboard. Attend to your duties with particular care. Those in authority may be keeping a close eye on you. It is possible that some doubt may fall on your honesty or reliability. Your actions are ilkely to be misinterpreted. What seems straightforward to you can appear devious to others. Scorpios may have to suffer some unjust accusations. Under the circumstances, denials could further incriminate you. It is better not to make any fuss. Get on with your work quietly. Allow time to inform people of their mistakes.

18. SATURDAY. Variable.   A good day for visiting exotic places with people you love. Journeys to places of particular interest or grandeur will be stimulating and enjoyable. Country homes and places will have appeal for all the family. Famous art and antique collections could have much to offer. Trips to the country will be a relief from the city air and dirt. Such excursions will serve to offset the moodiness of loved ones. Relatives could be rather lifeless and easily irritated. Discontent may give rise to angry reactions. Scorpios will have to be firm with self-indulgent people, but sympathy will be called for if the unhappiness of dear ones results from genuine deprivation.

19. SUNDAY. Frustrating. Scorpios may feel an urge to bridge any gaps that have opened up with loved ones. In an attempt to strengthen the ties of affection, you may want to show others how much you care. Efforts to involve them in your activities, outings or simply your conversations may be tried. But it is possible that no matter what you do to win others over and make them feel wanted, separation will increase rather than narrow. Partners are likely to see your actions in a bad light. They may resent your attempts to get closer. Invitations and suggestions can be rejected. This may be very hard for you to bear, but angry or emotional reactions will only make matters worse.

20. MONDAY. Stressful. Scorpios may feel like retreating into their shells today. Those around you are likely to seem noisy and interfering. You can overreact to quite modest demands or intrusions. You must try to curb the intensity of your responses. Others will be going on about their regular activities with the usual expectations. You are simply out of tune with the world. Let people know you are feeling off-color. Once you are on your own, your mood will probably calm down. You can then concentrate on work or interests that give satisfaction. You will find it easier to engage in study, reading or writing activities. You may need to attend to paper work concerning shared funds.

21. TUESDAY. Mixed. Shared savings can be put under strain. Scorpios will have to rein in free spenders. Loved ones may have the urge to go on shopping sprees. There may be a lot of indulgent buying. At the risk of arguments and upsets, Scorpio people must nip extravagance in the bud. Savings must not be allowed to go below a reasonable level. You should be doing all you can now to put finances on a firmer footing. Investments in modernizing your home will be a safe bet. Family assets can be increased by adding to the value of any property you own. House sales can reap handsome profits now that can be plowed back into smaller or more economic accommodations such as apartments or trailer homes.

22. WEDNESDAY. Good. Concealed moves are more likely to be appreciated by those who are in a position to give you backing. Surreptitious inquiries and approaches can bring you into contact with people who will be helpful to plans for utilizing joint capital. This is a time when working in the dark is very much to your advantage. Don't let others know of your intentions unless they are intimately connected with the business at hand. You may lose a head start by revealing too much. This is a good time to consider donations to charities and other organizations as a way of seeking tax relief. Arguments over divorce settlements can be more easily settled through confidential meetings, with lawyers present.

23. THURSDAY. Misleading. It will be difficult to convey accurate information to people far away. Letters, phone calls or messengers can easily give others the wrong impression. Messages communicated to you may also be misinterpreted. Double-check incoming news. Reassure those who have received important information from you recently. This is not a good time to approach people who are experts in their field for advice. Matters you discuss with them are likely to get more complicated. Neither will Scorpios have much luck in convincing others of their political or philosophical outlook. Conversations are best kept to less serious affairs. Attempts to broaden personal horizons can be successful.

24. FRIDAY. Rewarding. Scorpios can meet new emotional partners through activities at universities or training centers. Love and learning go together particularly well now. Accept invitations to attend social events at educational establishments. Scorpios will probably be exerting a strong magnetic pull. People from overseas or from other regions are likely to feel attraction for you. There is no need to hide the more assertive aspects of your nature now. These are the qualities that others will be drawn to. Your will and determination may prove a perfect complement to other natures. An interest in mysticism, the study of dreams or psychology may be rekindled now, almost forgotten in the pressures of today.

25. SATURDAY. Sensitive. You are likely to receive planning permission for house alterations or get other official go-aheads. Visas can be granted if you are planning an overseas trip. While you may get the bureaucratic assistance you need, others may be feeling less happy about your plans for travel or domestic changes. This is not a time to attempt to barge through with your ideas. Don't get carried away by the approval of authorities. It is especially important now to win the sympathy and support of those who are affected by the moves you propose. In professional spheres, resentment will be caused if you do not confer with partners and shareholders.

26. SUNDAY. Troubled. There could well be a clash between private and professional interests. Loved ones will be bitterly disappointed if you spend too much time attending to business concerns. Your domestic life can be made very uncomfortable by a disgruntled spouse or partner. If you have to work today, do not totally neglect your home responsibilities. Scorpio people involved in love affairs may also have some difficult choices to make. Opportunities to push ahead in your line of work may mean canceling appointments with sweethearts. You may be obliged to miss social events you have been looking forward to all week. Consider the feelings of others when changing plans.

27. MONDAY. Variable. The shoe may be on the other foot today. Involvement in personal affairs is likely to detract from time and energy that should be given to professional matters. Get your priorities right. Don't jeopardize business opportunities or hard-won positions. Ask friends or loved ones to help you out with private visits or purchases. Words must be carefully chosen. It will be easy to say or write the wrong thing. Repercussions can occur on a larger scale than you thought possible. You may stir up bad feelings in many people. Bringing lively ideas or artistic schemes to the attention of influential people can result in useful advice or financial backing; take advantage of this assistance.

28. TUESDAY. Useful. Let your friends know of problems or intentions you have concerning personal plans or projects. Help may be close at hand. You may be introduced to people or places that suit your purposes or further your aims. One of your buddies may be better connected than you had realized. It is very likely that an avenue to success will open up. Things can be made easier for you. Don't rely purely on your own resources and contacts. Follow the leads you are given. But when it comes to money you must stay wholly independent of your friends. Don't ask for loans or comply with requests for financial assistance. If you do, relationships and cash will both be jeopardized.

29. WEDNESDAY. Difficult. Do not count on anything working out for the best in commercial operations. You would do well to monitor each new development in detail. It will only take a small incident to upset the applecart. Alert others to the sensitive conditions. You may need support to keep an eye on progress. The chances of huge losses occurring are high. Fees and expenses must be taken into account when considering memberships in organized groups and societies. Try to get an idea of the cash outlay that will be involved before signing on. Financial commitments may be difficult to keep up with. Friends may bring pressure to bear on you in an attempt to force a loan. You must stand your ground.

30. THURSDAY. Demanding. This is a day when Scorpio people must consider their own welfare before that of others. Your inclination to give a hand may be rewarded by injury or illness. Don't take on anything that has a high degree of personal risk. Avoid ladders and cold places. Arrange for professionals to carry out difficult work if necessary. Conditions at work can be a little tricky. Work mates may have something up their sleeves. Give doubtful colleagues a wide berth. Don't be pushed into actions or decisions prematurely. It may be in the interests of others to get a quick answer or for things to get moving, but you must consider all possible outcomes before committing yourself.

31. FRIDAY. Good. You will move things along more quickly by working behind the scenes. Concealed moves and background research will yield the best results. Your finances will get a boost if you do business with people who are not in the limelight. Keep any inside information to yourself. You may learn things that will be to your advantage in the near future. Don't bypass commercial offers or opportunities that come your way, however unlikely these may seem on first inspection. The oddball schemes have the most chance of succeeding now. Once you have seen the viability of a project, you may have to go straight into action to gain the maximum advantage of the project.

NOVEMBER

1. SATURDAY. Fair. All activities that use the mind primarily will have a better chance of success today. The conditions are just right for study and research work. Difficult writing tasks will present less of a problem. It will be easier to bring a touch of flair and inspiration to projects connected with arts and crafts. Lively ideas and original solutions to problems are likely to crop up once you get started. You will find the necessary concentration to attend to work that requires fine judgment or a delicate touch. If you are passing the shopping center, take time off to look around for bargains. Useful items or commodities are likely to be on offer at very reasonable prices. But you don't save if you buy what you don't need.

2. SUNDAY. Variable. This can be a very lively day for amorous developments. Single Scorpios could find themselves swept off their feet. Without making any direct moves yourself, you may become involved in a whirlwind love affair. Keep an open mind and watch for opportunities. The more you hang back, the more attractive you will appear. Established relationships can be made more vital now. You can make plans and arrangements that break old routines. Partners will welcome the change and are likely to go along with adventurous ideas. But conditions at home regarding other family members are not so promising. Loved ones may be difficult to please. Heavy demands may be placed on you and angry reactions are likely.

3. MONDAY. Useful. Moving around will be to your advantage today. Opportunities will be missed if you stay put. Beneficial contacts are easier to make. It will be possible to meet people who can bring the realization of private aims and ambitions closer. Let others in on your current projects. No good will come from keeping quiet. You will find yourself able to communicate even quite complicated ideas with much greater ease. Others are likely to be impressed by your forceful and precise presentation of interests and plans. Sympathy and support will be forthcoming as a result. Don't be too put out by impending financial problems. They will sort themselves out soon enough.

4. TUESDAY. Uneventful. Any spare cash will be wisely used if invested in house modernization or redecoration. This can be a very sensible way of putting your money to work. Improvements will represent an increase in family assets. The resulting rise in value of your property will stand you in good stead in the future. Non-essential spending must be kept to an absolute minimum. Your outlays on pleasure and recreation should be moderated. Extravagant spending or shopping sprees are out of the question. Social gatherings you have planned may be best postponed until you can make a good job of them. Wait until you can afford a self-respecting spread. You may have to keep an eye on your partner's impulse to indulge later on.

5. WEDNESDAY. Pleasant. Your plans could get a boost from an unlikely source. Family members can make contact with just the kind of supporters you need. Chance remarks can make meaningful connections, or loved ones may do some campaigning on your behalf. A project that is close to your heart may receive the finances needed to put it into operation. This is a good day to treat your sweetheart to a special outing, candlelit dinner or gift. Demonstrations of affection will be warmly appreciated. Relationships can be more closely cemented. You may hear something that really cheers you up later. But before you get too jubilant, check all information. Mistakes in communication are possible.

6. THURSDAY. Happy. The go-ahead from people in authority may be closer than you thought. If you are waiting for planning permission or acceptance of plans, contact those who are dealing with them. A visit or phone call may save you weeks of waiting. Decisions are likely to go in your favor. Financial transactions will be easier to handle. If risks of loss are not too great, Scorpios would do well to go ahead with business deals they have had doubts about. Luck is on your side now. Commercial enterprises are more likely to work out for you. This will be a good night on the town with your sweetheart. Shared outings with other couples will be great fun. Everybody will have a ball.

7. FRIDAY. Good.   Make an early start. You will gain advantage by informing potential supporters of your ideas and intentions during the first part of the day. Minds will be fresh and more easily influenced. It will be easier to win sympathy early on. Your enthusiasm will probably be answered with active participation. Dreams you have nurtured for a long time will come closer to realization. Self-employed people or those who are always on the lookout for extra work should keep on their toes now. There are likely to be excellent short-term opportunities for increasing earnings, but you will have to keep your ear to the ground for the right information. Half the battle will be in knowing where to look.

8. SATURDAY. Difficult.   The morning will be a time for taking care of loose ends. Get everything out of the way so you can leave the remainder of the weekend free. It would be better to alter other plans so that you can concentrate fully on business that needs completion. You must bring order into your affairs now. Untidiness or backlogs will make efficiency difficult in the time ahead. Although you may have received planning permission or the all clear sign from official sources, your plans may meet opposition from the people who are close to you. Loved ones may have quite a different outlook from yours. Attempts to force the issue can result in ugly scenes and ruffled feelings.

9. SUNDAY. Variable.   The first part of the day may be marred by domestic tensions. Loved ones will not be seeing eye-to-eye with you. They may seem to be purposely misinterpreting your intentions or what you feel and say. Scorpios may have to work hard and patiently to get things straight. If you are gently persistent, you will break through any resistance or bad feeling. By the afternoon, it should be possible to achieve a more harmonious state. In the absence of pressures and difficulties, you will be able to take some well-earned rest and relaxation. A special evening out with your partner will help to bury the memory of unpleasant times. Relationships will become more loving.

10. MONDAY. Pleasant. Your artistic plans and projects are likely to get some unforeseen assistance. You can take a risk or two with creative ideas. Take the plunge. Chances are you will land on your feet and make a success of imaginative schemes. Time spent with children can be enjoyable and instructive. Their spontaneity will give much pleasure. Young people may have good reports of exam results or other affairs to tell you. Scorpio people will appear most attractive and pleasing to others. Sweethearts and spouses will be very happy in your company. Finances need conservative handling. Losses resulting from risks and gambles can be ruinous if you are not careful.

11. TUESDAY. Good. You have everything to gain from bringing commercial operations to a speedy conclusion. The sooner they are rounded off, the greater the profits or gains will be. Don't dither over last-minute details. Attempts to save small amounts of money may mean much greater losses in the overall picture. Recreational activities that involve long journeys will be successful. Your boss is likely to be sympathetic if you ask for time off to watch or play in a sports event. Special outings to theaters, cinemas or social gatherings will be enjoyed by all involved. A good day for visiting parks or places of special interest. All in all, a successful day.

12. WEDNESDAY. Mixed. Those around you at home will be particularly touchy today. Watch what you say. It won't take much to start unpleasant arguments. Things you say about family members are likely to get back to them. Even uncritical remarks will trigger tense situations. The less said, the better. As this can be a very productive day work-wise, you may do well to spend less time than usual at home. Plunge into your professional duties. Channel all the energy you can into increasing your output. It could be that the eyes of employers are on you and other employees now. Your efficiency drive could win you pay raises and promotion.

13. THURSDAY. Fair. Another day when hard work and application will pay dividends. Get small and irritating jobs out of the way. Bring projects that have been hanging about for too long to a quick conclusion. You need as much order and clarity around you as possible. Clutter and distractions can be the cause of missed opportunities. There will be chances for taking on new work that involves quick and lucrative returns. You will need to be on the ball and uncommitted elsewhere to take full advantage of offers that come your way. This is not the time for sweeping difficulties under the carpet in emotional affairs. All parties concerned should make a clean breast of their gripes. Everyone will feel better for facing up squarely to problems.

14. FRIDAY. Variable. Professional contacts may come up with some exotic but effective ideas for bringing your products or services to the attention of a wider public. Don't be hasty in rejecting outlandish and original schemes. A zany approach is more likely to be successful now. Don't allow the fixed and conservative side of the Scorpio nature to block exciting developments. Associates may also produce imaginative solutions to contract problems. You would do well to follow their lead. The known and tried methods can lead into a dead end. Don't expect too much from your sweetheart this evening; he or she may not be feeling romantic.

15. SATURDAY. Manageable. The skills of people working for or alongside you may stand you in good stead. They are likely to have just the right touch to handle risky commercial operations. They will know when to hold back and when to make the final push. Negotiations are likely to be delicate. You are better off to allow others to be fully in control of events. Your interference will only distract them. Sweethearts and spouses will be affectionate and responsive. Make a point of including them in your plans. There may be a temptation for Scorpio people to go it alone, but shared outings will be enjoyable. Relatives can be obstinate and unhelpful. But if they are elderly and insecure, they can't help it.

16. SUNDAY. Troubled. There could be a clash between emotional demands and ambitious drives today. People close to you may interfere with your plans to meet and discuss ideas with potential backers. Arrangements to present the outlines of a pet scheme to influential persons may have to be shelved. This is not the time to stick rigidly to your guns. You may be obliged to take into account the feelings and needs of loved ones. Dreams you have been nurturing may have to be put on ice for the time being. Don't draw back into yourself too much. Scorpios may have a tendency to hold off and keep certain advantages to themselves. Let others have a piece of the pie.

17. MONDAY. Disturbing. There could be trouble brewing between you and people you share finances with. It will be up to you to rein in free spenders. You will amost certainly find yourself in deep water if you allow extravagance to go unchecked. Friction with emotional or business partners is preferable to the economic upheaval that will result from misuse of funds. Try to make others see reason. Communicate the seriousness of the situation to them. Schemes that are likely to drain your reserves should be put off until more prosperous times. Scorpios may be tempted to spend too much on pleasure and recreational pursuits. Economies must be made across the board.

18. TUESDAY. Mixed. Personal savings may be in danger today. Partners may be drawing too freely on shared funds. Bills and financial payments are likely to come showering in. The mail may bring bad news from tax authorities. Insurance premiums may need renewing. Unfortunate coincidences can mean you have to meet many monetary demands at one time. Conversely, in business transactions, capital you have allowed to accumulate may prove invaluable now. Extremely profitable offers are likely to come up. Property dealing in particular can pay dividends. Having the cash ready at hand will give you a great advantage. Immediate decisions will be called for. You must be ready to take charge.

19. WEDNESDAY. Disconcerting. Various practices you may have taken up as a means of self-improvement could lead to some raised eyebrows. Conventional people are likely to think that you are going around the bend. Others can be frightened or confused by activities they do not immediately comprehend. If other people's view of you gives rise to concern, you could help the situation by some simple explanations. If you are involved in yoga or other physical disciplines, try to give some idea of the historical background and the resulting benefits. Even though you come up against incomprehension, the attempt to explain will give some reassurance. Relatives and locals may be very difficult to enlighten.

20. THURSDAY. Satisfactory. Now is the time to be planning Christmas holidays. If you can afford it, visits abroad will suit Scorpios well. Pick up brochures and information from the travel agent. Those of you who are artistically inclined could consider trips to ancient sites or ruins. Excursions to foreign museums and collections may prove to be a great inspiration to your own work and imagination. Plan to take a camera or sketching materials to record places of interest. Misunderstandings can easily occur in love affairs. But problems can be avoided if you make special efforts to convey your thoughts and feelings directly. Lovers will get to know each other better by taking care in communications.

21. FRIDAY. Good. You will have a better grasp of business or emotional situations that are occurring in other cities or regions. Your words and actions will hit the nail on the head. Events can be assisted by your intervention. Commercial operations will move more quickly as a result. Relationship problems can be sorted out. Background research into matters connected with your work will give knowledge that can be used to advantage in the near future. Sounding out business contacts on likely future trends will stand you in good stead. People who are experts in their fields may have much to offer you now. Sources of finance for carrying out your plans could become available in unexpected ways.

22. SATURDAY. Manageable. This is a day for keeping a low profile. Scorpios should try to stay in the background. Your ideas and drive are unlikely to be appreciated, especially in working situations. You may feel you have much to offer, but others can see your efforts as interference. Better to let others get on with it alone than to cause unpleasant repercussions. Even when you have decided to stay out of the action, you must guard against becoming verbally involved. You can easily overstep the mark when putting your views forward. You will attract angry reactions by speaking out. If you play your cards right, there will be opportunities for making economic gains. Your standing with others can be enhanced.

23. SUNDAY. Successful. You are likely to be too busy today to take much rest. Opportunities to advance career prospects may be too good to miss. Your best chances can come through not playing by the rules. Approaches that have not been tried before can pay off. Don't shy away from original and imaginative methods; but you must also be careful not to annoy those who are used to more traditional ways. Avenues to further business may be closed to you if you overlook the values of others. Any unexpected cash that comes your way should be put into backing professional projects. Developments that occur today can win you much personal distinction. This may lead in turn to higher income.

24. MONDAY. Productive. You are likely to get a helping hand from people in authority. Permissions, information, work or contacts you receive should reflect profitably on your finances. Nevertheless, it will be necessary to contain your delight. Good news must be kept to yourself. Others will all too readily jump on the bandwagon. Friends in particular may try to take advantage of situations you have engineered or been offered. You will lose the upper hand if you tell all before making use of what you have received. Others can be given a piece of the pie when you have things well under way. Congenial gatherings will provide exciting contact and exchanges. You might find a new romantic partner.

25. TUESDAY. Good. Friends may be in a position to ease pressures on your private life. They can make introductions to people that you will find very helpful. Their understanding or knowledge may help you to gain greater insight into problems or possibilities. You may be given inside information on new accommodations that are coming up. The idealism of Scorpio people could find outlets today. Your ability to express the situation and the needs of the oppressed and underprivileged will be at a peak. Your words are likely to carry real conviction. Others will be persuaded and moved to action. A conservative approach to money matters is more recommended at this time as the holiday season draws near.

26. WEDNESDAY. Deceptive. There won't be much going on today. In spite of slow conditions, you may run into situations that catch you unawares or cause unease. The less you push yourself forward, the safer you will be. Your work or activities should be carried out unobtrusively. Don't make trips or visits that can wait until better times. Facing up to difficult people or events should also be postponed. Attend to routine matters and order your current affairs. Attempts to solve problems can result in further complications. You may lose track of your own intentions later. Scorpios may end up chasing their own tails. It could be difficult to stick to the decisions that you yourself made just recently.

27. THURSDAY. Good. Scorpios may feel like withdrawing into their shells. Once on your own, you should find it easier to get on with some serious work. Without distractions, you will cover plenty of ground. The results of your accomplishments may have greater rewards than you imagine. Future security can be put on a firmer footing. Don't be dissuaded from focusing your attention where you think it is most needed. There may be some quirky developments in commercial affairs. Give all business proposals that come your way a thorough examination. Don't dismiss oddball suggestions out of hand. The more extraordinary schemes are the ones most likely to pay off in a big way.

28. FRIDAY. Rewarding. Old faces are likely to turn up today. People who have helped you out in the past may do so again now. Projects or affairs that have been hanging around for too long may be brought to a speedy end with the assistance of old acquaintances. Clear up as much business as possible now. It looks as though you are going to need order and a free hand to cope with busy times ahead. The less there is to weigh you down or cause distractions, the more efficient and single-minded you will be. All overdue mail should be attended to promptly. Relatives are likely to offer their services to look after sick or injured people. You will be able to share responsibilities.

29. SATURDAY. Fair. Events in your personal life should take a turn for the better now. Any problems with family members or close relationships will ease up. Some fundamental changes of attitude could be required. This is a good time to take stock of your situation. Are the ambitions you are chasing worthwhile? Is too much time being devoted to worldly affairs at the expense of domestic responsibilities? It could be that you have to set yourself more realistic aims. Any new approach to life should include more balance between emotional and professional affairs. Be ready to grasp any lucky breaks the day provides. New fields of activity can open up.

30. SUNDAY. Restful. You will be left to your own devices today. Very few demands will be made of you. You will be able to put business and financial problems out of your mind for the time being. Catch up on some rest. Let the batteries recharge. While you are relaxing, cast your mind over creative work and pastimes. You will probably find the energy and interest to get started. You may have the urge to get going on jobs around the house that you enjoy. Pleasurable activity will be more relaxing than sitting around. You may also find time to review the uses to which you are putting your skills and abilities. It could be that you are not stretching your talents sufficiently. Don't let them go to waste.

DECEMBER

1. MONDAY. Disquieting. You may feel it is time to make some changes in money matters. Even if you are not in the mood to do so, circumstances may make it necessary. Certain investments may need concluding, and more lucrative uses for your money can be found. Much patience will be required. Capital channeled into new projects will take some time to show returns. Commercial schemes may need a lot of preparation. They will not be easily or quickly started, but efforts put into laying firm foundations will show profitable results in time. Borrowing money to add to existing capital should not be considered. Keep your cash out of risky ventures. Gambles will not pay off.

2. TUESDAY. Variable. You should be ready for some ups and downs. People who are backing business projects or other financial associates may give you the runaround. They may leave you not knowing where you stand. Commitments and forward steps will be impossible in the face of so much uncertainty. Decisions can be made and undone in rapid succession. You had better draw back and wait for conditions to settle down. You will probably have more success in creative spheres. The artist in you could be bursting to come out. You will soon get into an inventive and productive mood once you get started. Work that requires the use of the imagination will be handled with some ease.

3. WEDNESDAY. Good. Go all out to advertise your wares, services or abilities now. Much good can come from letting others know what you are doing or what you are capable of. Take the products of creative work around to prospective buyers or people who will display them. Approaches to people for the purpose of enlarging personal projects can pay off. You can organize a little more spare time by asking other family members to babysit with children, if you are usually responsible for their care. Work mates may be prepared to stand in for you and cover your duties. This should allow you more time for recreational activities or personal errands. Outings with sweethearts will give much pleasure.

4. THURSDAY. Unsettled. You will gain more by keeping on the move today. Do the rounds of your contacts and acquaintances. Find out what is coming through the grapevine. You are likely to pick up news and knowledge that will be of use to your private dreams and ambitions. Plans you have been nurturing for a while could be put into operation at last as a result. This is a favorable time for putting the finishing touches on negotiations and contracts. People who are in a position to make life easier for you won't be inclined to do so. Potential backers may go cold on you. Projects can be left up in the air. Bureaucrats may need some persuading to handle your affairs quickly.

5. FRIDAY. Manageable. There could be some conflict between household and personal demands. You may have to give up plans for recreation and enjoyment to attend to responsibilities at home. Try to see your duties through with good grace. Sourness won't make anybody's life more bearable. Relatives are unlikely to take to a new partner in a love affair. Family and romance are best kept apart now. If you come in for criticism over a sweetheart, don't be put off. This is a starred day for romantic meetings, and outings should be most successful. Get professional advice if you are involved in land or property transactions. Profits may be made greater than you had expected.

6. SATURDAY. Disquieting. This is a good day to dispose of old pictures, furniture and silver. Antique items will be much in demand. High prices can be obtained, but don't get carried away during negotiations. Too domineering an attitude in bargaining is likely to put people off. You may end up having to accept smaller sums. A more subtle approach is called for. You must appear casual and less than eager to part with your goods. In business, hard-headed and realistic thinking is necessary. Commercial operations with a high risk of loss must not be entertained. You won't get the backing you require. Wait a while before asking your boss for time off in the near future.

7. SUNDAY. Sensitive. Feelings will be running high today. It will be easy to go over the top. Reactions may get out of hand. If you can gain the upper hand and keep emotions in check, relationships will have a creative intensity. Love affairs will be particularly passionate and volatile. It can be difficult to avoid doing or saying the wrong thing, but with adroitness, harmony can be maintained. A good day for getting away from the grime of towns and cities. A trip to the countryside will make you feel a lot healthier. Beautiful scenery and fresh air will lift your spirits. Bricks and mortar can have a suffocating effect after a while and may even stifle you.

8. MONDAY. Variable. The affairs of children can prove to be rather costly. Scorpios with offspring may be obliged to pay out more than was anticipated. Bills for school fees, clothing and other essential items are likely to take you by surprise. Outings to plays or movies may provide a further source of expense. If Scorpio people are engaged in mechanical and uninteresting work, it could be time to cast around for alternatives. It could be that you have creative potential that is going unused. Take stock of your skills, talents and artistic tendencies. If you are single-minded, you can find ways of applying your abilities to a much greater extent. More satisfying work can be found, and perhaps an increase in earnings.

9. TUESDAY. Deceptive. Both self-employed and salaried people may run into difficult working conditions. People you work with or rely on for materials, services or assistance may be the source of your problems. Delays or bad feeling may mean that you cannot reach the targets you have set for the day. The less you react negatively to the lack of efficiency or awkwardness of others, the less time and energy you will lose. Get along as best you can. Any loss of temper will further aggravate the situation. Don't allow yourself to be distracted by thoughts and worries. Travel will be particularly hazardous if you let your mind wander. Keep on the alert. Accidents can happen.

10. WEDNESDAY. Fair. It could be that you are worried about your health problems and the best way to get them treated. Help may be at hand. This is a good time to approach well-off friends or relatives to ask for financial assistance. Even small contributions can help to lessen the burden. There may be some welcome developments at work later on. Conditions are likely to improve one way or another. New and compatible colleagues may be appointed. Remunerations may be increased. Some strain may be placed on love affairs. Scorpios will need to keep firmly in control of matters. Relationships can be jeopardized if you vacillate. Let others know exactly where you stand.

11. THURSDAY. Good. This is not a time to go steaming ahead on your own. You are likely to require the support of those around you at home and at work. Neither must their needs and pleasures be overlooked. You should do all you can to make life a little easier for those who are close to you. Cooperation is the keynote for the day. Make sure you have the full backing of partners before putting personal plans into operation. Charitable or selfless gestures will mean a lot to others later on. Putting aside your own desires in order to be of service can make a huge difference to someone. You may be asked to undertake a rather arduous journey. Try to find something worthwhile about the place you visit.

12. FRIDAY. Variable. Time spent with sweethearts or spouses will give even more pleasure than usual. You will be in good company and many laughs and much fun can be expected. Outings with friends and acquaintances will likewise be most successful. This is a day for throwing off the shackles and living it up a little. Visits to places of entertainment, restaurants and night spots will fill the bill. Scorpios may have a tendency to crowd others out. Take care not to be too heavy-handed or overbearing. Your energy will probably be very high and concentrated. Others may think you are trying to be the center of attention. Hold yourself in check. Let others have their say.

13. SATURDAY. Quiet. There won't be too much going on today. Scorpios will not have much initiative or urge to busy themselves. You should look around to see who is in need of a helping hand. You may be able to relieve family members of some burdens or chores. Undertaking even small jobs will give others a break. You will win thanks and affection for your efforts. Family feeling and harmony can be strengthened. Scorpios who share business responsibilities with others could review working procedures and job delegation. Perhaps your organization can be made more effective if more emphasis is put on cooperation and joint decision-making.

14. SUNDAY. Difficult. Trouble may be brewing at home. Ideas for making money will not mix well with loved ones.

Discussions on ways and means to increase earnings are likely to make spouses and sweethearts see red. Avoid such subjects if you can. If the matter proves unavoidable, don't be too dogmatic. Put suggestions forward tentatively. Ask others for their opinions. If opposition mounts, you may have to make some concealed moves. It seems that you won't have much luck in sharing other problems with those around you either. Affairs of yours that are in the hands of bureaucrats or officials are likely to be a cause of concern. Others won't have much time to listen to your worries.

15. MONDAY. Sensitive. Play it safe where finances are concerned. Joint savings must not be used in commercial operations that are not assured of success. Risks and gambles are not worth taking. Be content with regular souces of income. Take it easy with pleasure and entertainment spending. You can blow a hole in domestic resources very quickly. Moderate your appetites and expectations. You are likely to be needing ready cash for more essential matters. Scorpio parents may have big bills to meet stemming from the affairs of children. These are best paid immediately. Don't let debts pile up. It is not a good time for borrowing money.

16. TUESDAY. Satisfying. There won't be much that demands attention in public spheres. The world can be left to run by itself today. You will have plenty of time to attend to your favorite subjects or abiding interests. A very rewarding day is in store for you on this count. Study, hobbies and personal creative work can be engaged in with success and enjoyment. Visits to libraries or museums are likely to assist your inquiries. People who are experts in their fields can give much insight and inspiration. New knowledge can come to light. It may be worth your while to give attention to one area of worldly affairs. If tax and insurance payments are overdue, they should be brought up to date at once.

17. WEDNESDAY. Good. Journeys to distant parts are likely to go without a hitch. You should put the finishing touches to preparations for trips during the Christmas period. Hotel and flight reservations should be checked. Contact relatives you will be staying with to ensure that all is well. Scorpio people may be taking too narrow a view of events in love affairs. This is a time for being more open-minded. Don't restrict yourself to a small circle of friends and contacts. Be more adventurous. It may be time to end a relationship and look further afield. Stand back from events a little. More objectivity is required. You may meet a new partner during evening revels; the time is right, so don't be shy.

18. THURSDAY. Disquieting. The day may not get off to a very good start. Last night's enjoyments may have got the better of you. If you have the blues or are hung over, treat yourself gently. Don't expect more indulgence to make you feel better. Take things slowly until you regain your balance. Rich food and drink may be best avoided for the time being. Don't take on any heavy work. Leave jobs that are not strictly urgent till another time. It could be that you have overlooked something related to visits you are intending to make to distant places. Go over the details of arrangements and the gifts you are taking or sending. A little forethought may save you time and embarrassment.

19. FRIDAY. Demanding. It seems that you have been mulling over certain decisions in your professional life for long enough. Now is the time to come to positive decisions. More thinking is unlikely to make the position any clearer. Action is called for. You must take a stand. Prolonged hesitation will leave you in an impossible situation. But do not base your moves on idealized notions. Don't fall back on tired old dogmas and theories. These may seem vital to you, but others will find them tiresome and foolish. People will be looking for action based on a realistic assessment of the facts. Airing ideologies at this stage may do great harm to your reputation, leaving you no closer to a solution.

20. SATURDAY. Variable. Personality games won't cut much ice in professional spheres. Attempts to flatter people will fail miserably. A new job, pay raise or promotion must be won by more direct means. You are dealing with people who have both feet on the ground. They are in business to make money. Personal magnetism will be of very little account in their reckoning. Straightforwardness must be met with a down-to-earth approach. Facts, figures and efficiency will count. Since Scorpios can be hardworking and determined, they should be able to adopt a more realistic attitude. Commercial operations are likely to show good profits, but you must advance cautiously. Others may not keep their word.

21. SUNDAY. Useful. This is an especially good day for being with people you like. Outings and recreational activities shared with friends will be most enjoyable. Accept any invitations to parties or gatherings you receive. On a day when being with others is so easy, you are likely to make important new contacts. You may meet new companions, people who are in a position to give assistance to your personal or professional plans. You have much to gain by getting out and about. It would be more sensible to keep details of your financial situation to yourself now. Letting others know of your good luck in money matters can have unfavorable results.

22. MONDAY. Favorable. Although business operations are probably slowing down as the holiday draws near, there will be excellent opportunities today for making things happen. By taking advantage of the current situation, you are likely to win handsome profits, but you must restrict yourself to using your own resources. This is not a good time to consider borrowing. Any projects you begin must be practical. Don't take risks with shaky ideas and operations. Gambles should be avoided. If pressures build up in your personal life, you may have to turn to a friend for advice or support. Love affairs promise to be very happy. An important occurrence may take place that will stay with you for some time.

23. TUESDAY. Disquieting. Friends could be making unreasonable demands on Scorpio people now. You may have to make some awkward decisions. You have to be clear in your own mind when to draw the line. Lending an ear to problems and offering advice and assistance is part of friendship, but requests for financial support are probably best refused. Complications can follow. Your own resources may not take the additional strain. Loans may be a long time in being returned. Further requests may occur. Conditions in commercial spheres can be rocky. It may be difficult to make the right decisions in such a changeable climate. Set your targets at the beginning of the day, and stick to them.

24. WEDNESDAY. Deceptive. A cautious approach is necessary in close relationships. Do not divulge your thoughts to family members. Secrets are best kept to yourself now. Others may react in unexpected ways to confidential matters. Reactions can be extremely violent and destructive. Bonds of a lifetime can be broken. Keep associations on a lighter and more frivolous level. You may come into contact with dark horses in commercial dealings. Doubts about the trustworthiness of business partners may undermine your decision-making ability. Plans may have to be held in check while you look into the reliability of those you are dealing with. A cautious approach may save you a lot of trouble.

25. THURSDAY. Merry Christmas. Although you will probably be surrounded by people today, material things will make the most impact. Friends and relations may seem less important. Your mind will be on other things. Some surprise gifts from long-lost acquaintances will give you much pleasure. Sums of money may be involved. This may set the trend of your thinking for the rest of the day. The financial demands of the season may be weighing rather heavily on you. It may be necessary to give more presents than you had anticipated. More strains can be placed on your resources. Try not to worry. Join in the good cheer around you.

26. FRIDAY. Fair.   If you have some time off from work, you can catch up on matters relating to your personal life. Outstanding jobs or visits should be attended to. Friends and relatives you haven't seen for some time will appreciate a call. This is a good day for getting on with reading or study activities you enjoy. Scorpios are likely to be in a persuasive mood, so meetings with people whose support you need can be very productive. You will do a good job of selling your ideas or winning sympathy. Employers or those in authority will be open to inventive proposals. You may be given the go-ahead for creative projects, but you must keep a realistic approach. Don't pretend to yourself or others that you can handle more than is actually the case.

27. SATURDAY. Mixed.   You may not get your way with people who hold power or control public events. Employers and officials may prove to be very slippery customers. They are unlikely to make commitments or clear statements. You may be left not knowing quite where you stand. There could be attempts to fob you off. Don't be content with mere catch phrases and clichés. You will have to be both calm and firm if you are to have hope of making any headway. This can be a marvelous day for love affairs. Scorpios will be radiating a very special quality. Others will find you particularly attractive. Passions will be running high between you and existing or new romantic partners.

28. SUNDAY. Quiet.   A day when conditions should allow you to rest after the hectic holiday period. Put your feet up and do as little as possible. Unfortunately, money matters are likely to flood into your mind as soon as you settle down. You are probably well situated to bring your mind to bear on financial problems. Take stock of the way things stand. Go over your accounts and payment records. Get some idea of what you have spent and what expenses are still to come. Economic pressures may have a quickening effect on the mind. You may have some bright ideas for bringing in more money. With a more relaxing day, you should be feeling in pretty good shape.

29. MONDAY. Disturbing.   Attempts to put bright ideas for making money into operation now are likely to fail dismally. Efforts to alleviate your financial situation can lead to more depression. Hold your ideas over for the time being. Wait for more conducive conditions. You will not get the support you require at the moment. Those you are relying on for a helping hand will be unwilling to give it. Scorpio people will find it hard to win the confidence of others. Don't react to economic constraints by blowing the resources you do have. Spending your money indiscriminately will provide only short-lived satisfaction; but sensible and well-planned shopping expeditions are recommended.

30. TUESDAY. Misleading. You may have the urge to be on the move today. Journeys and visits may seem to offer the solutions to a number of outstanding problems, but don't expect to realize all your plans or aims. Things are unlikely to work out quite as you had intended. Others may let you down. Don't put your faith in the words of others, particularly shop personnel. Recommendations, advice or information may be misleading or incorrect. Queries are best taken to the highest-ranking officials you can contact within the organization you are dealing with. You may be able to play a decisive role in events taking place in your vicinity later on in the day. These may relate to some public building or park.

31. WEDNESDAY. Good. Plenty of positive events are occurring to see the old year out. Relationships are likely to give much pleasure. Visits to or communications with old friends will be warmly appreciated. Affectionate links can be strengthened. You may have more people to visit than your leisure time allows, but requests to bosses for time off from work should be successful. The evening will see love affairs blooming. Occasions spent with loved ones will be most happy. Single Scorpios will find it easier to team up with new partners. This is not the time to hold back. If somebody has caught your fancy, you should not lose any more time. Take the plunge.